MANGA MANIA

COLORING BOOK

OVER 100 CUTE CHARACTERS TO COLOR

Christopher Hart

 **Get Creative 6**

New York

Get Creative 6

An imprint of Mixed Media Resources LLC
19 W. 21st Street Suite 601
New York, NY 10010
mixedmediaresources.com

Editor
PAM KINGSLEY

Creative Director
IRENE LEDWITH

Art Director
JENNIFER MARKSON

....

Chief Executive Officer
CAROLINE KILMER

President
ART JOINNIDES

Chairman
JAY STEIN

Background illustrations by ANZU
The art is based on the following books: *The Big Book of Drawing Anime, Manga 100,
Manga 100: The Cute Collection, The Master Guide to Drawing Anime, The Master Guide
to Drawing Anime: Amazing Girls, The Master Guide to Drawing Anime: Romance, The
Master Guide to Drawing Anime: 5-Minute Characters, The Master Guide to Drawing
Anime: Tips & Tricks, Manga Mania Romance, Manga Mania Girl Power,* and *Manga
Mania Shonen* The credits for the contributing artists are included in those books.

ISBN: 978-1-68462-086-9

Manufactured in China

1 3 5 7 9 10 8 6 4 2

First Edition

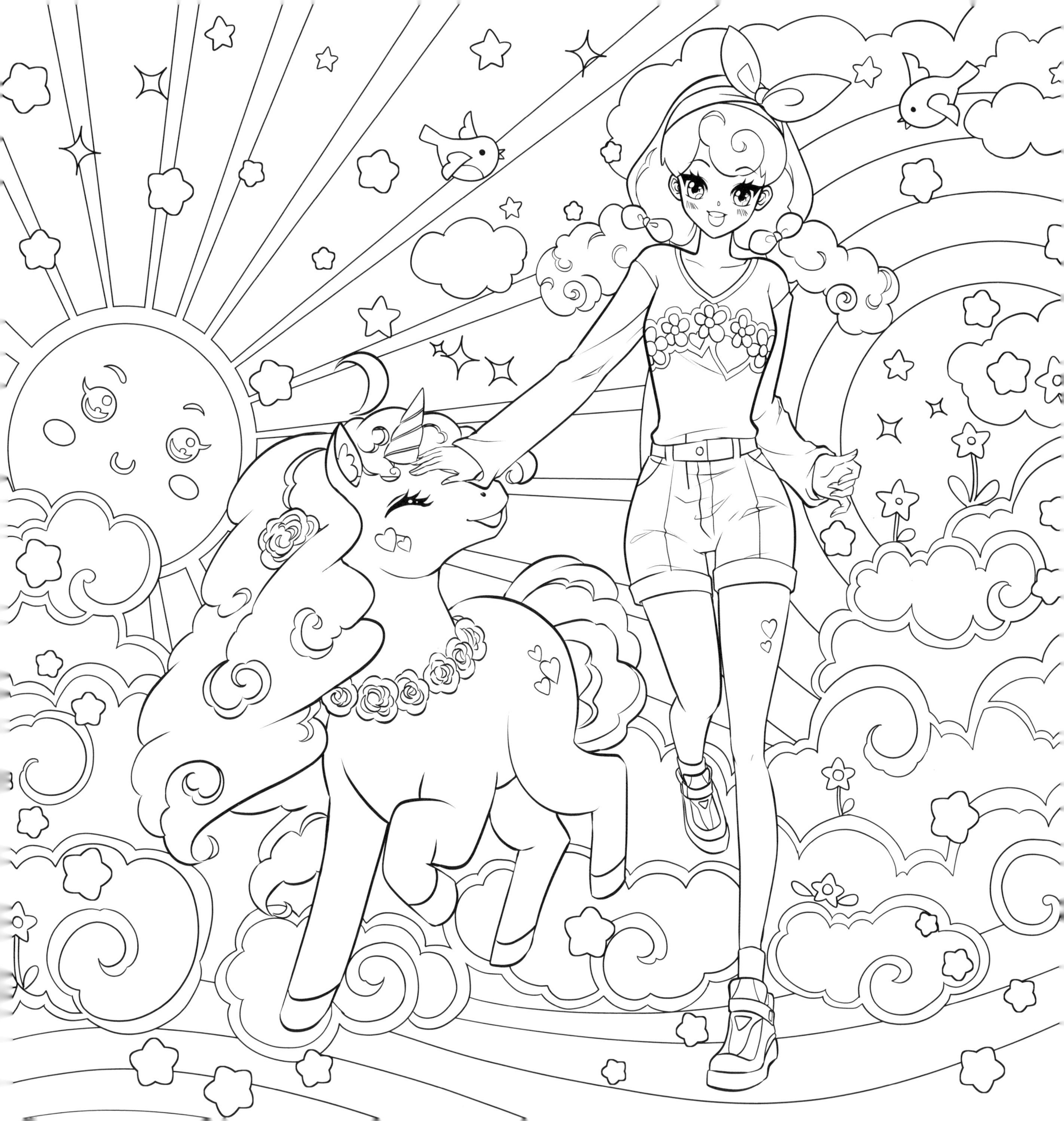

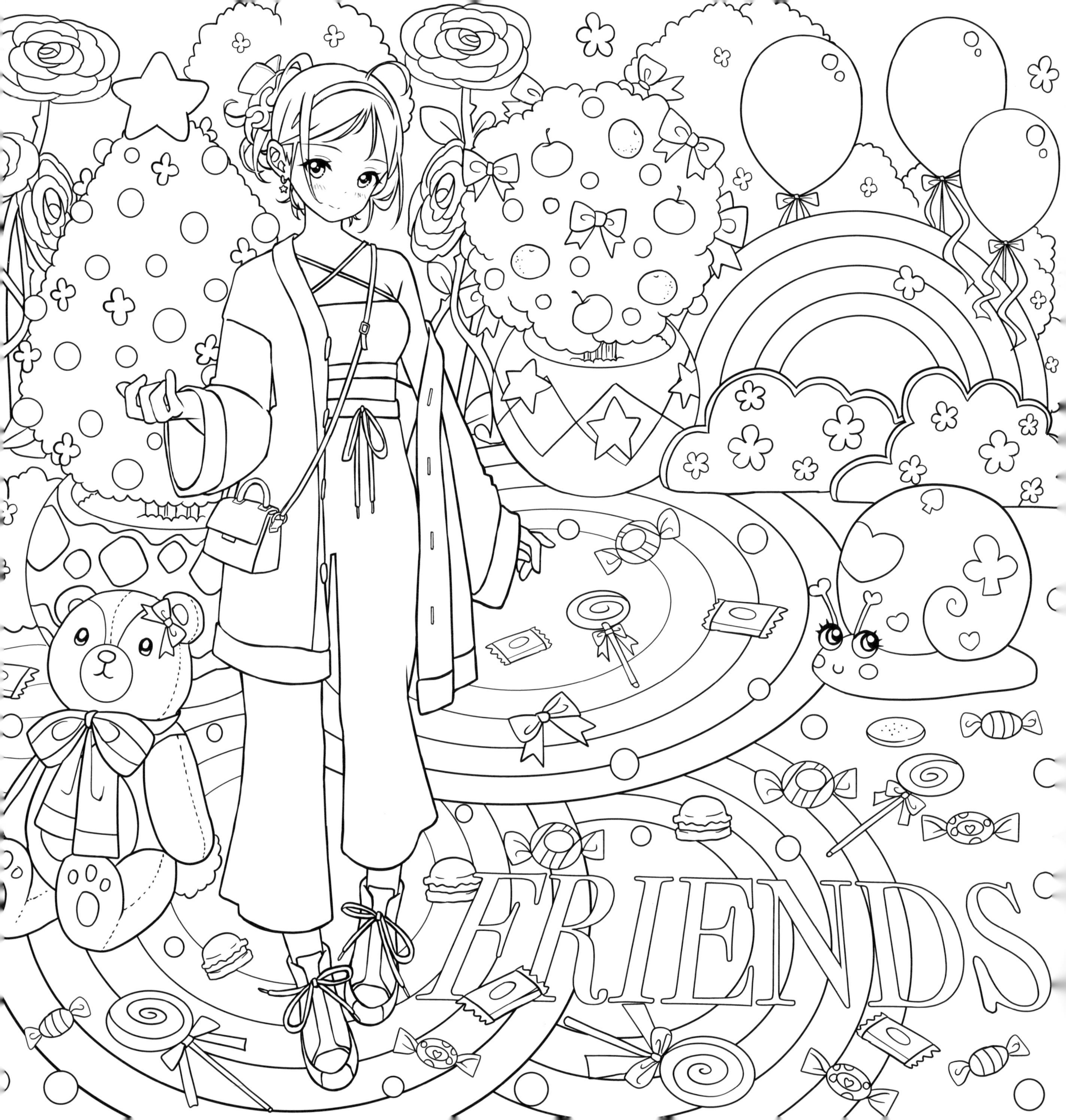
FRIENDS

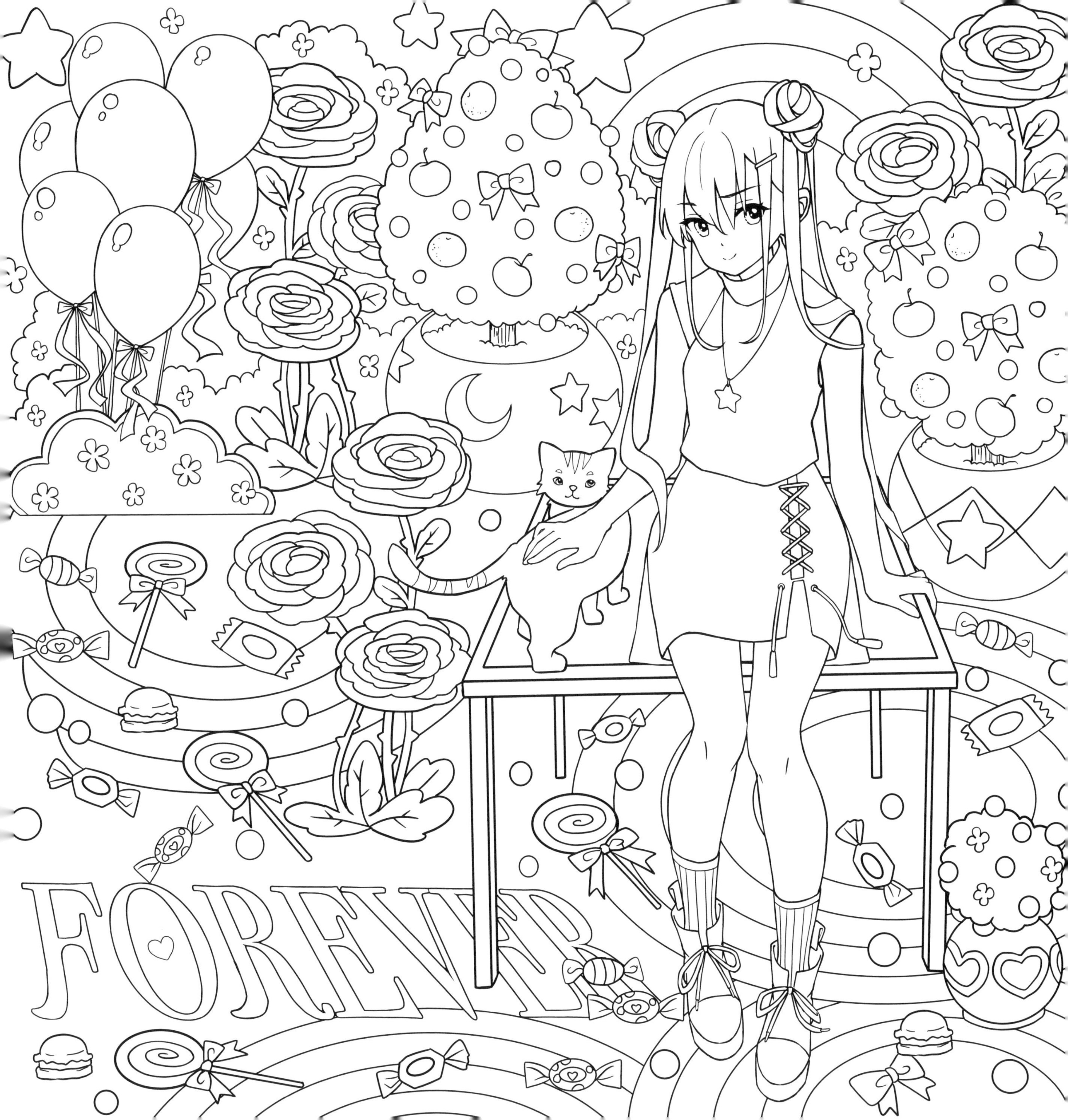
FOREVER

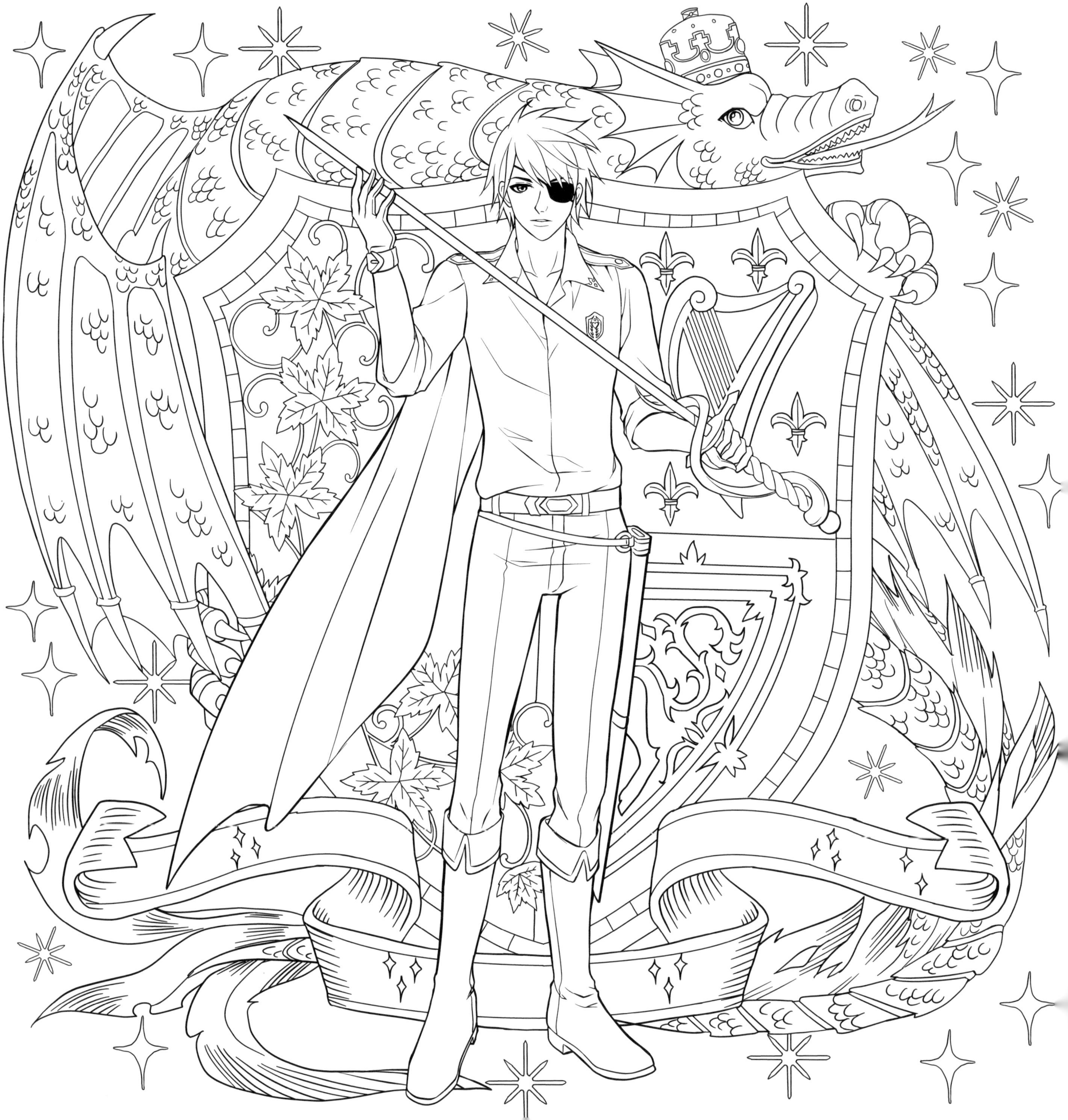

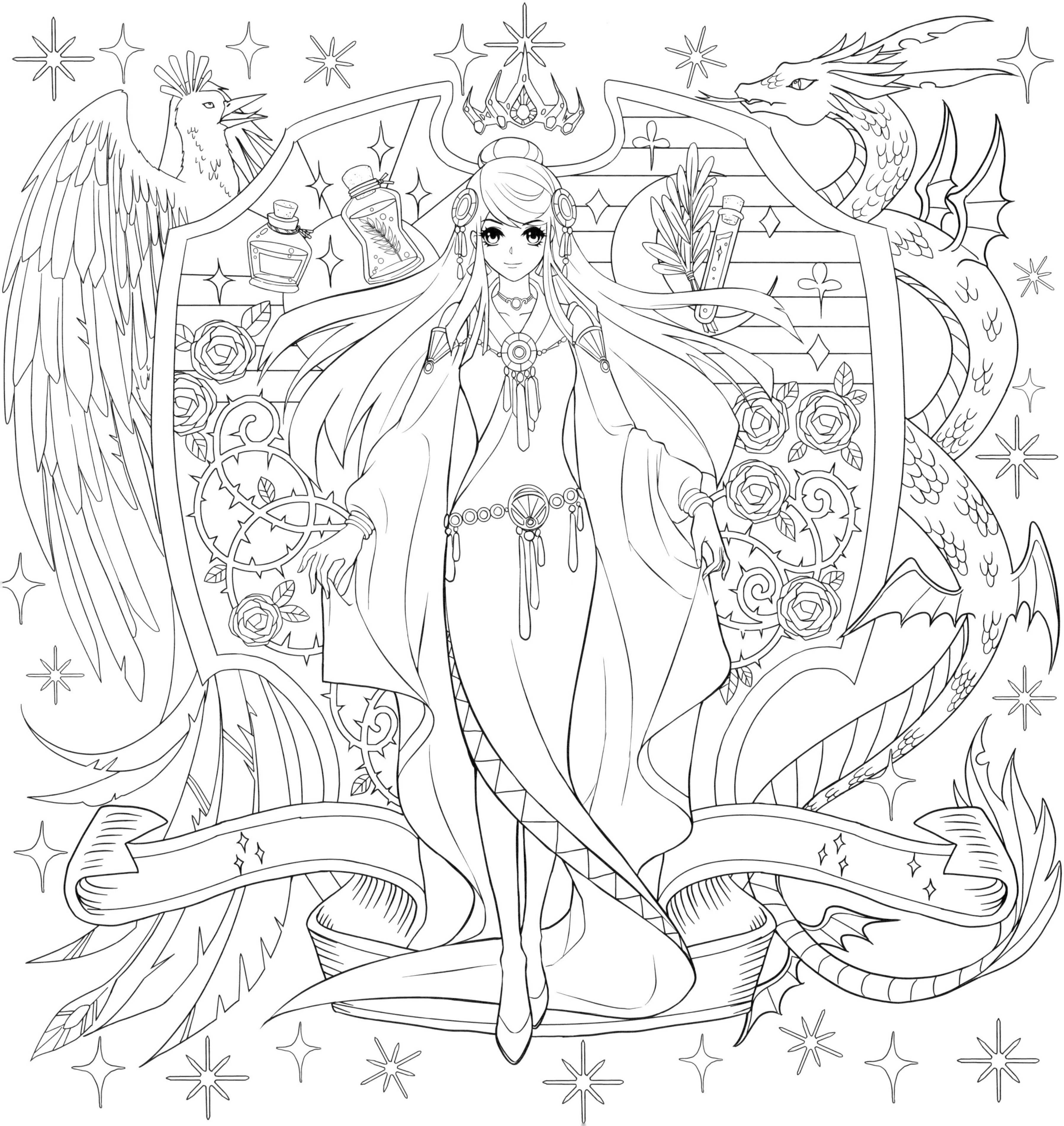

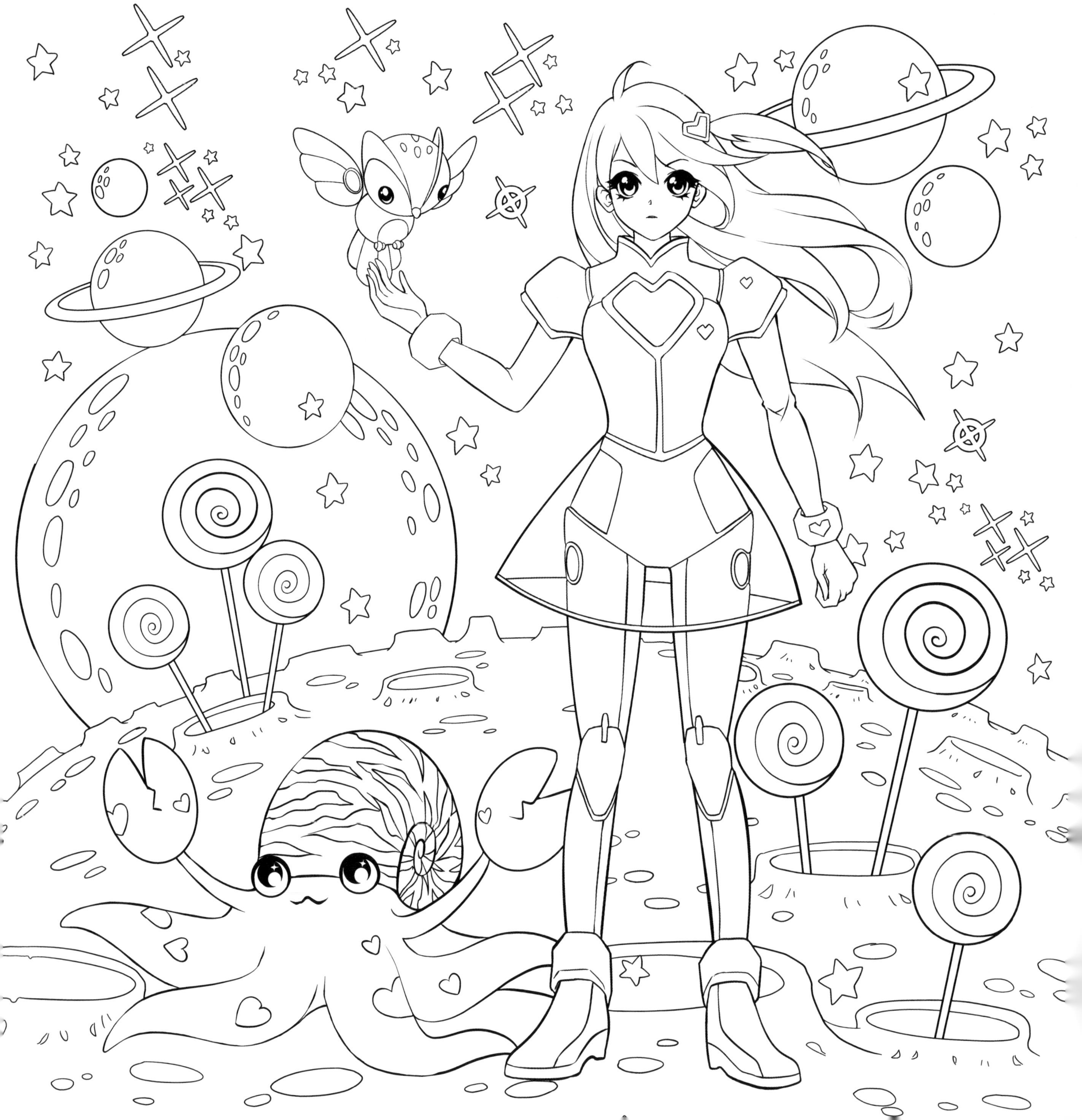

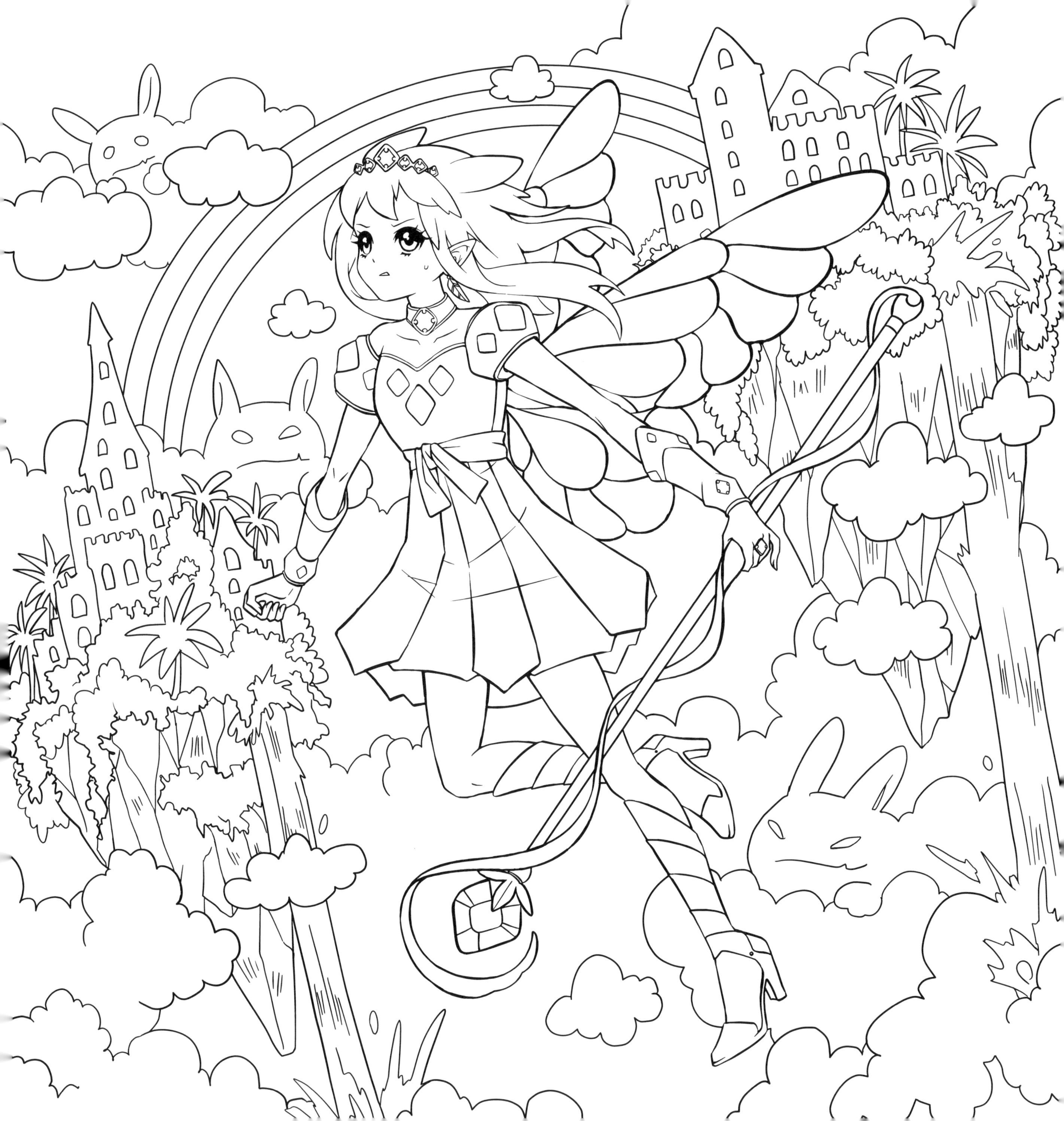

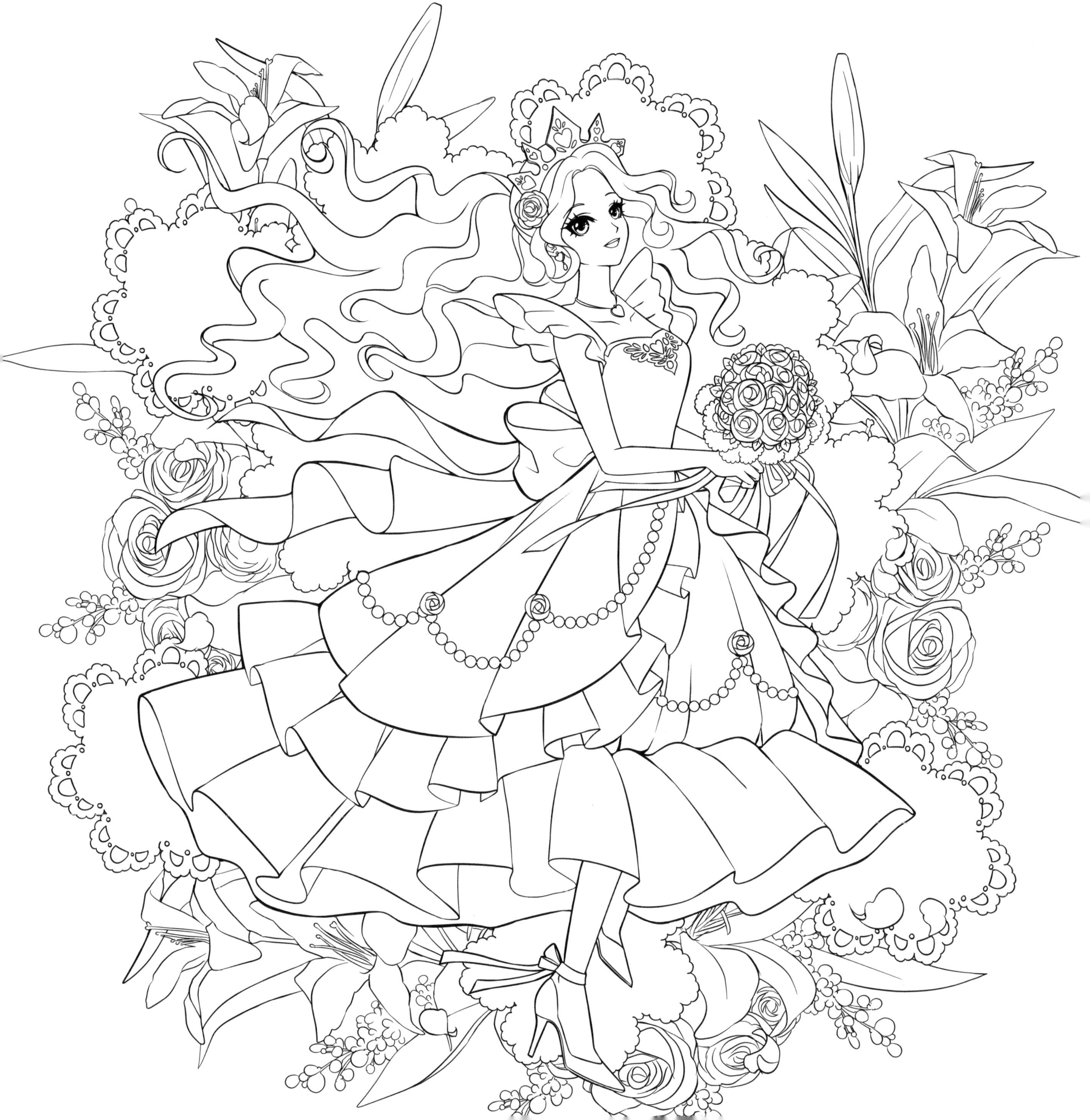

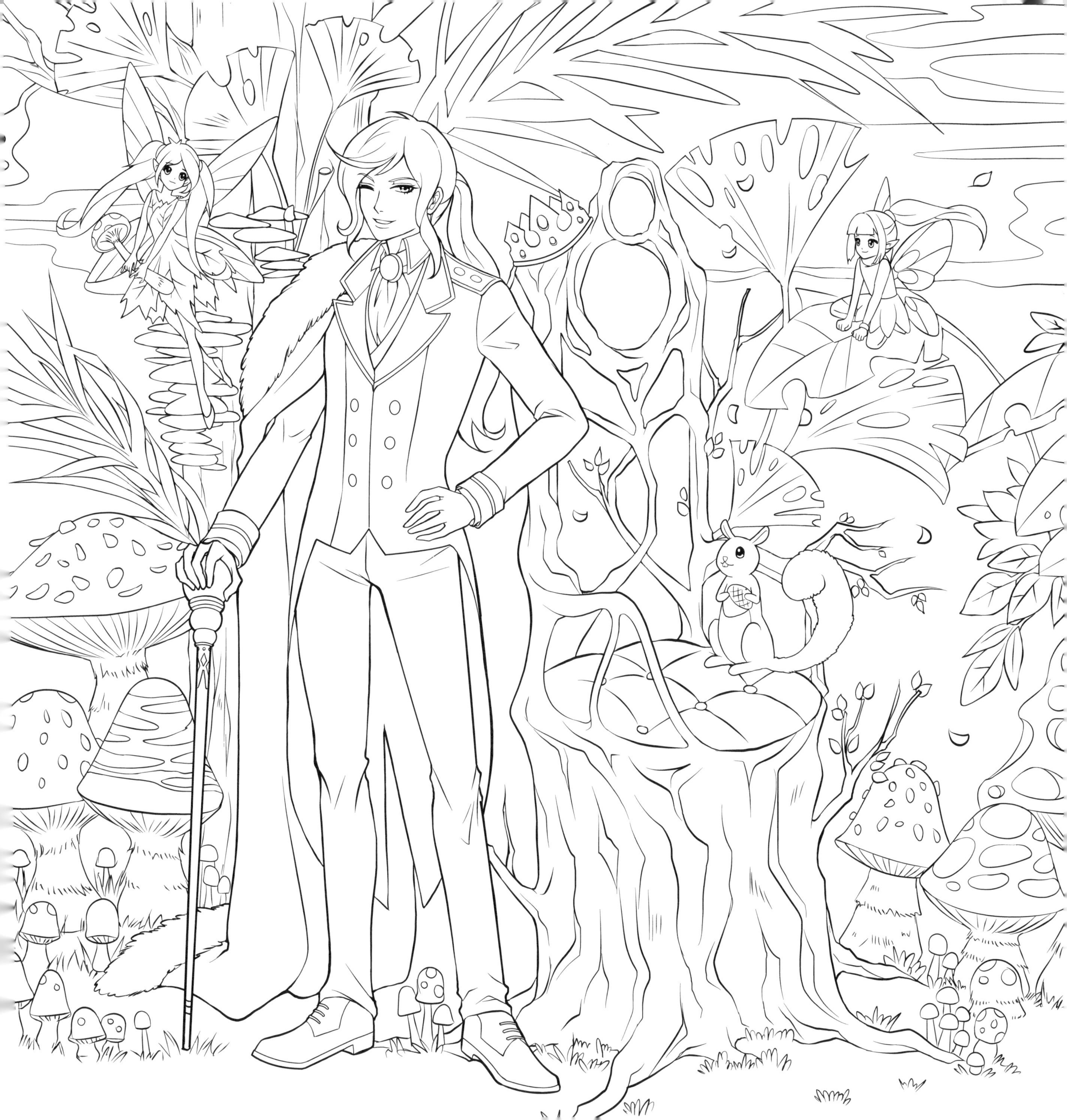

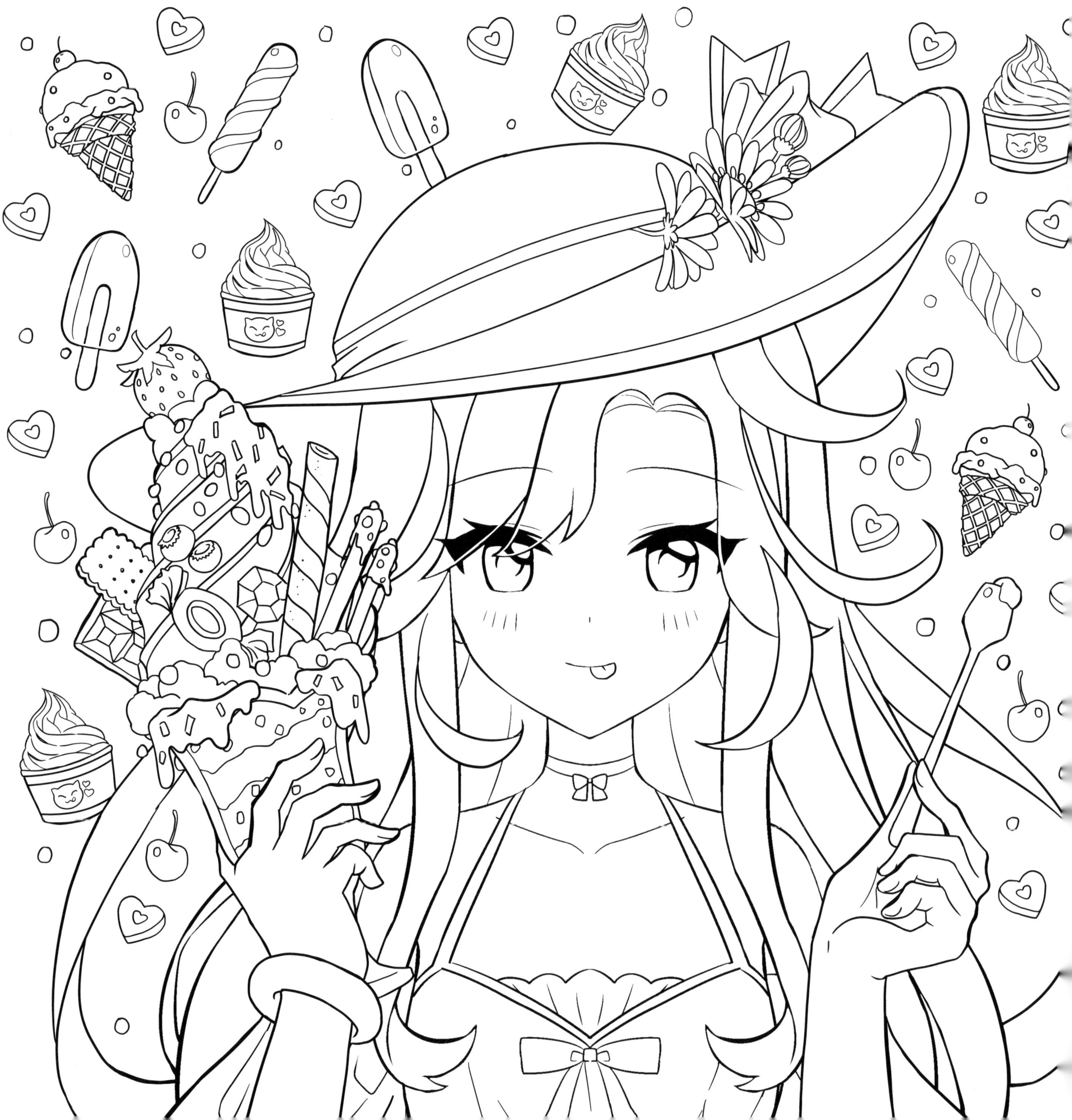

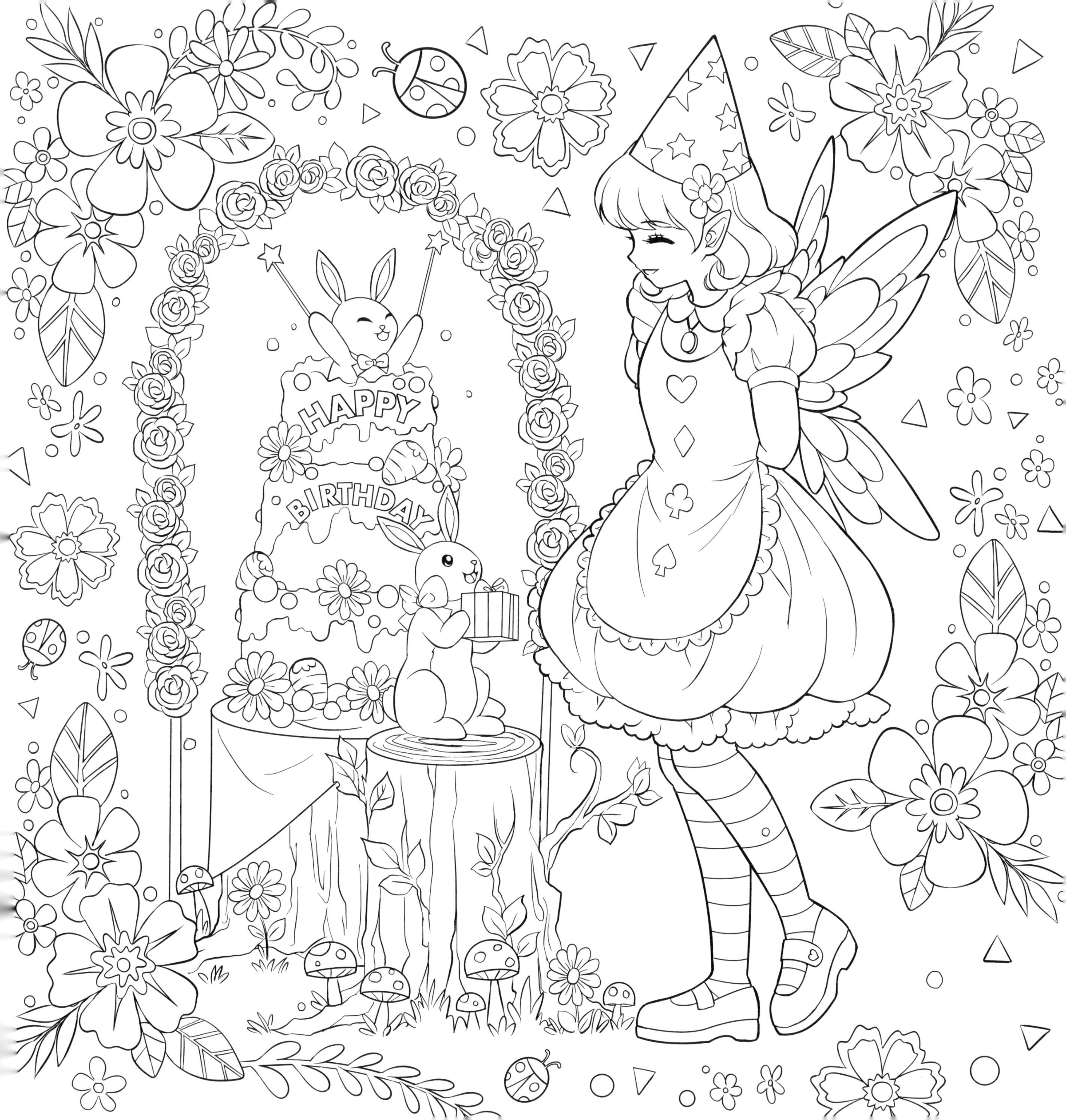
HAPPY
BIRTHDAY

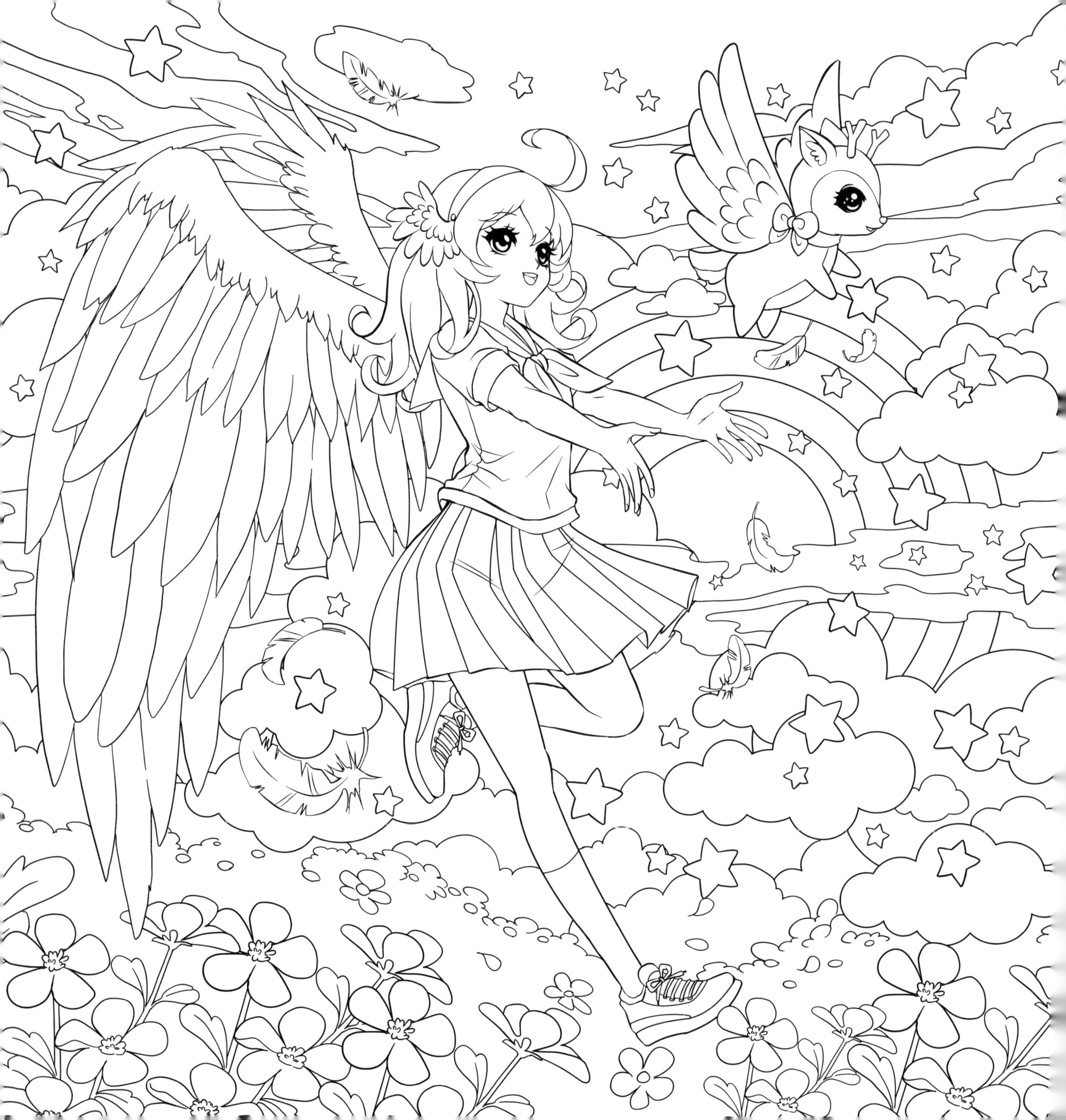

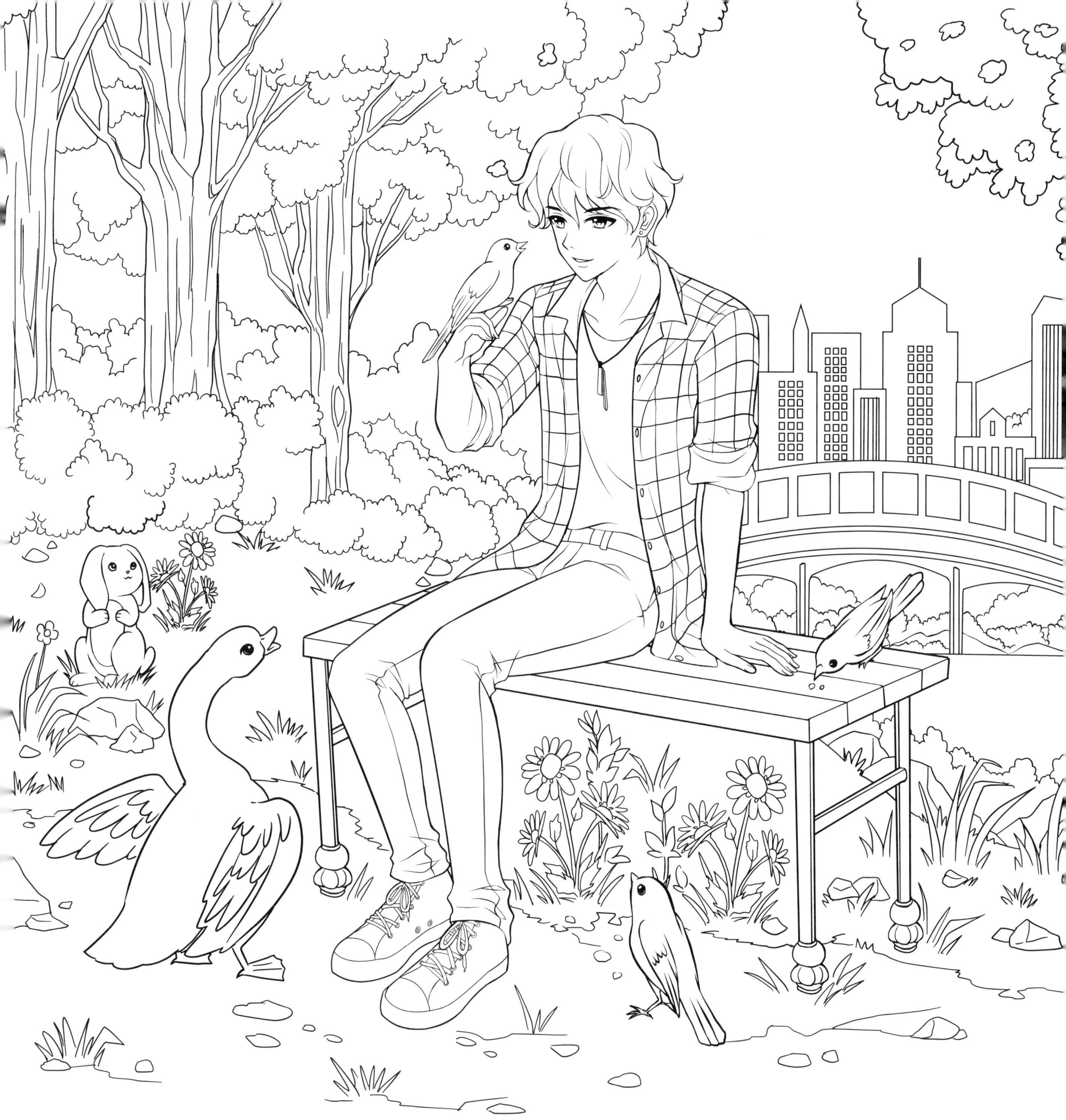

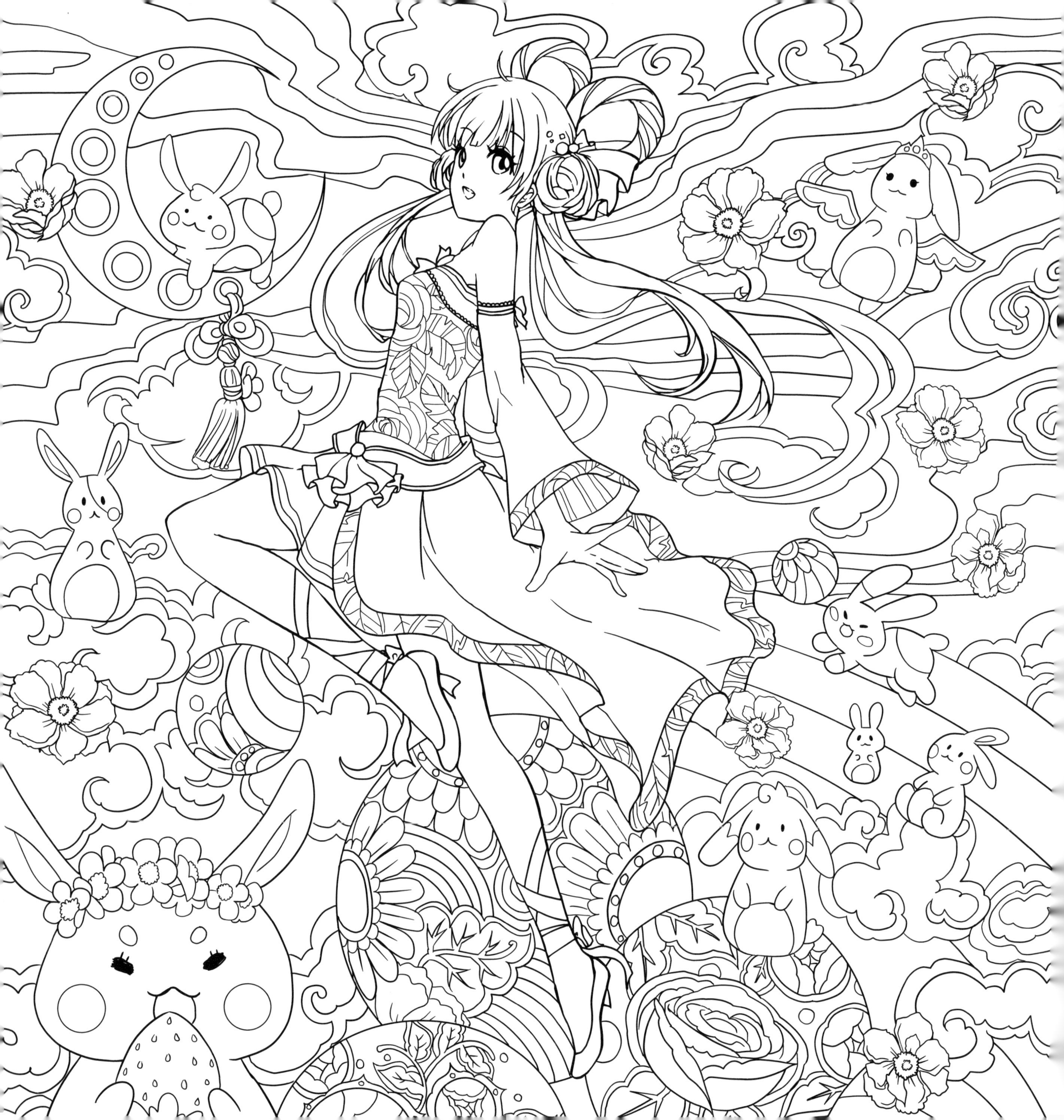

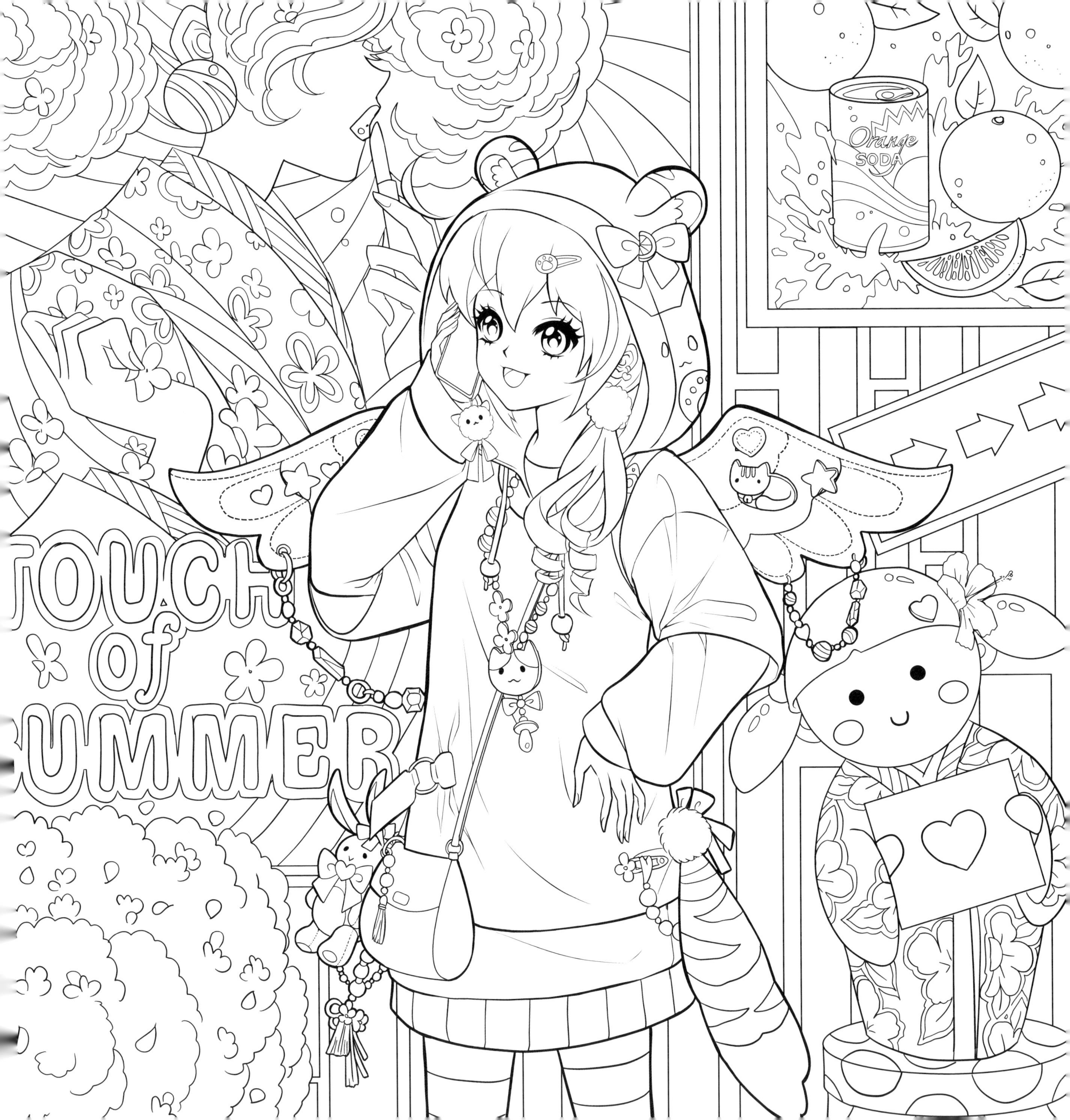

Orange
SODA
TOUCH
of
UMMER

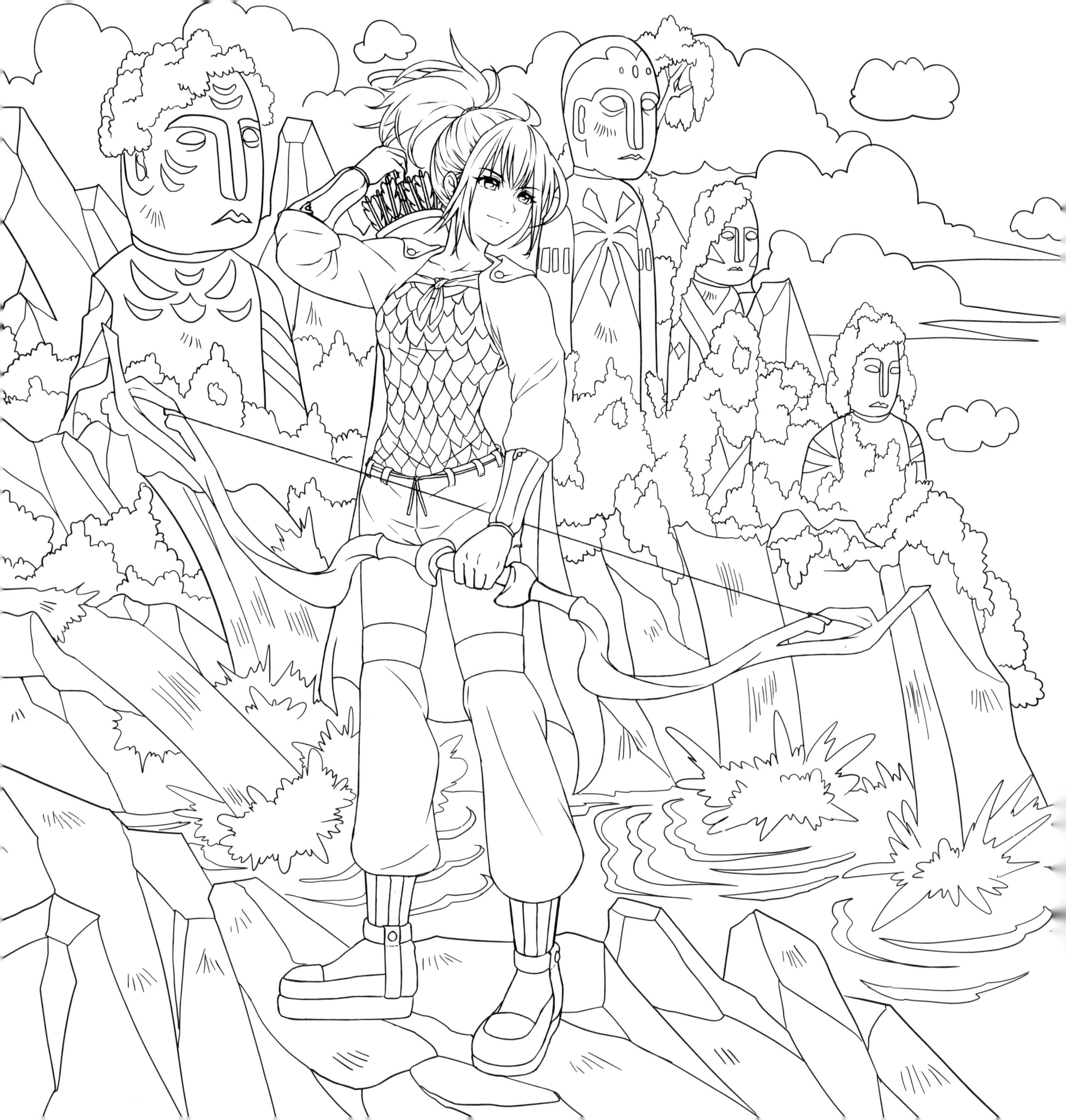

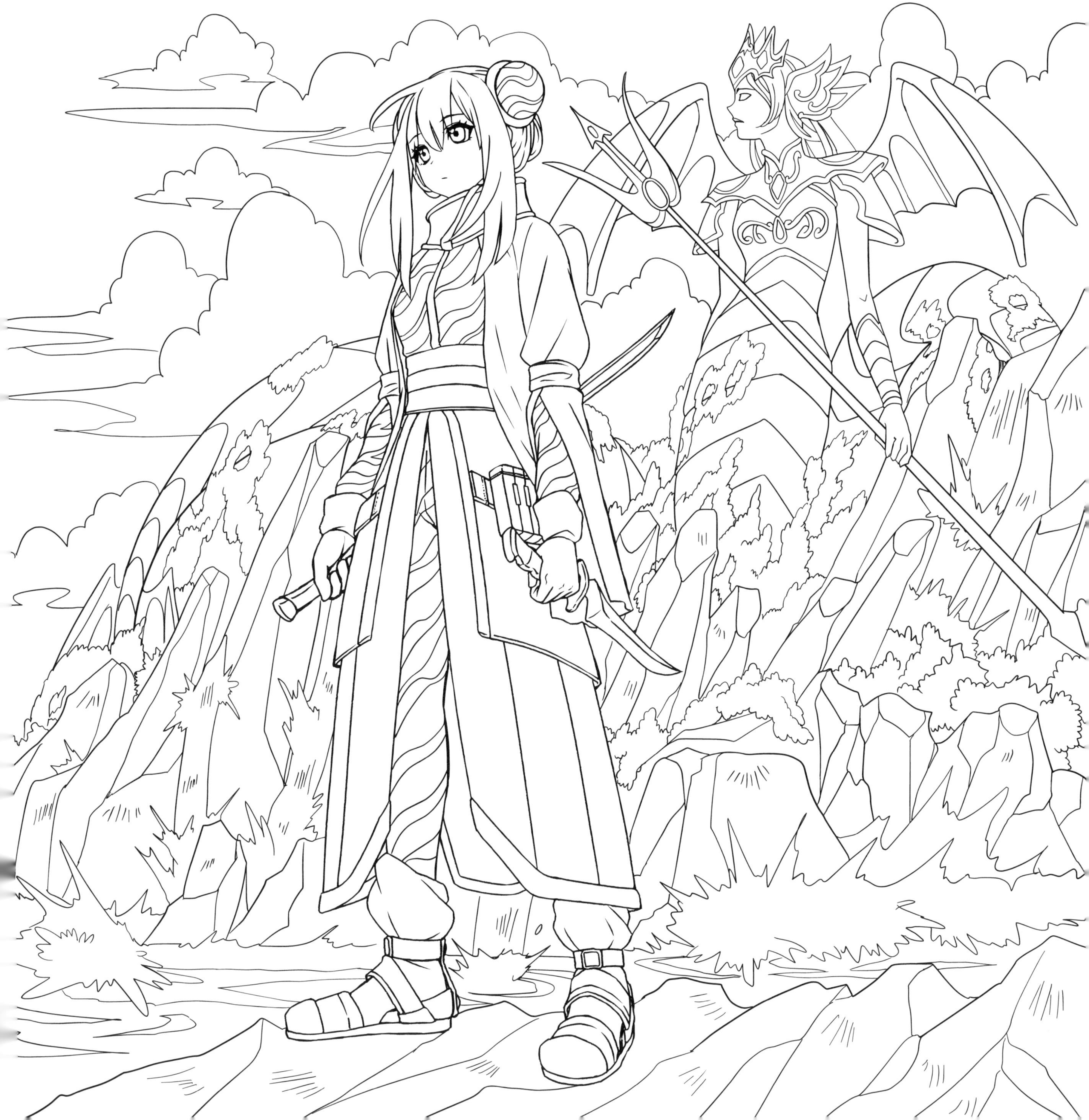

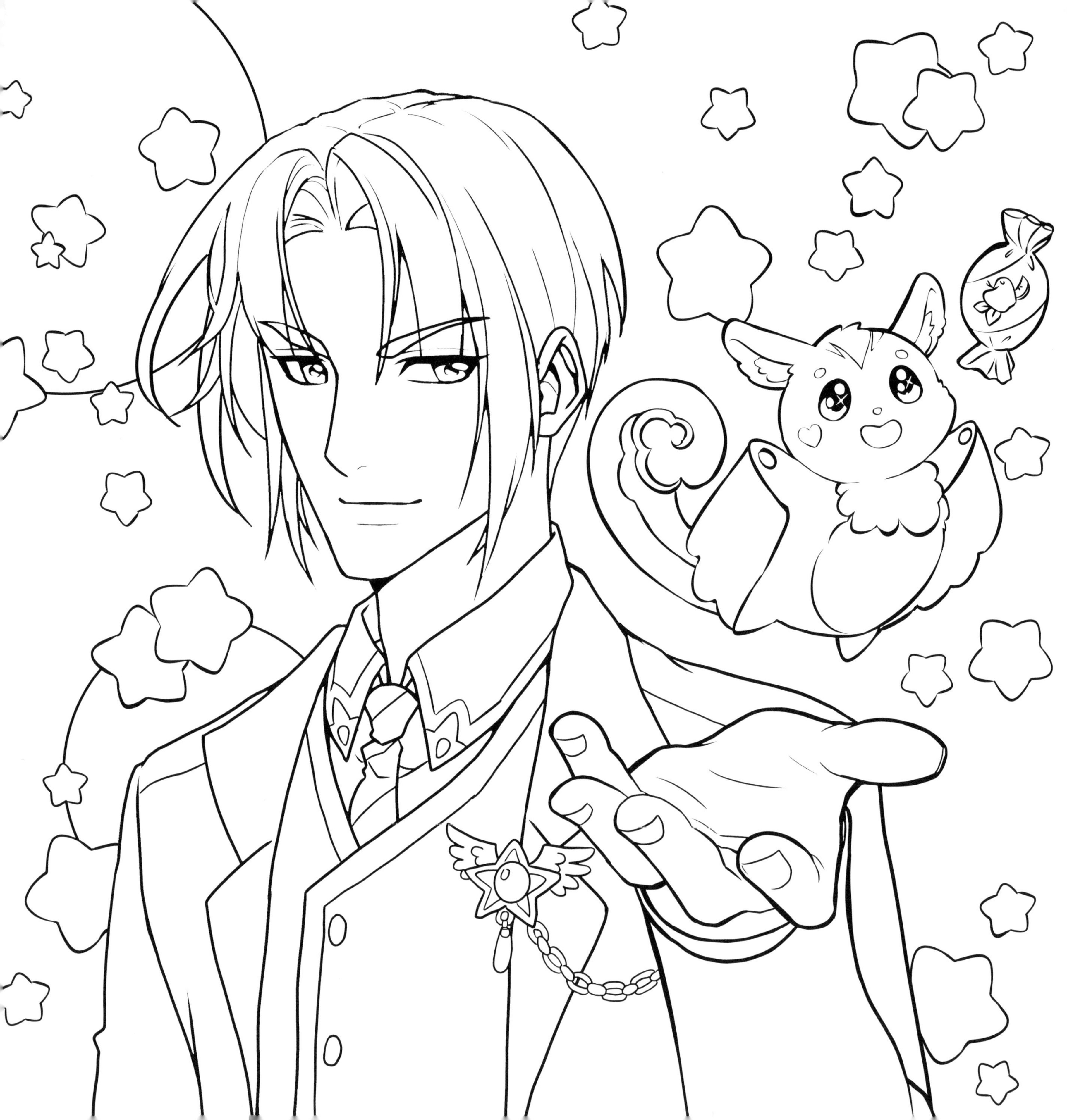

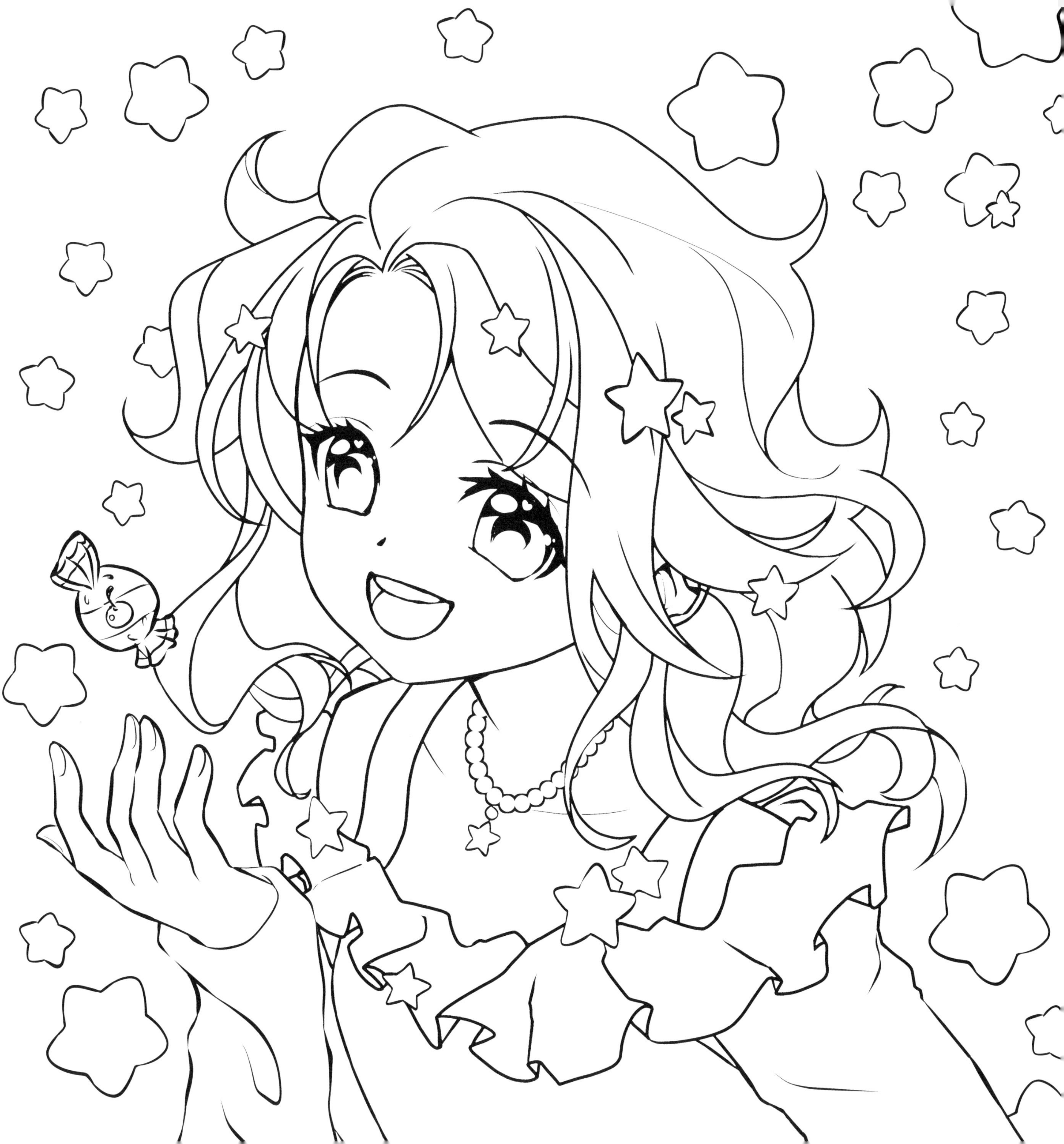

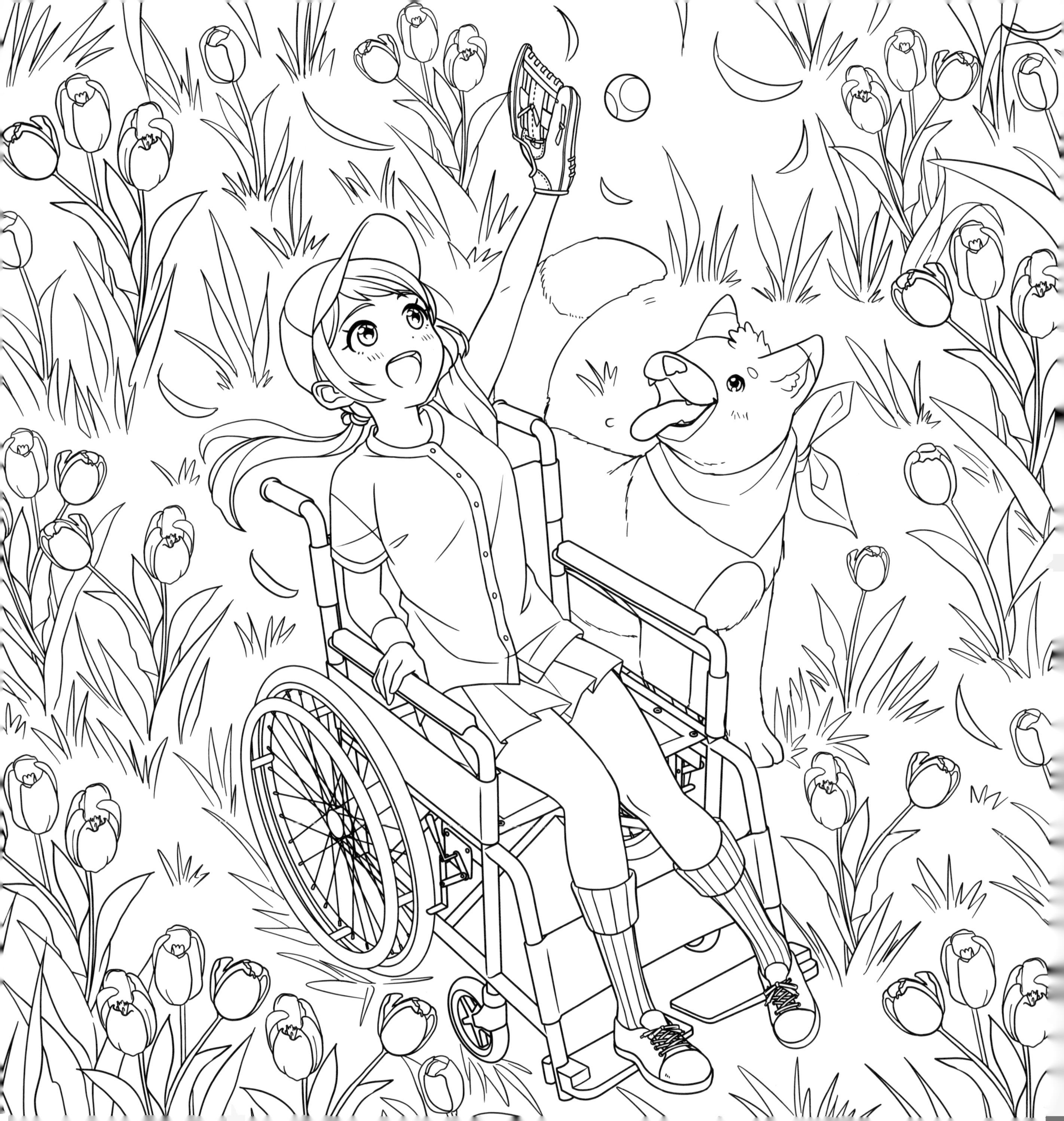

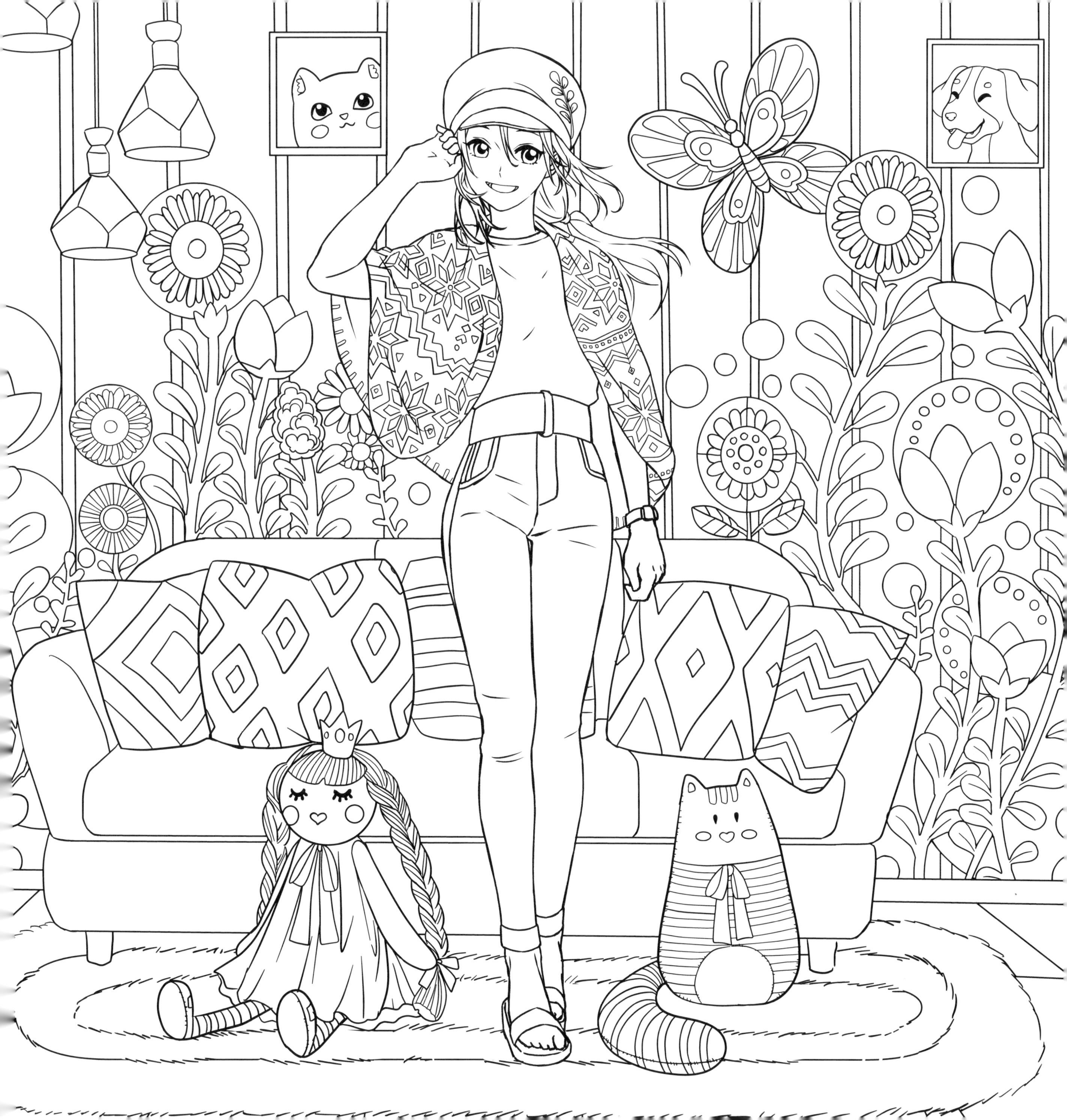

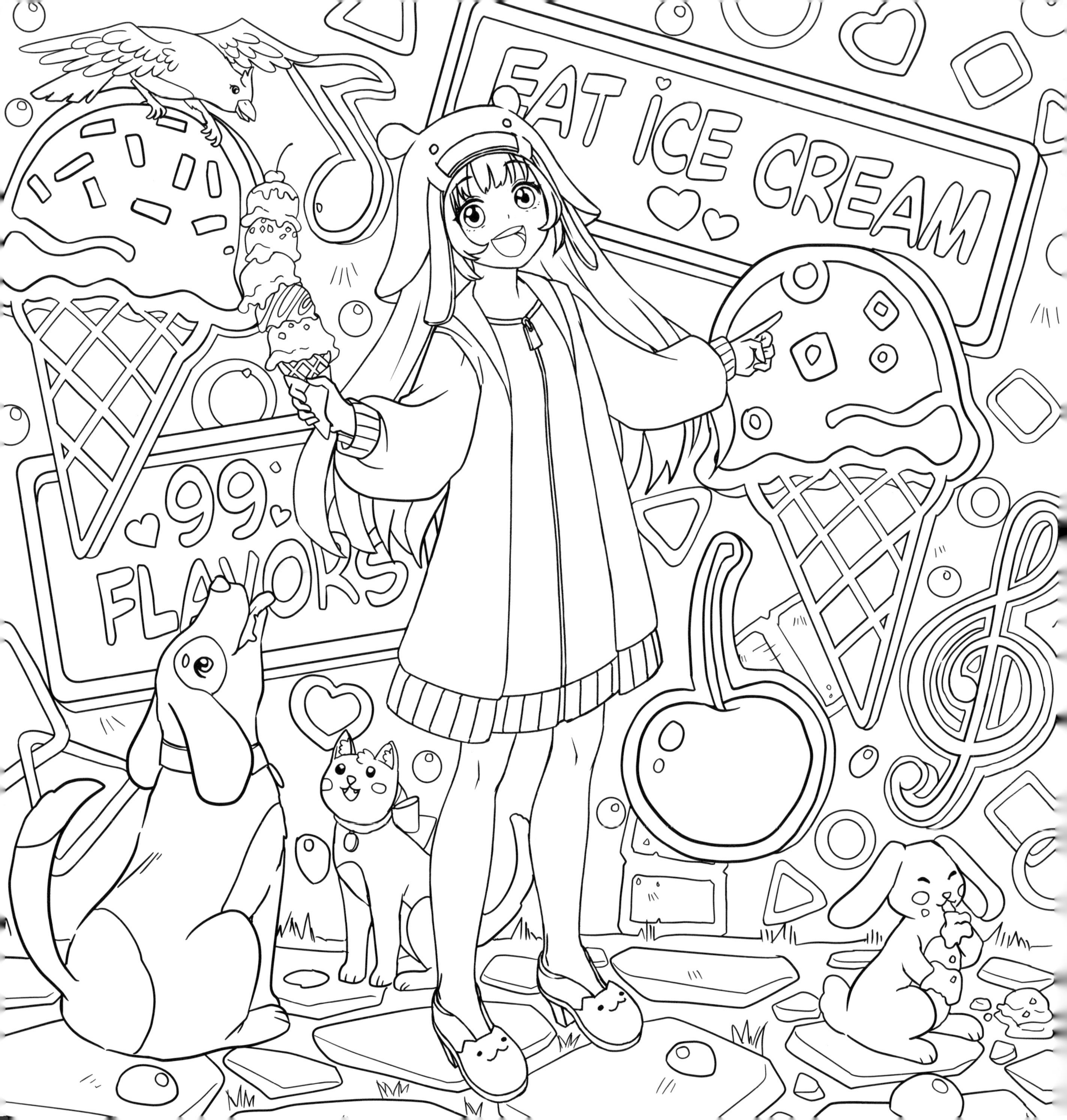
EAT ICE CREAM
99 FLAVORS

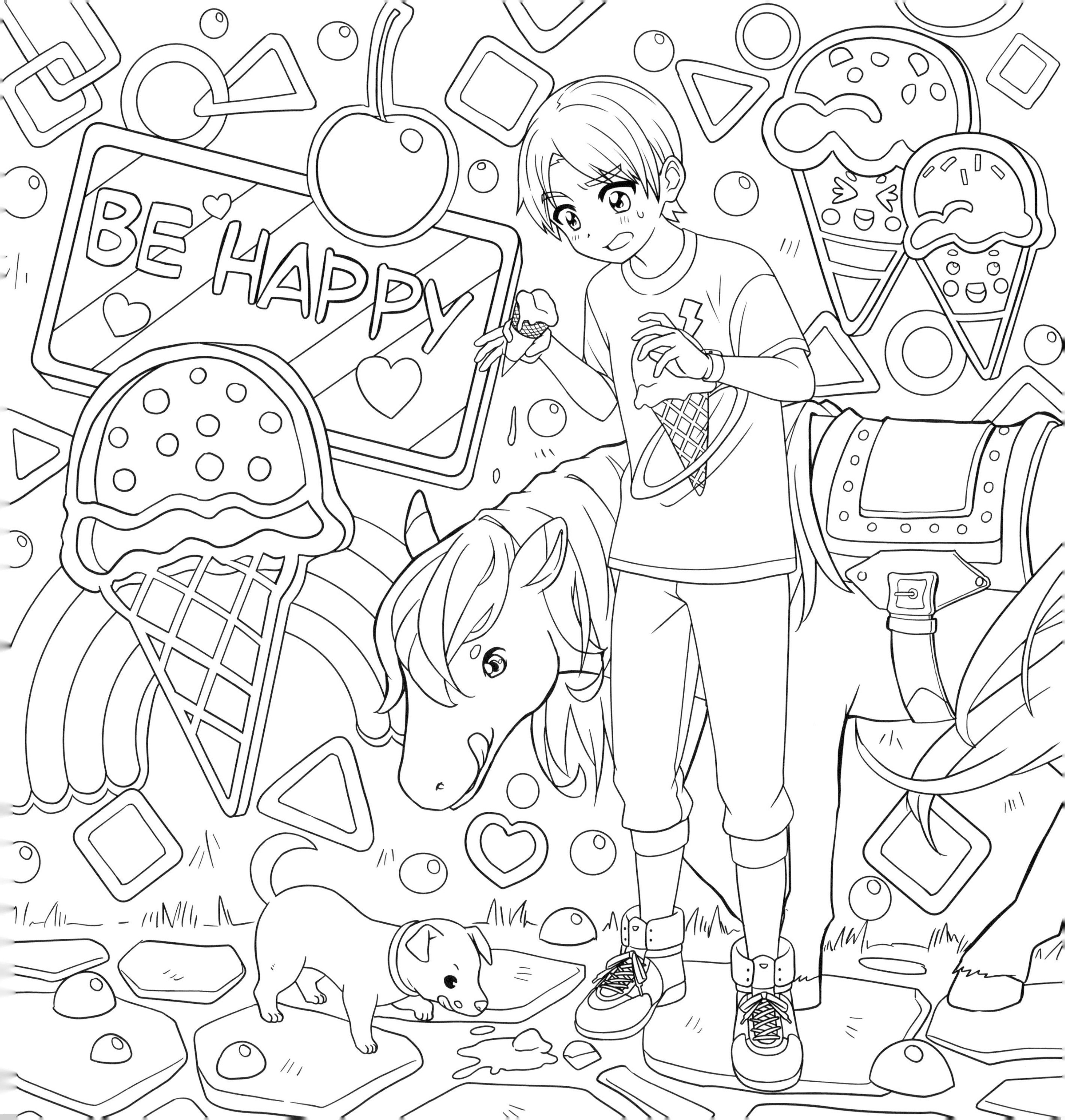
BE HAPPY

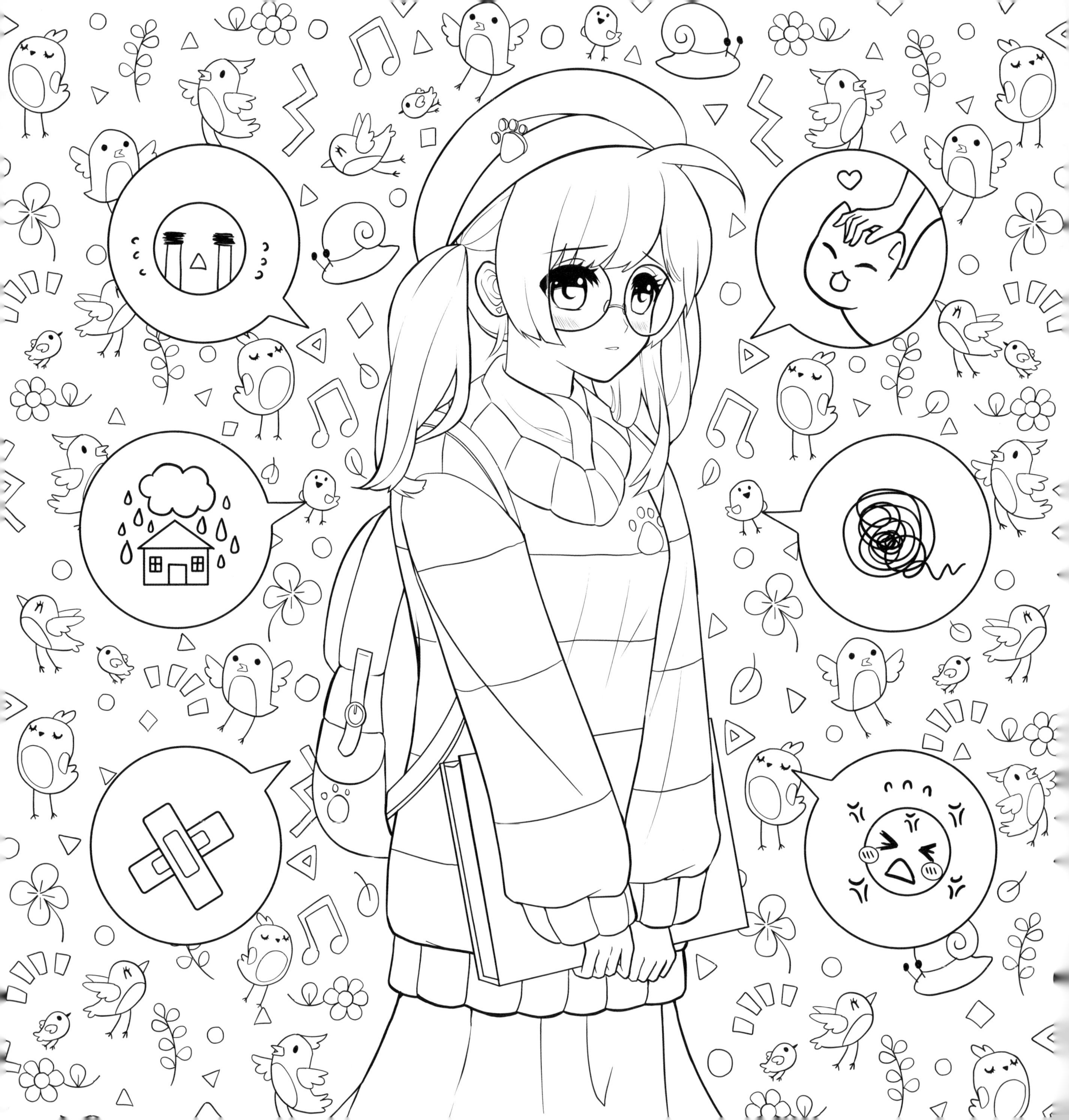

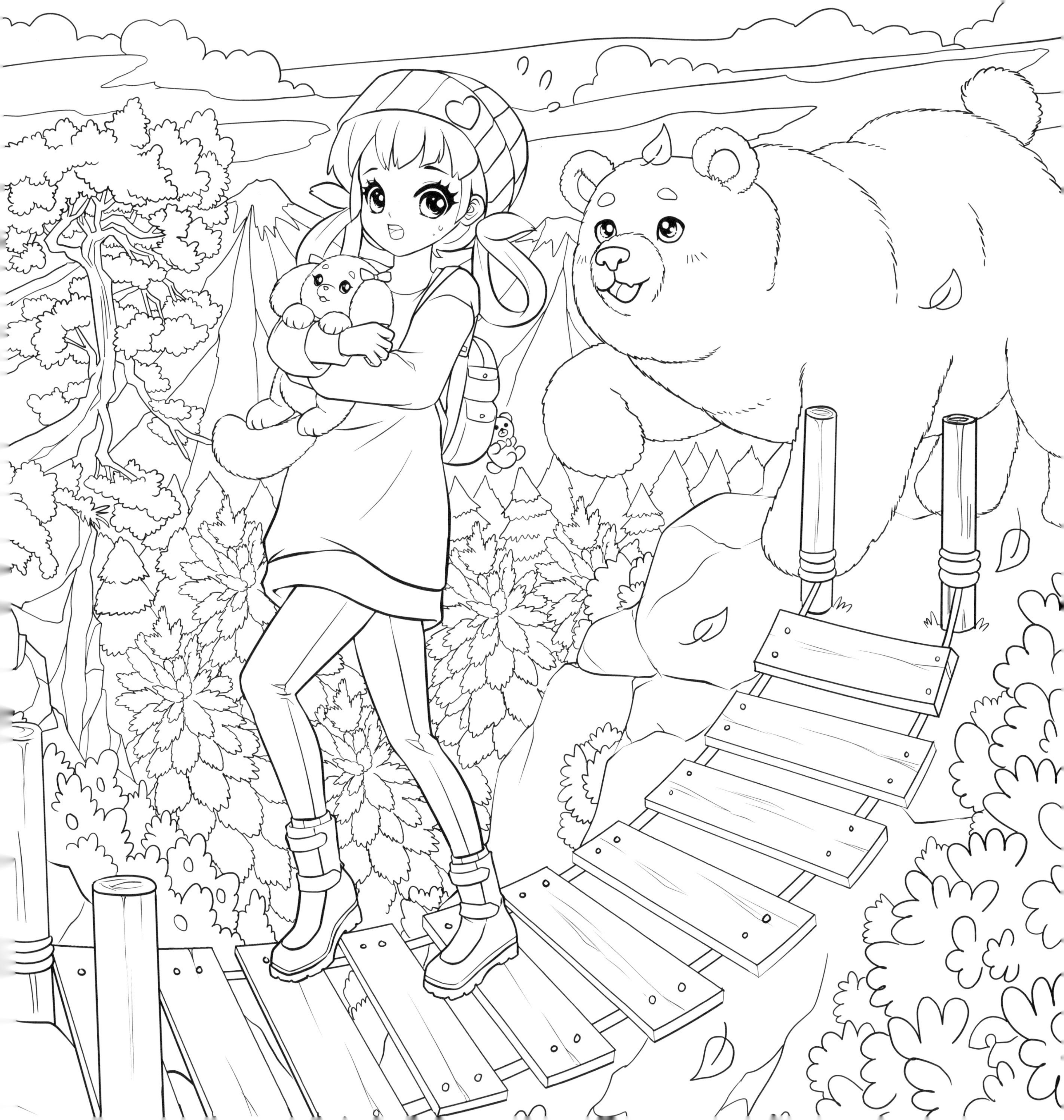

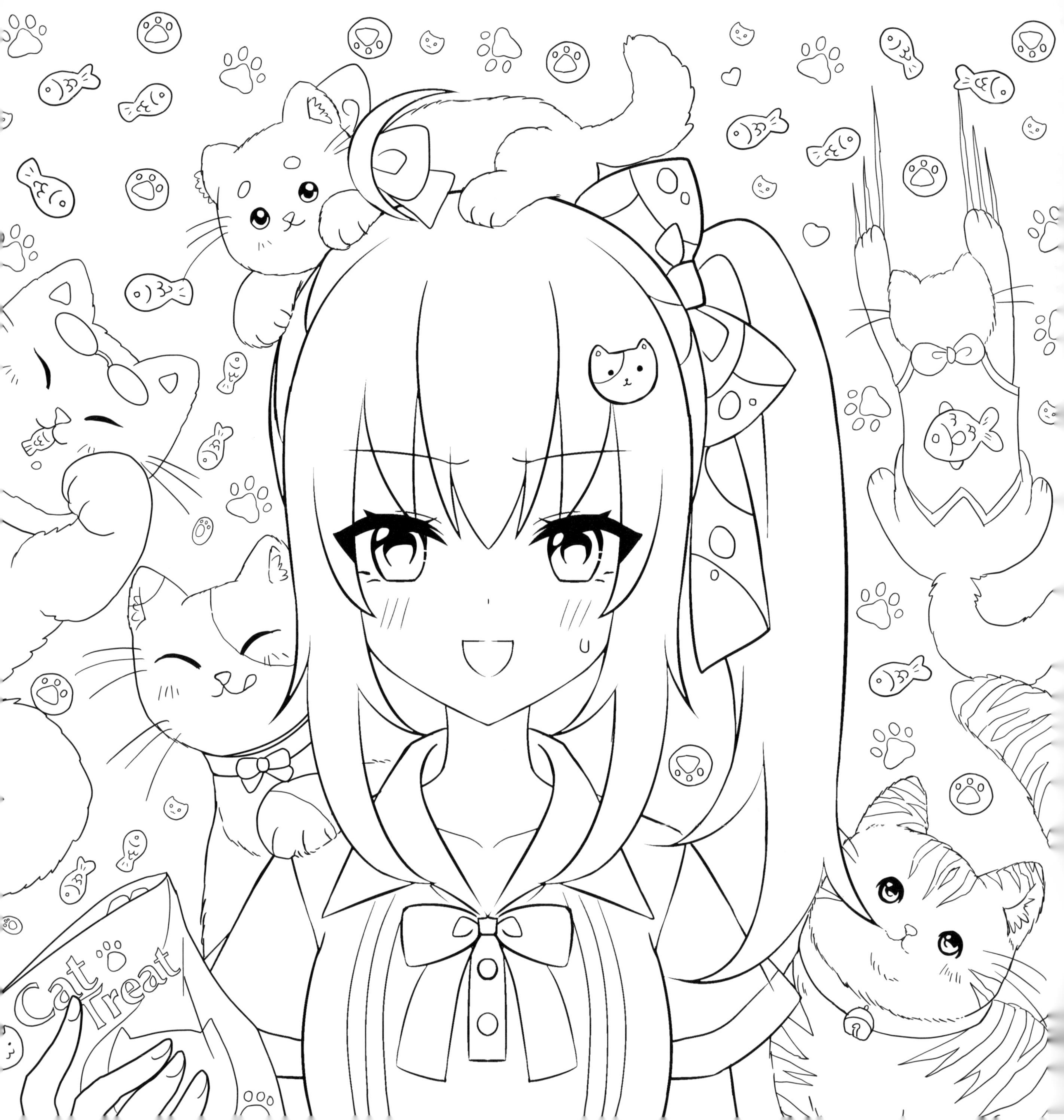
Cat
Treat

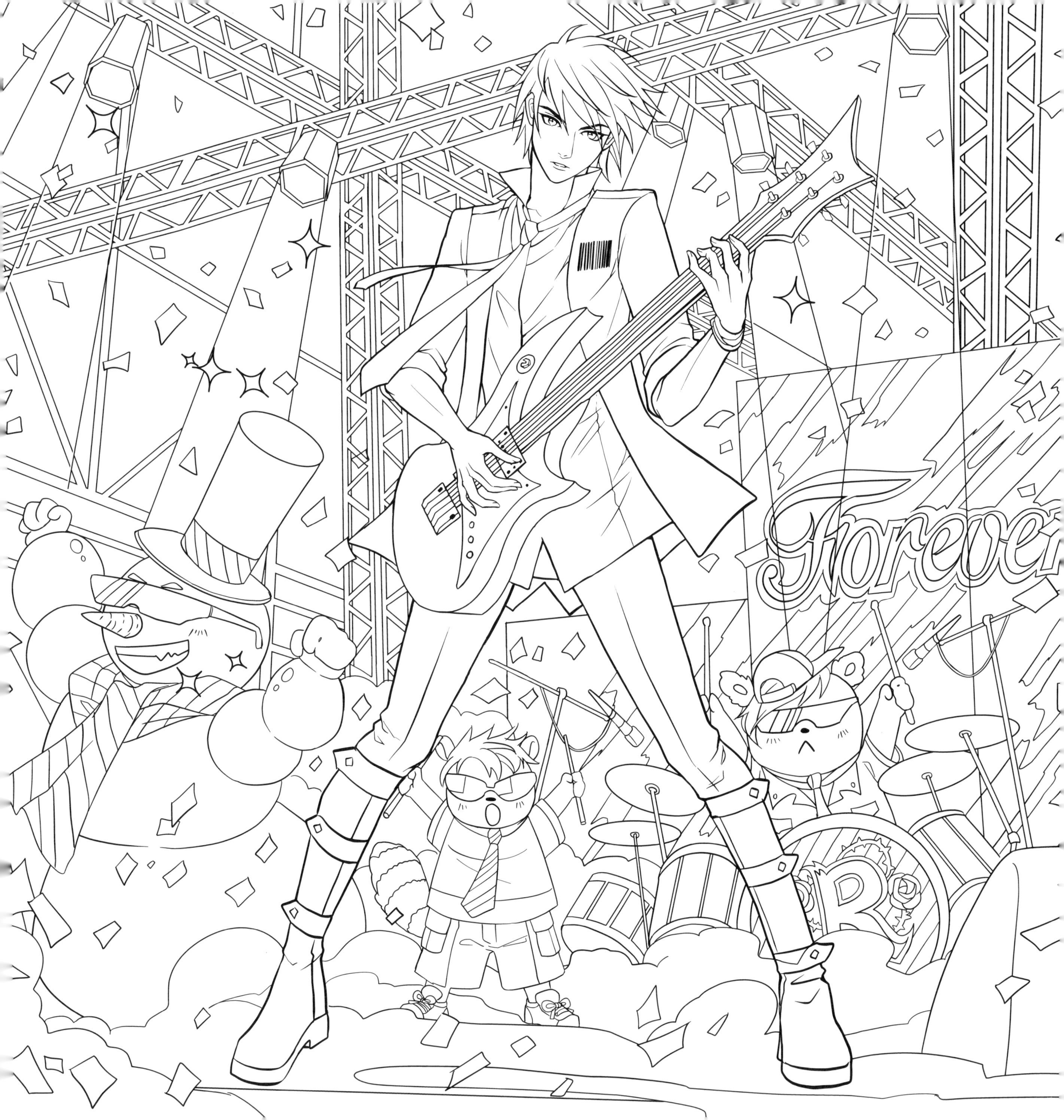
Foreve

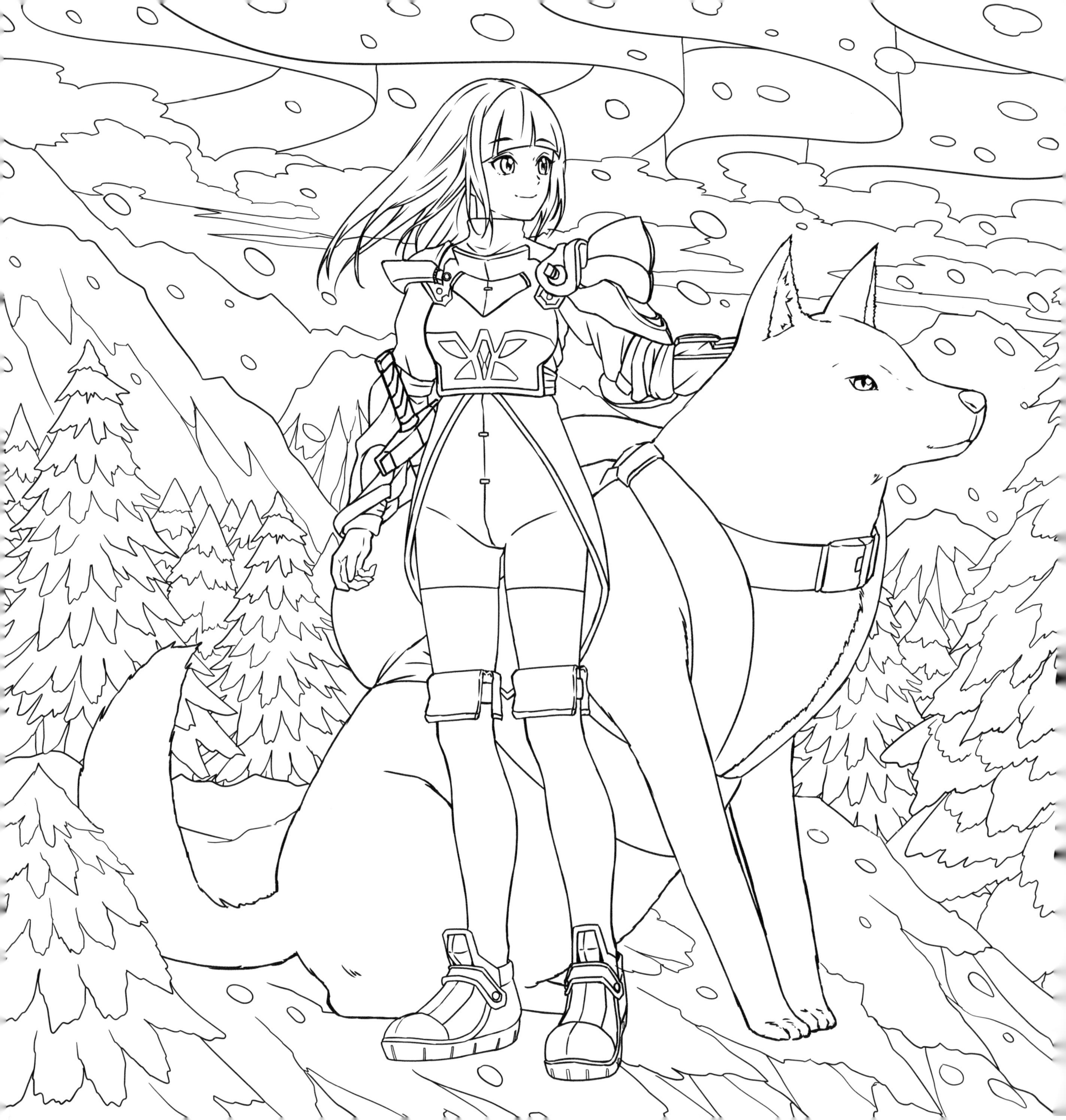

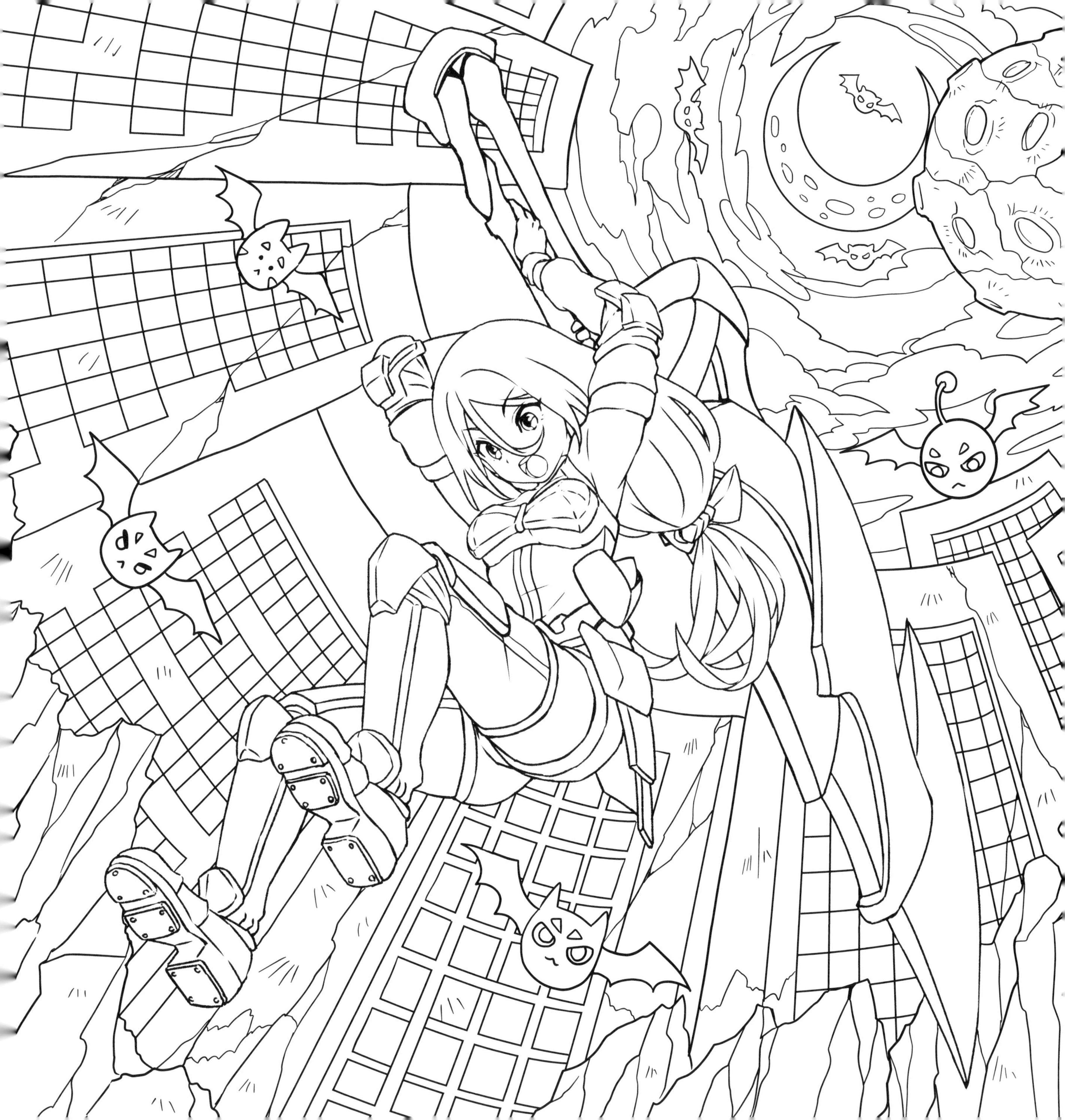

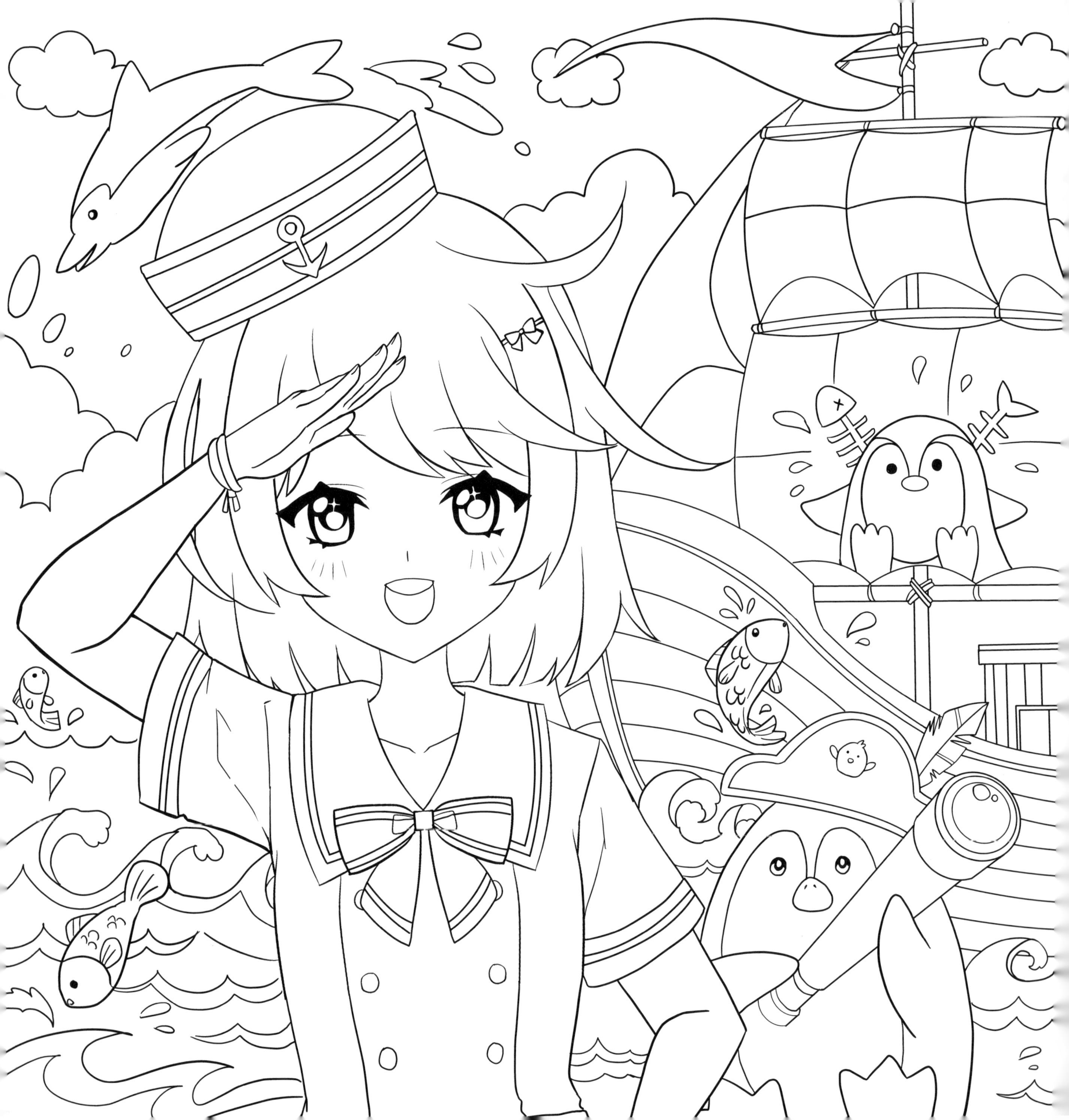

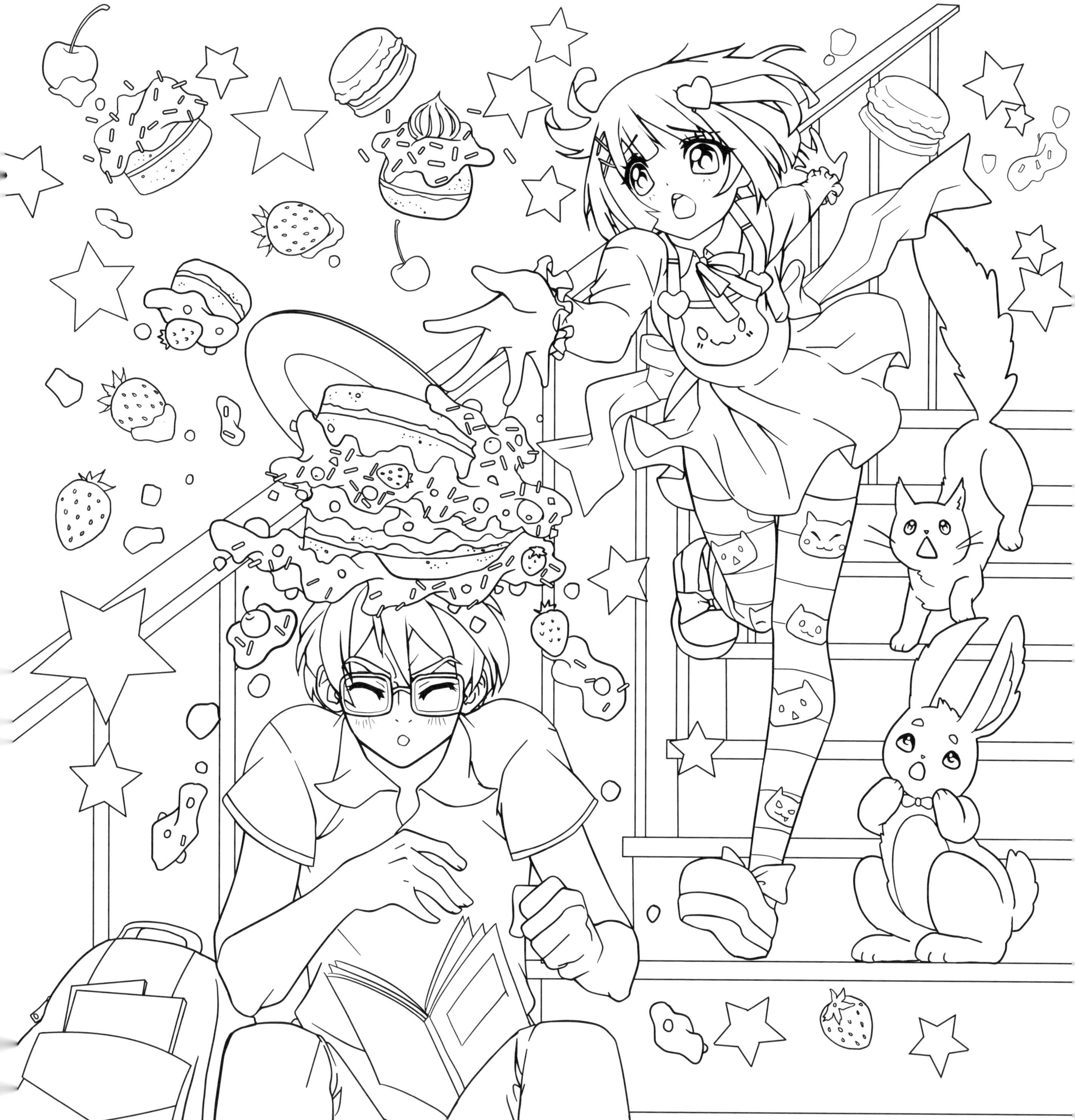

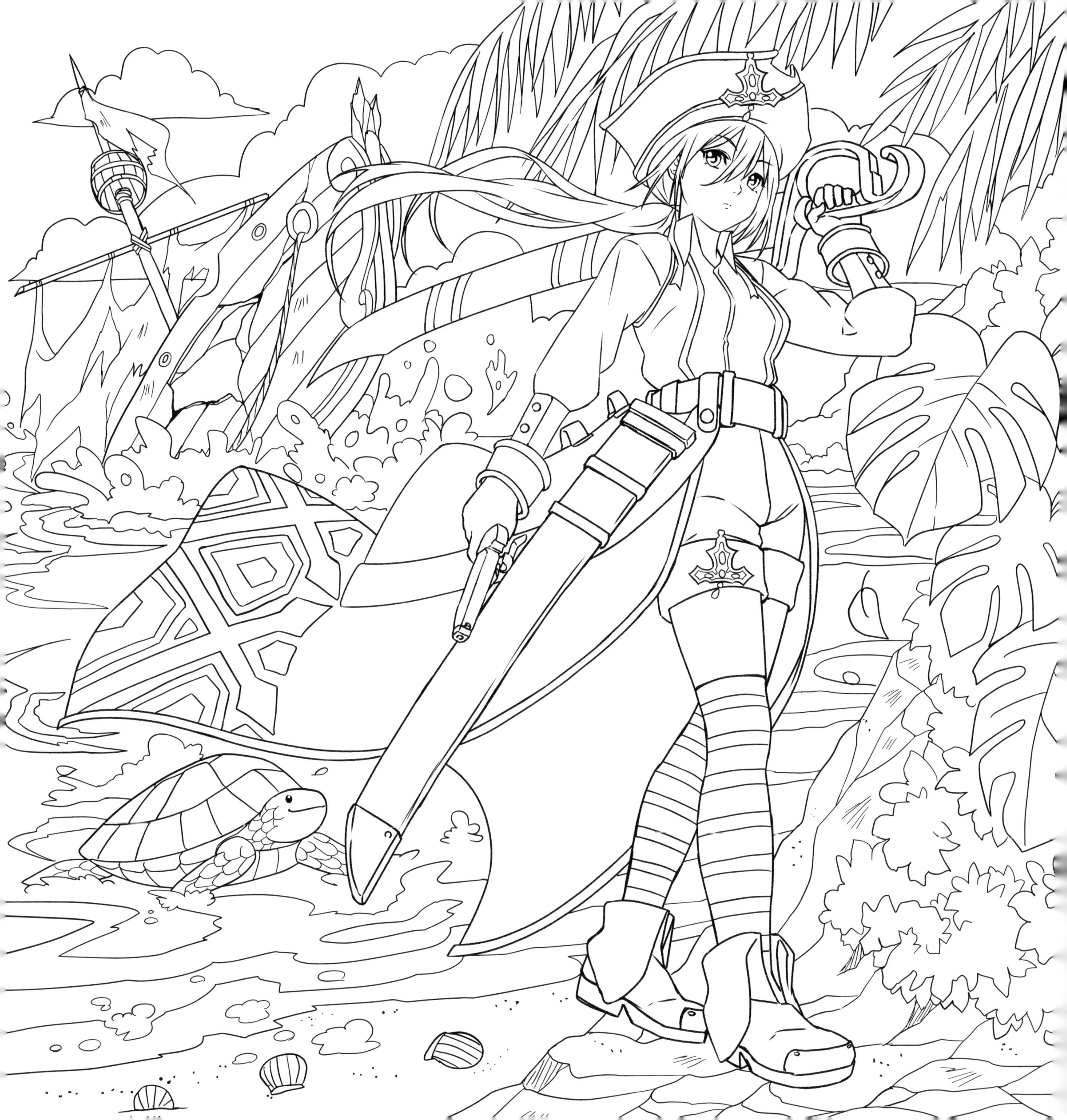

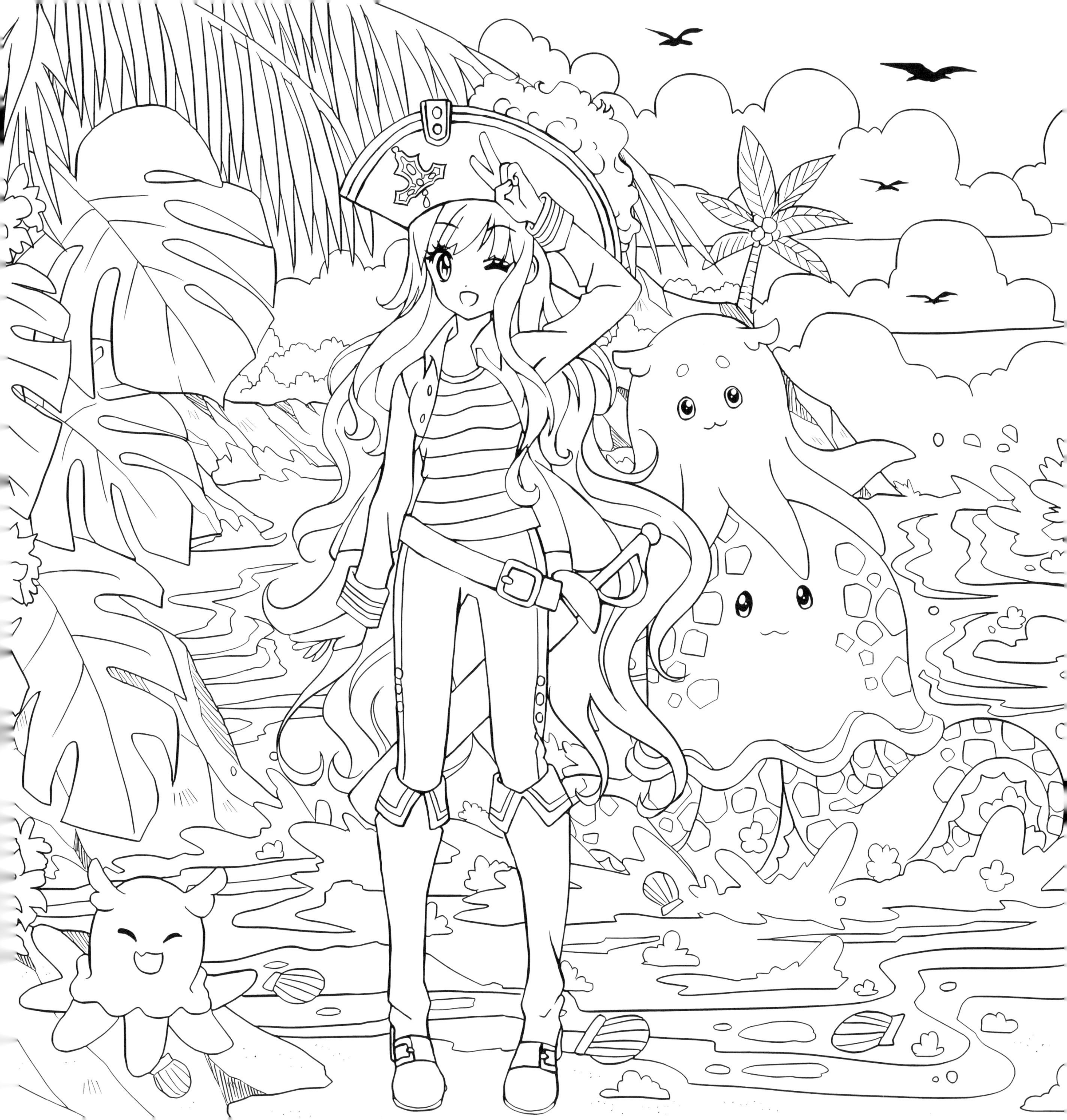

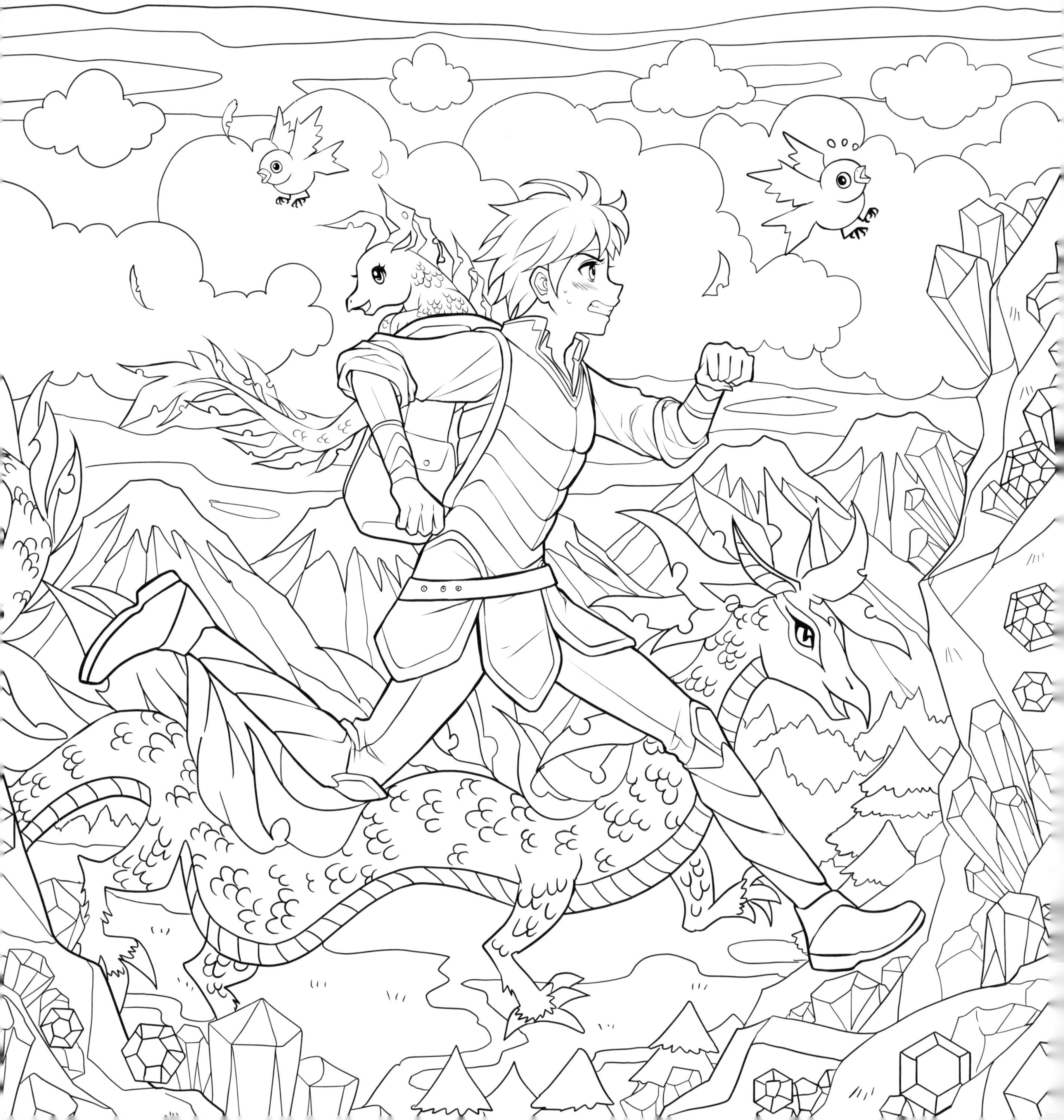

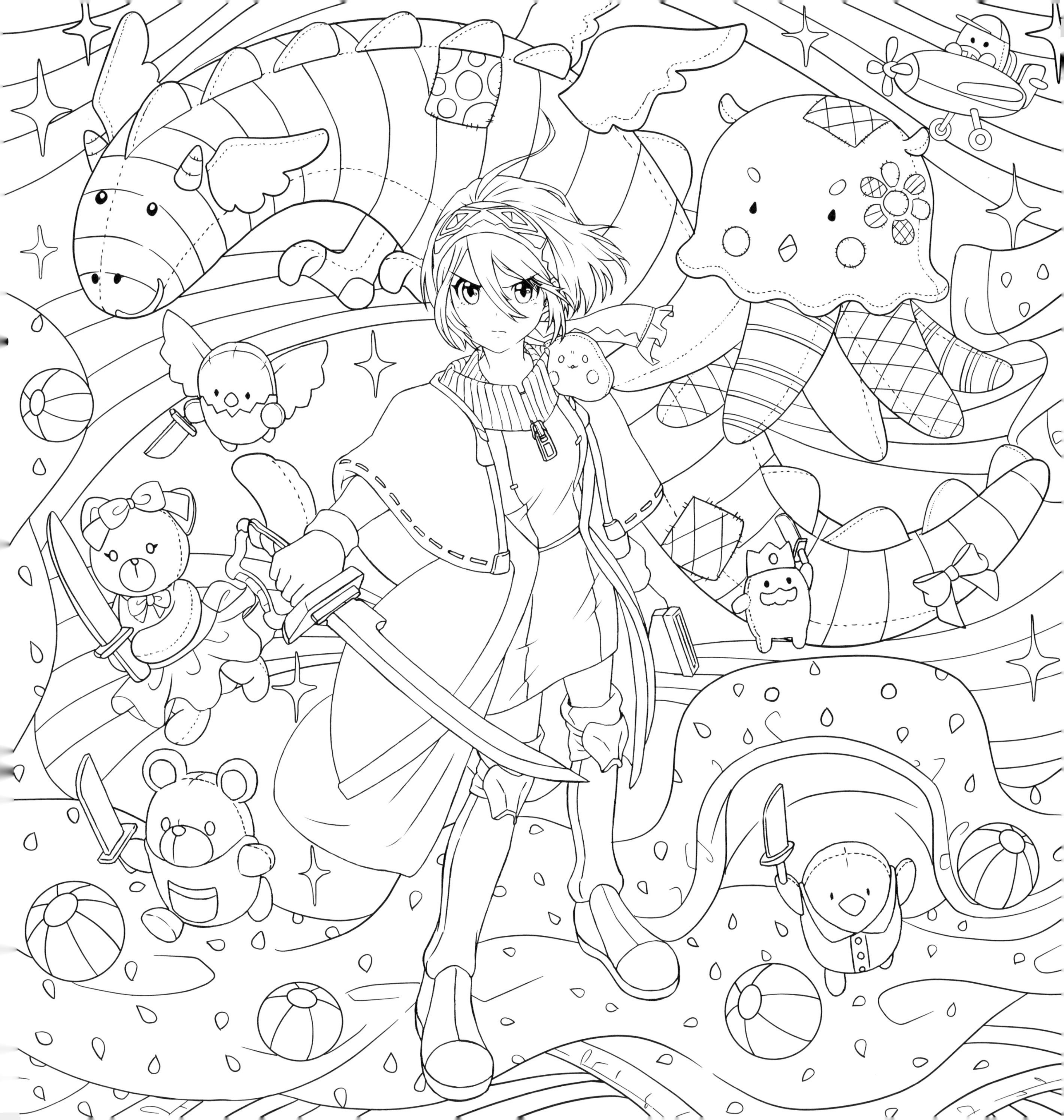

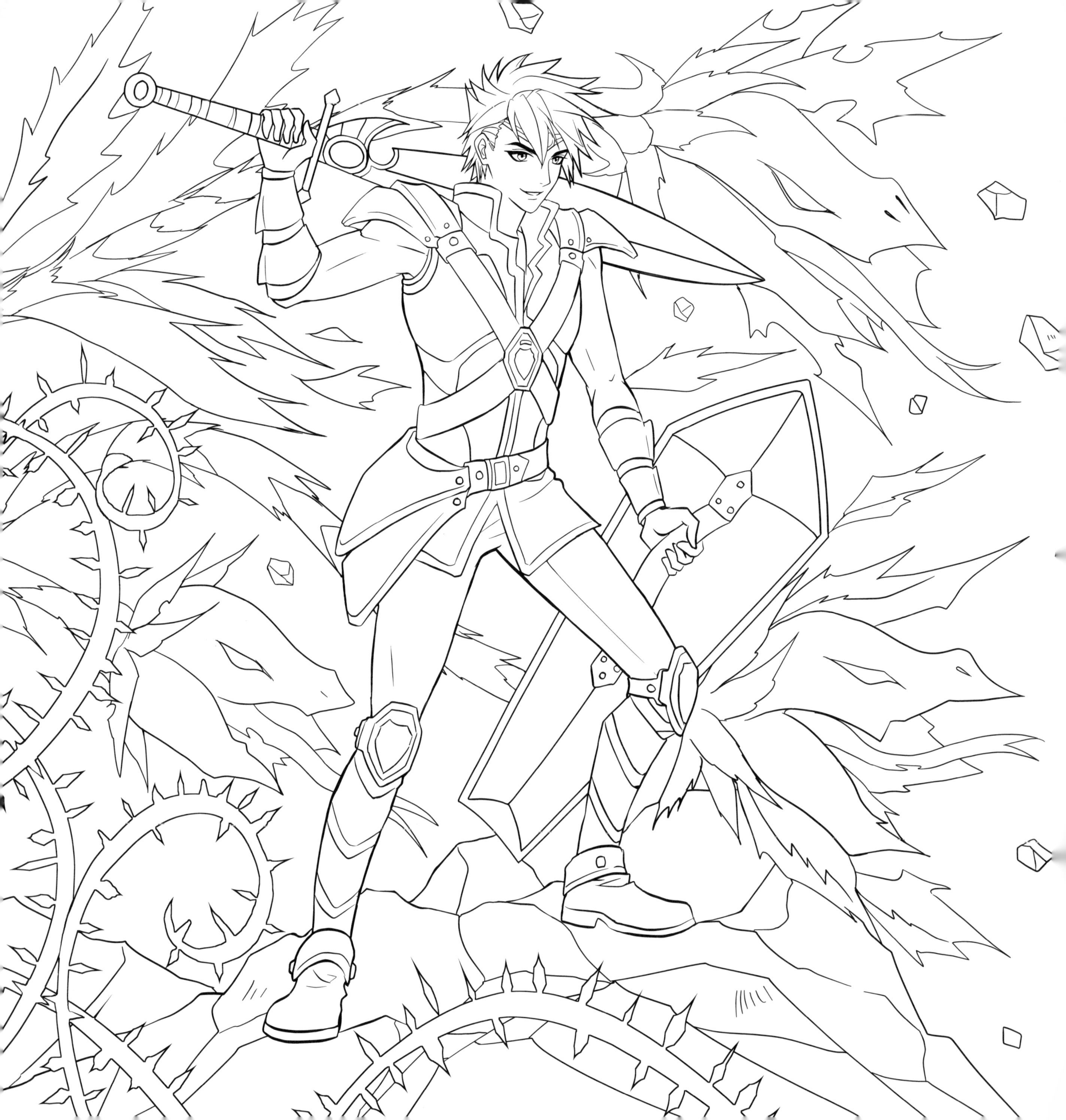

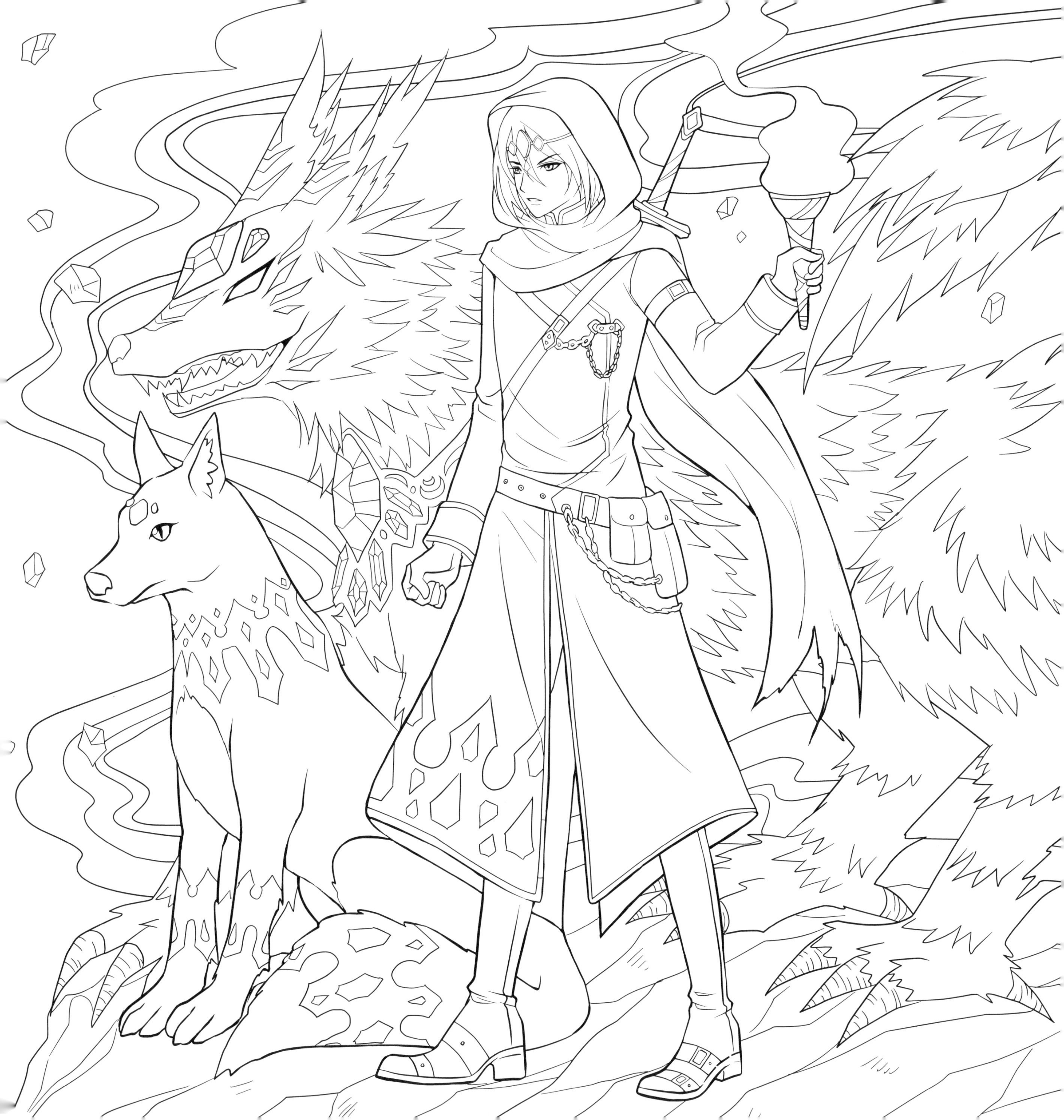

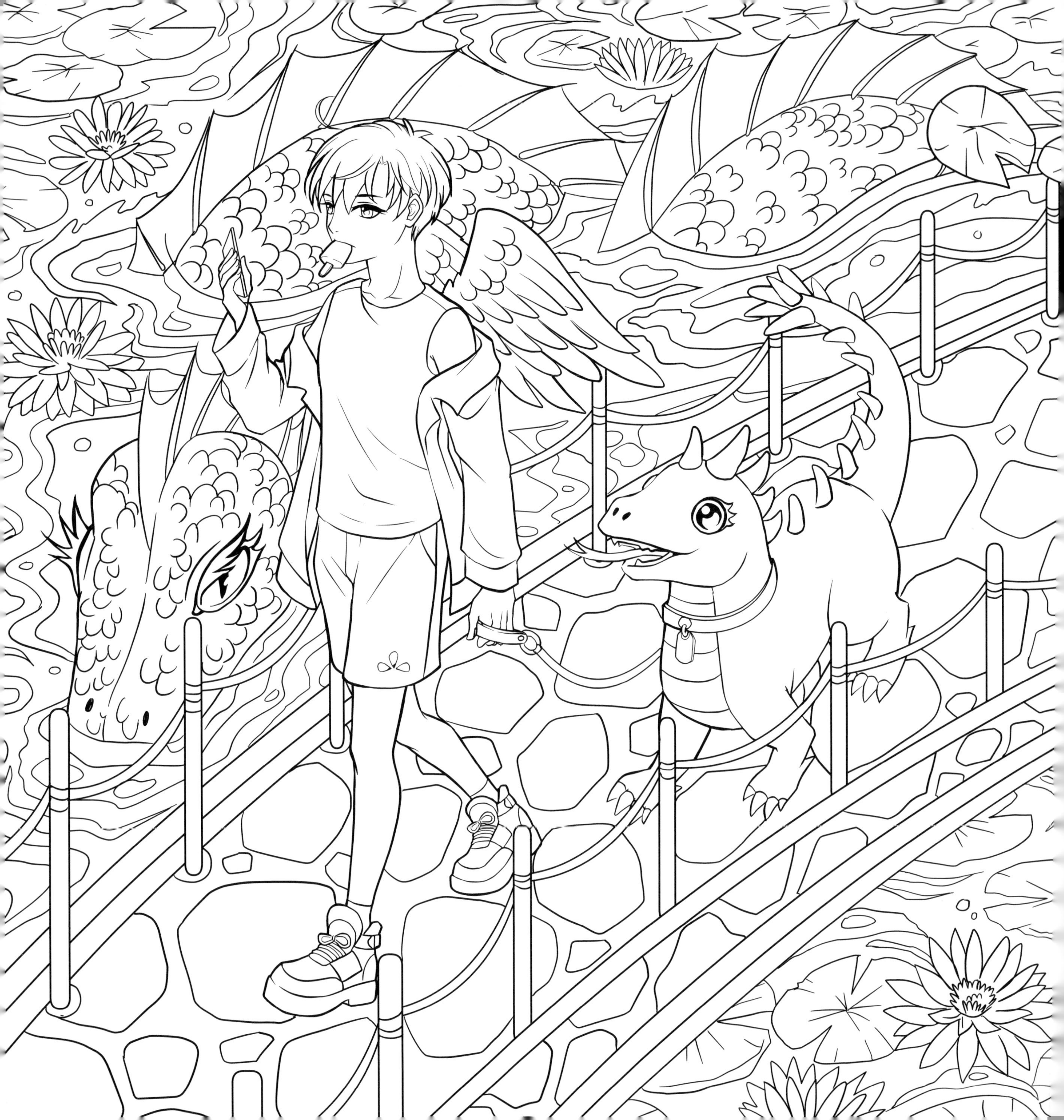

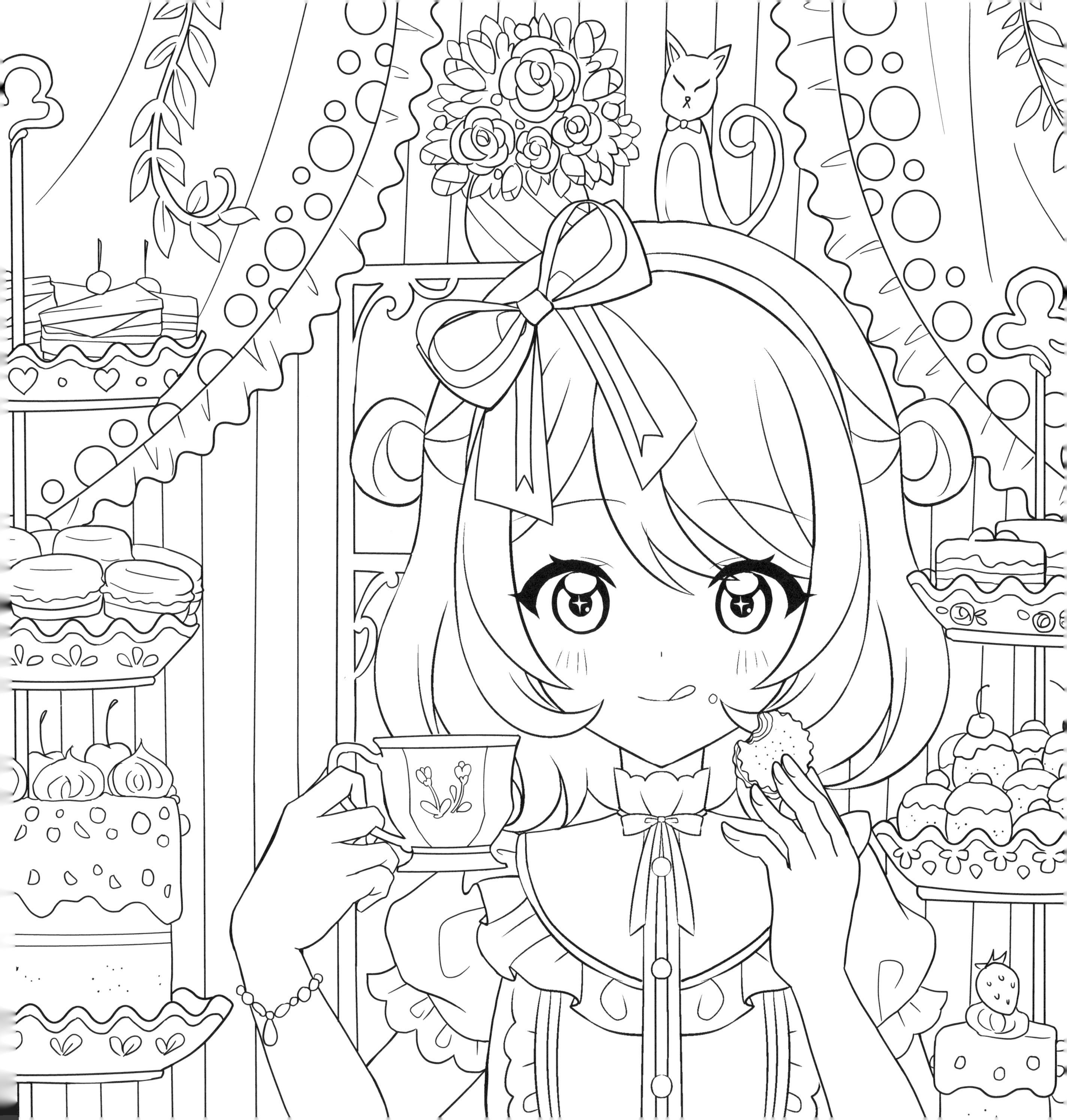

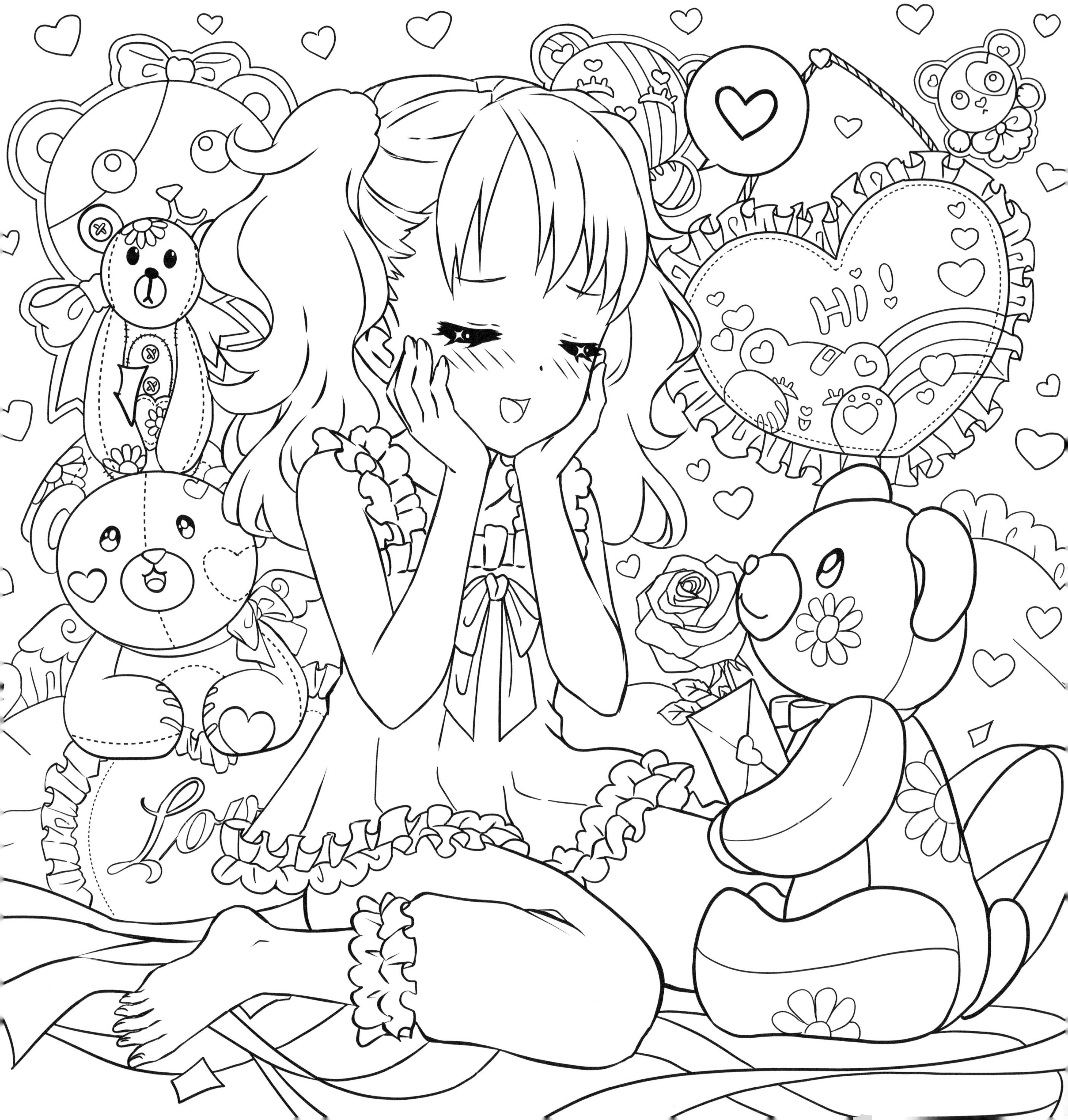
HI !

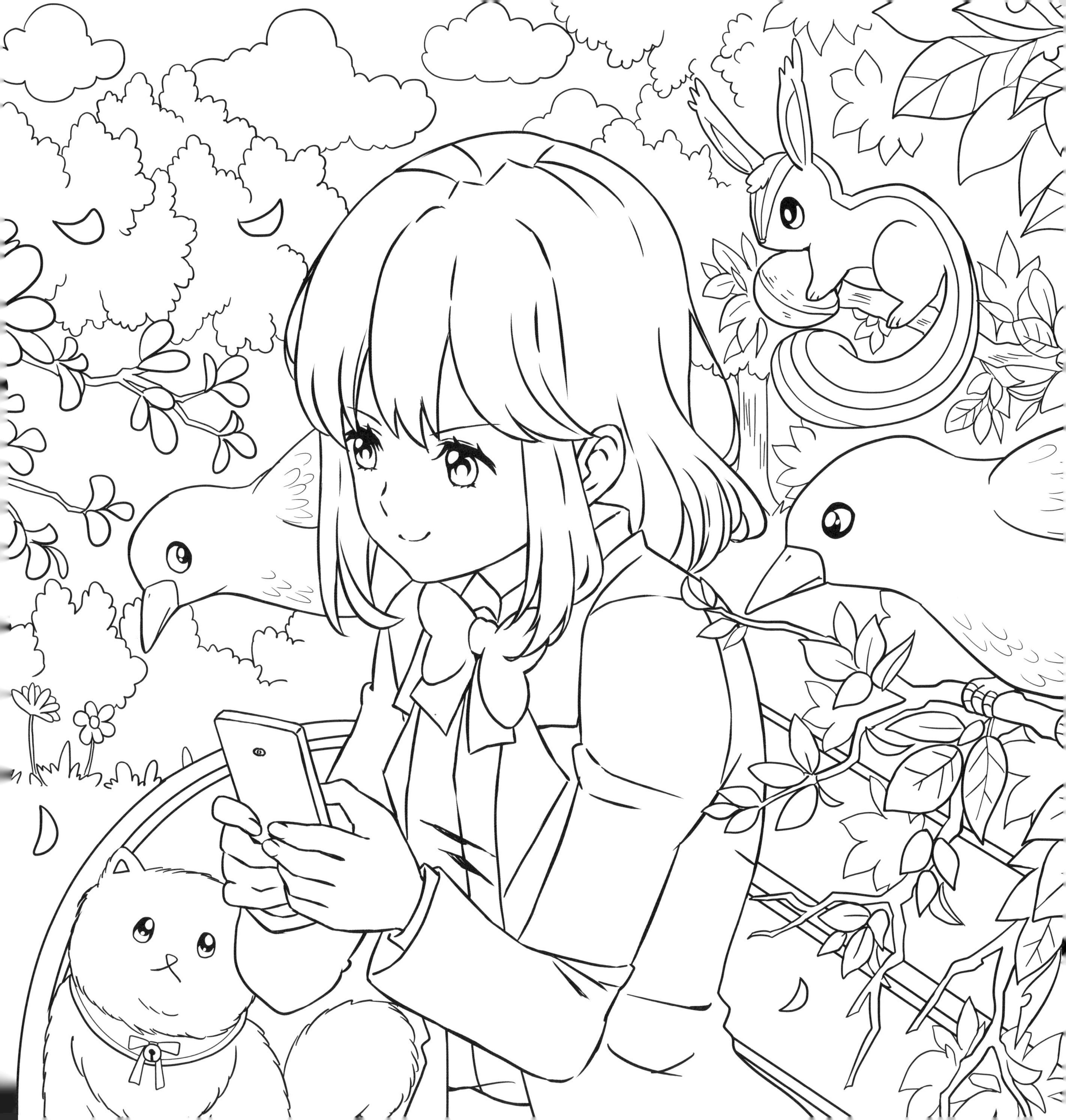

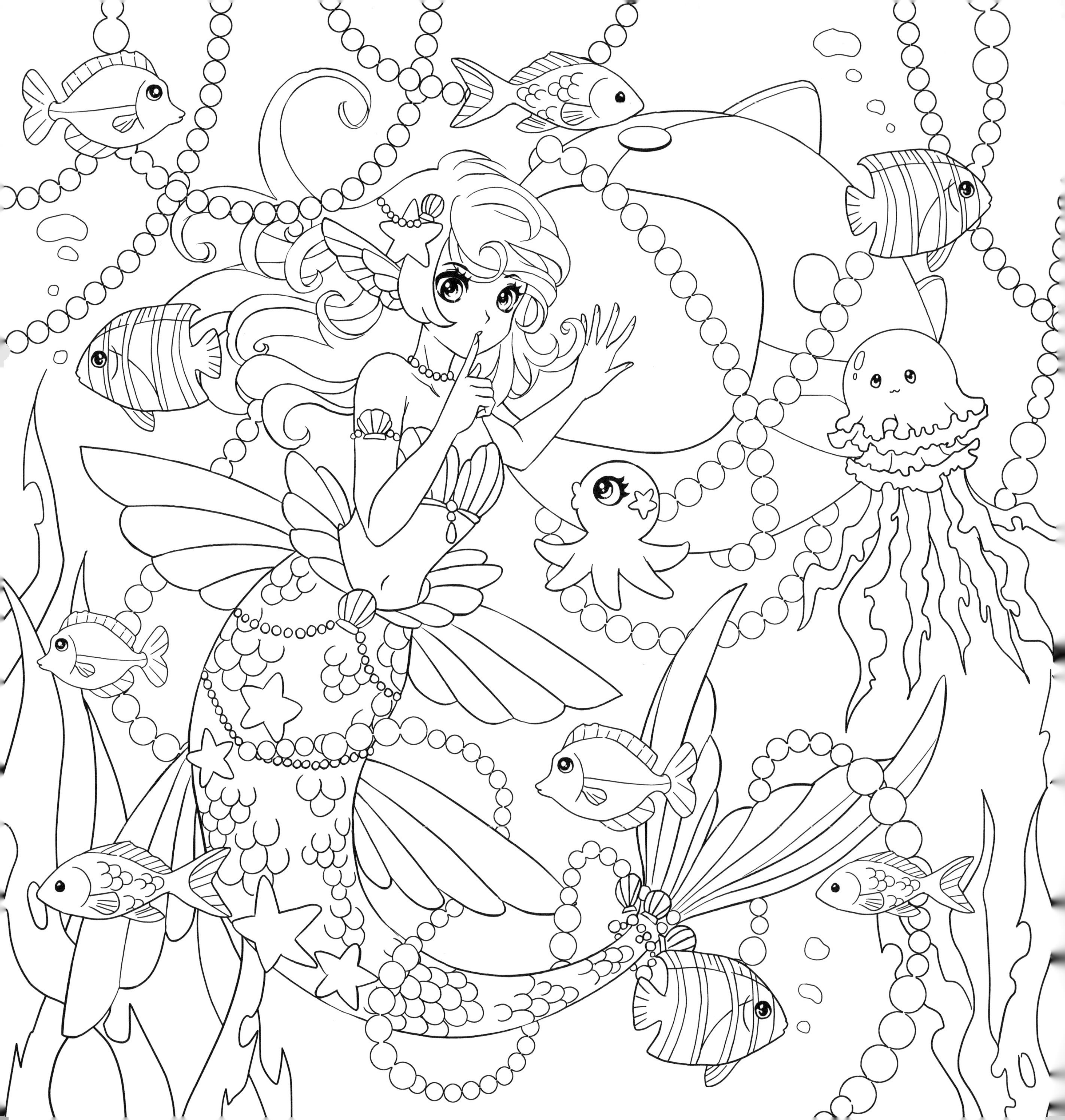

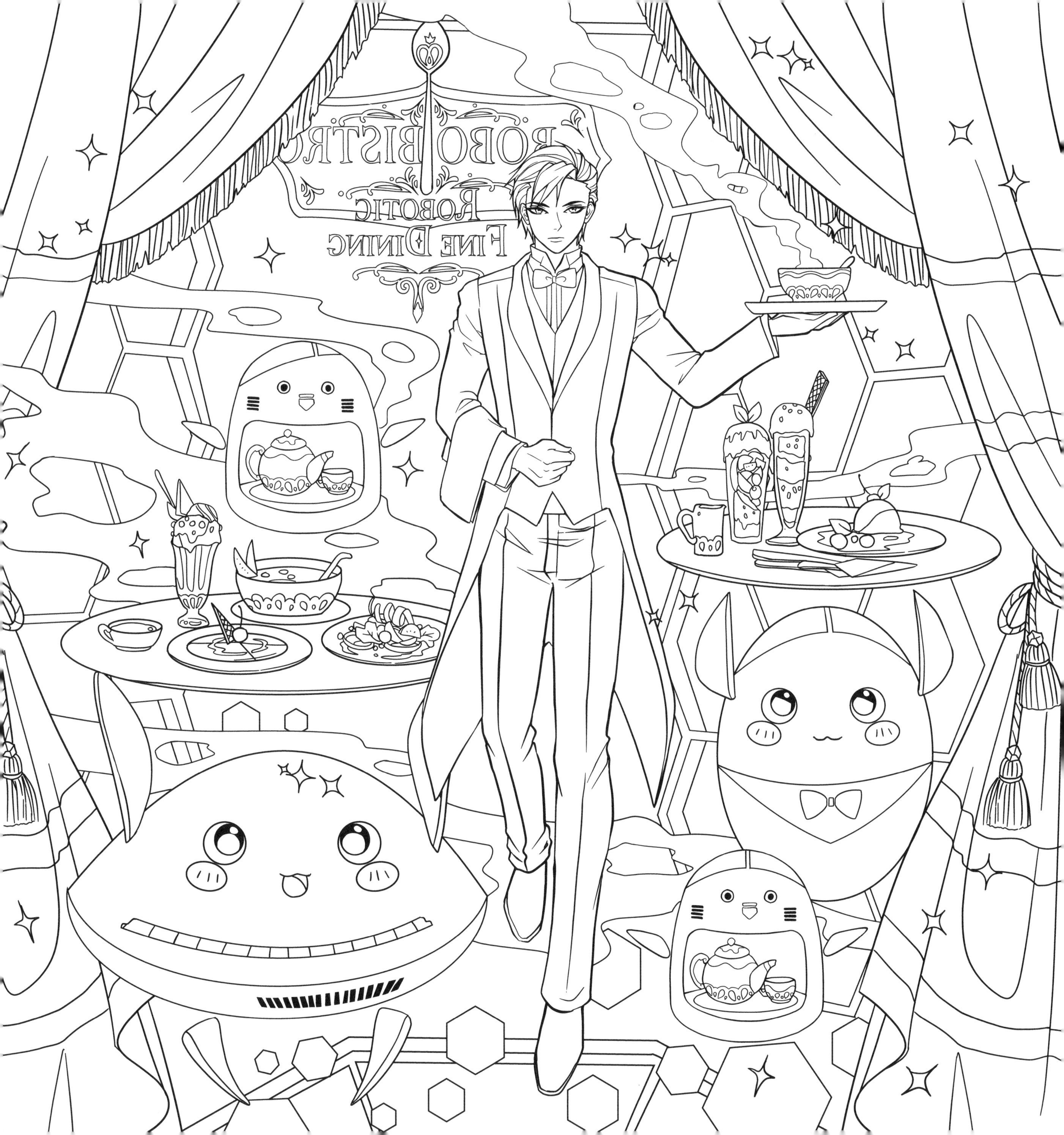
ROBO BISTRO
ROBOTIC
FINE DINING

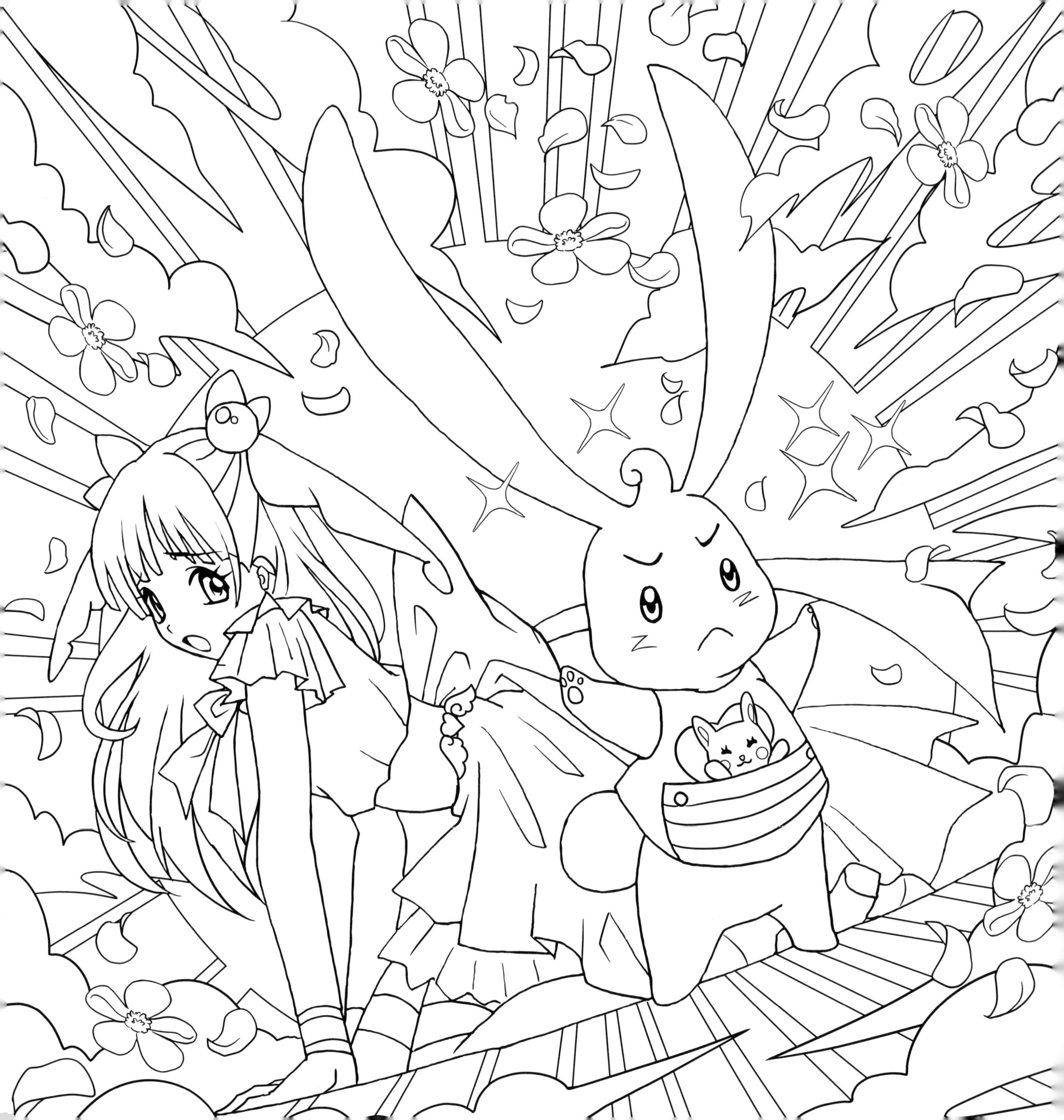

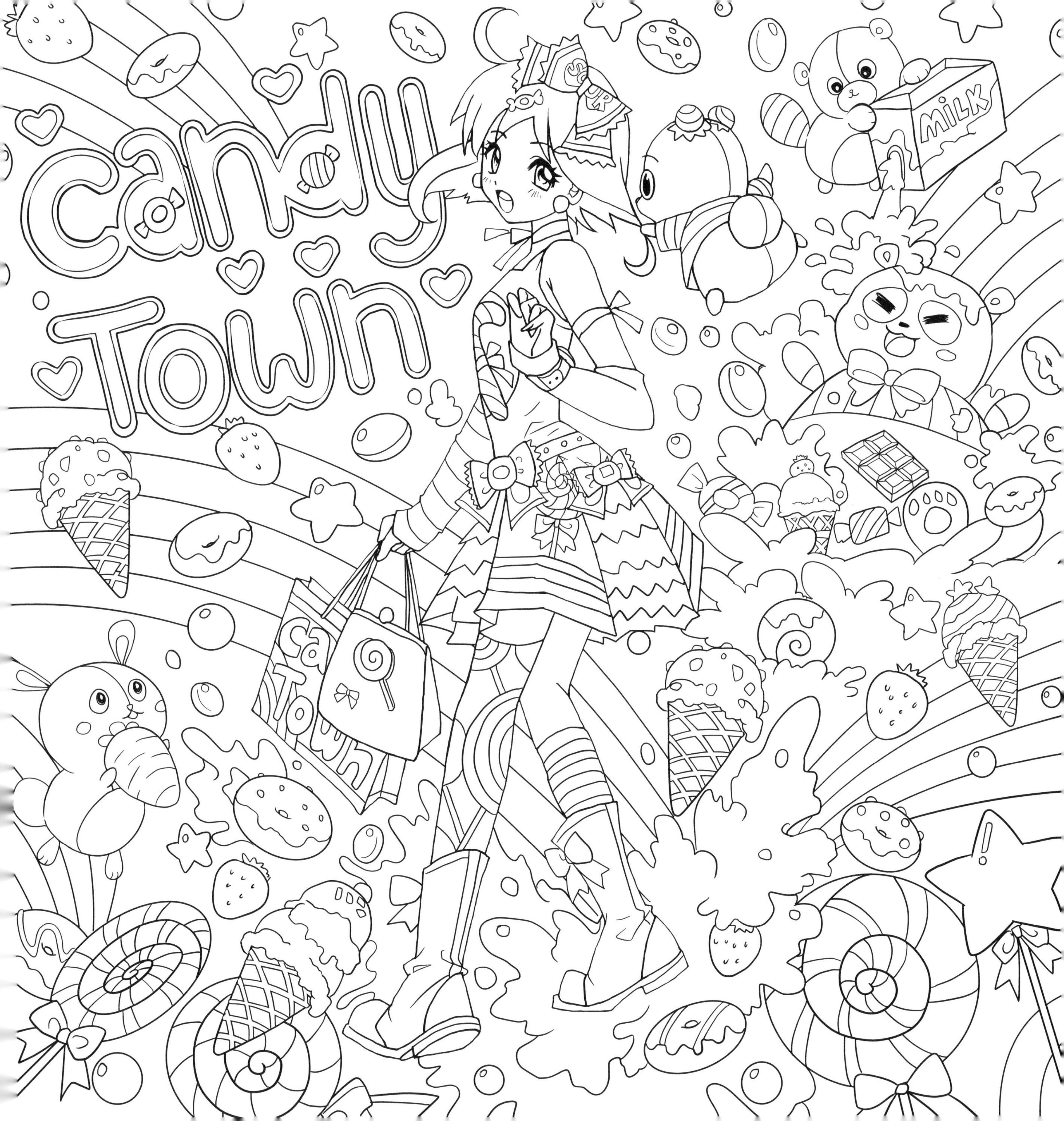
Candy
Town
MILK

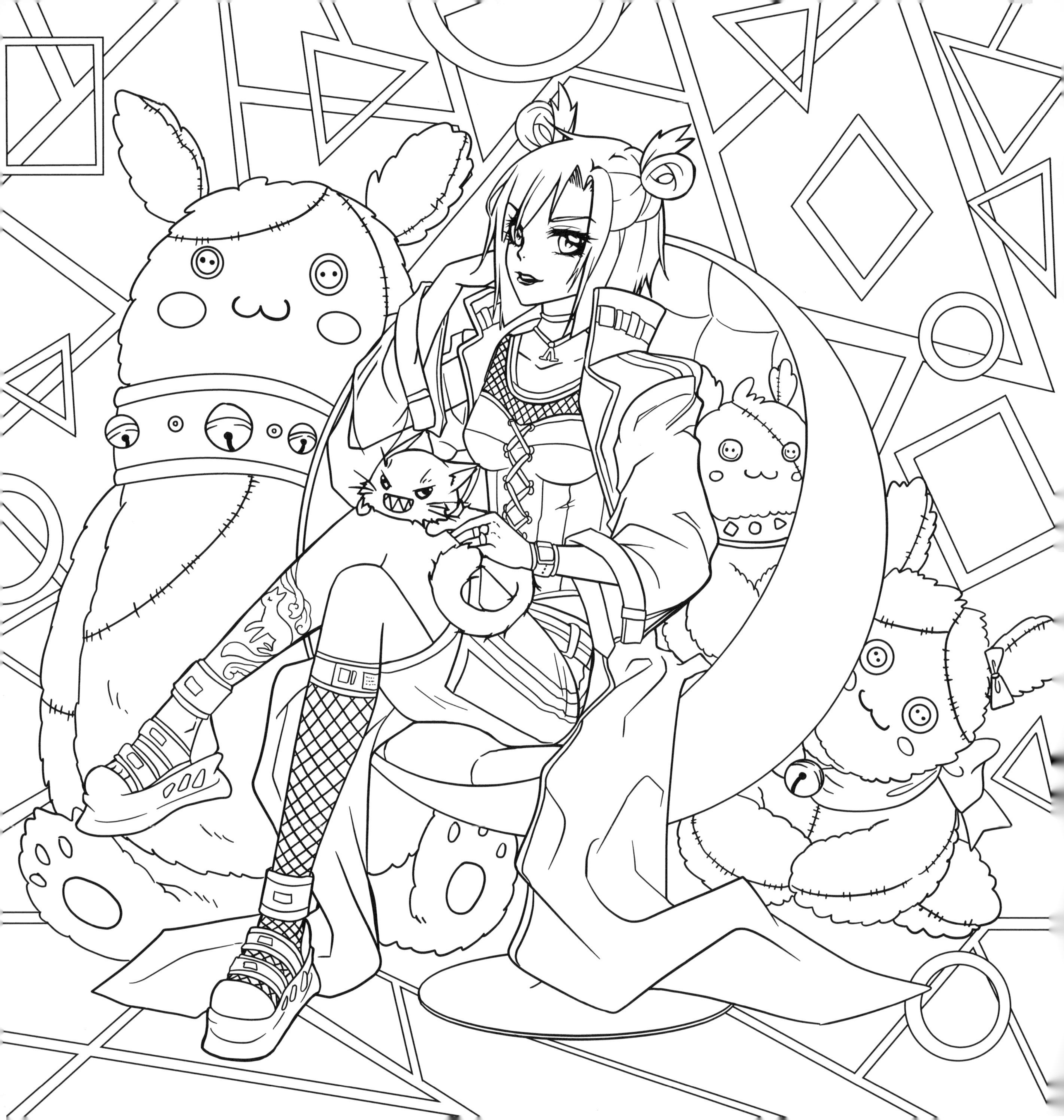

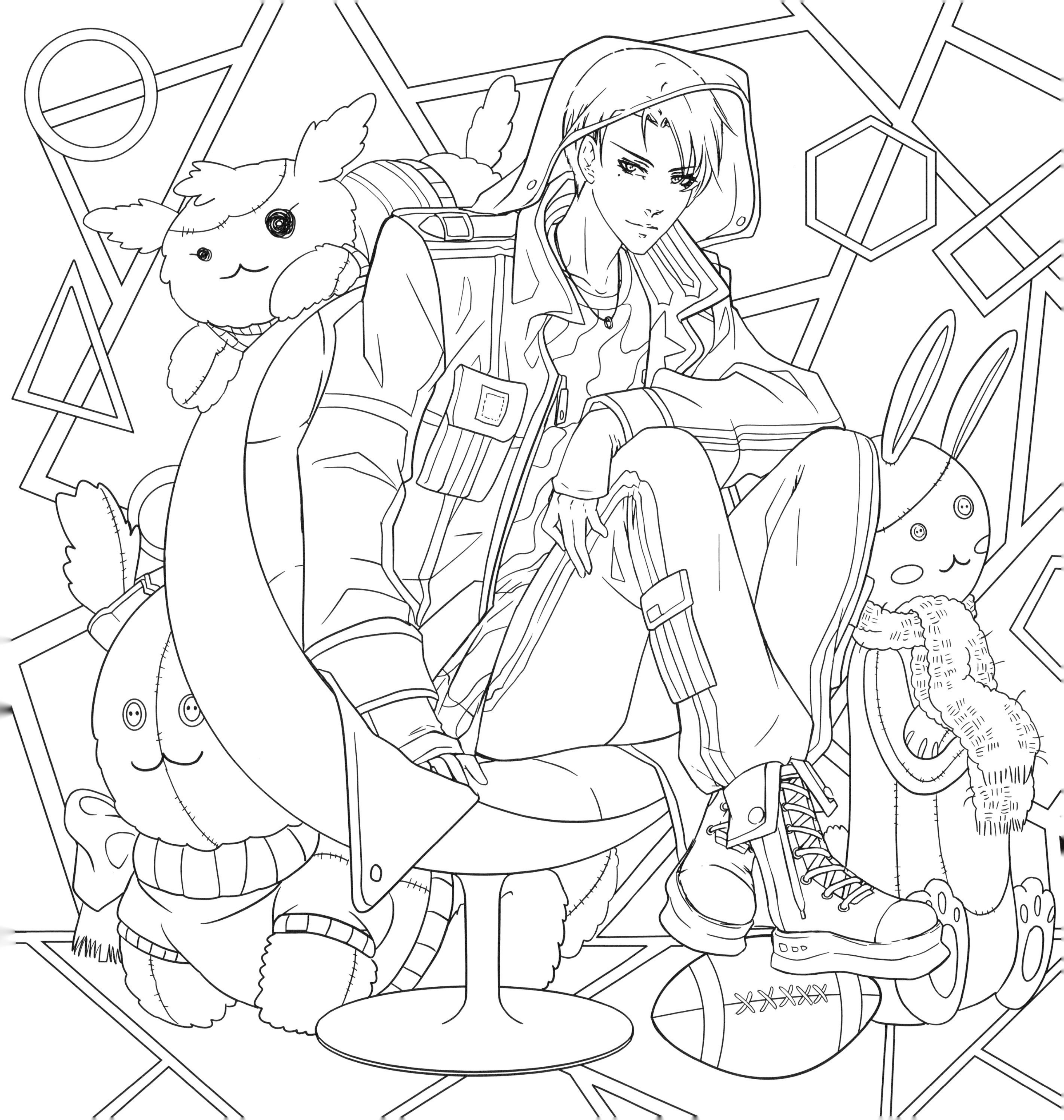

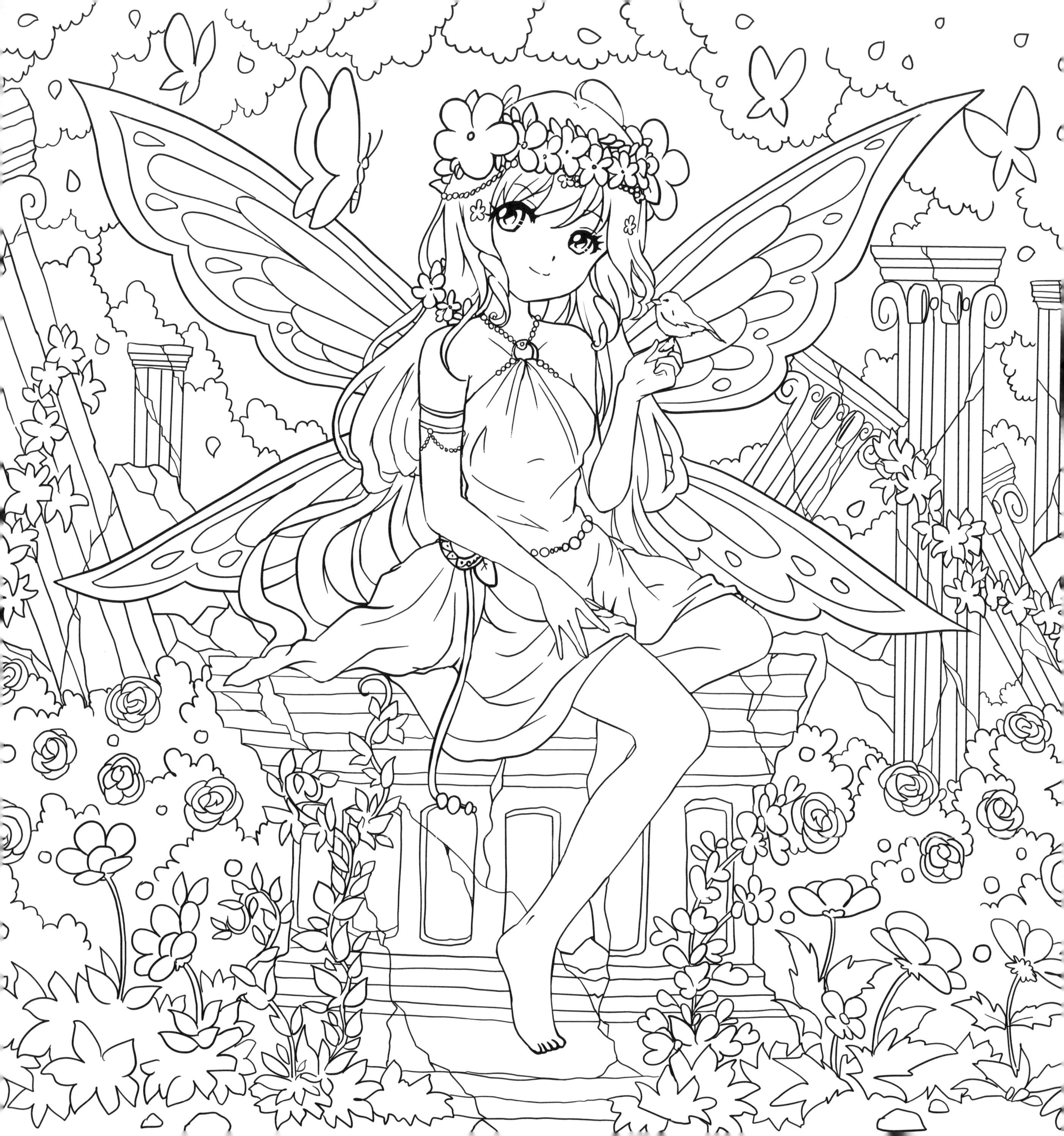

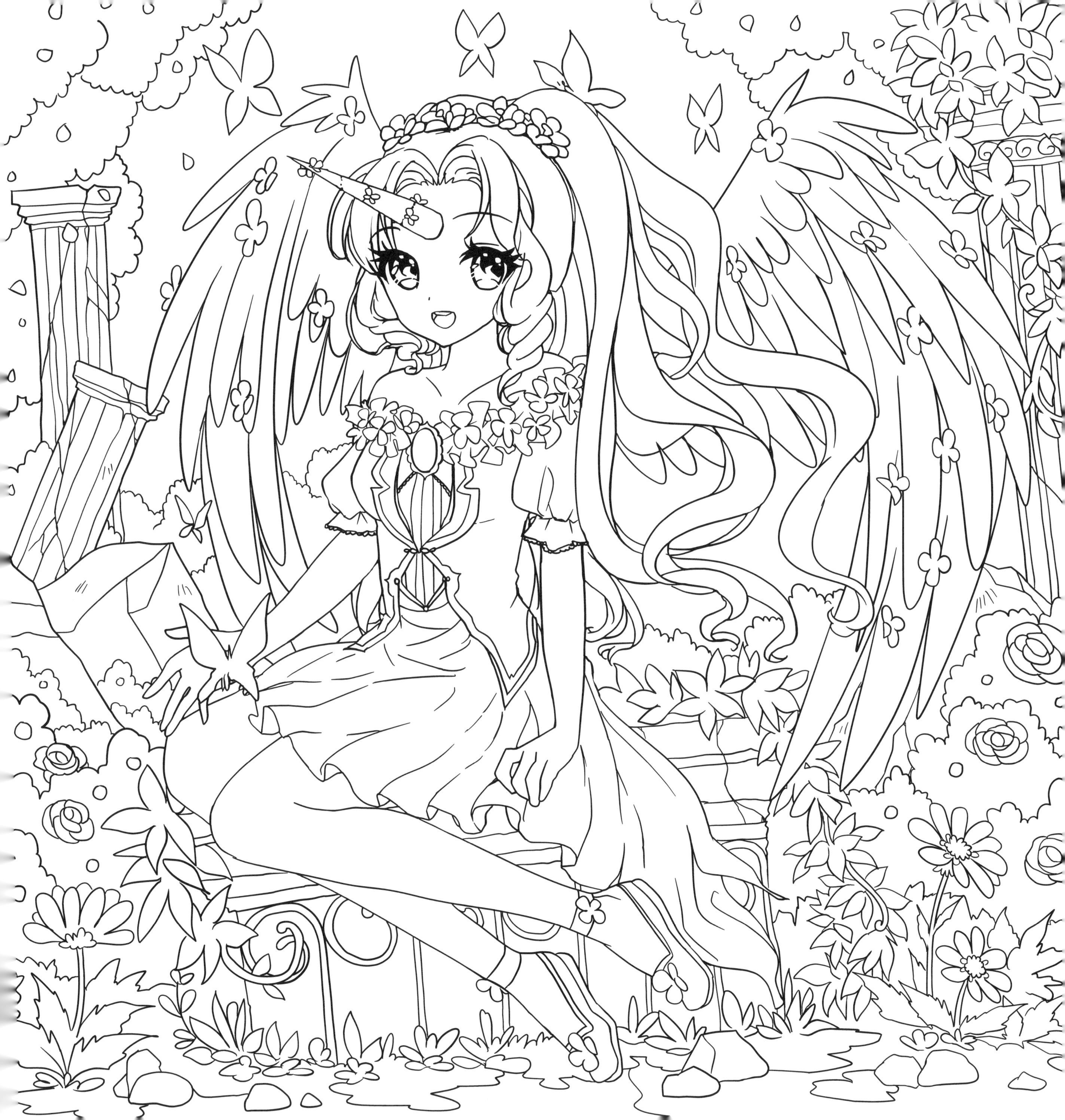

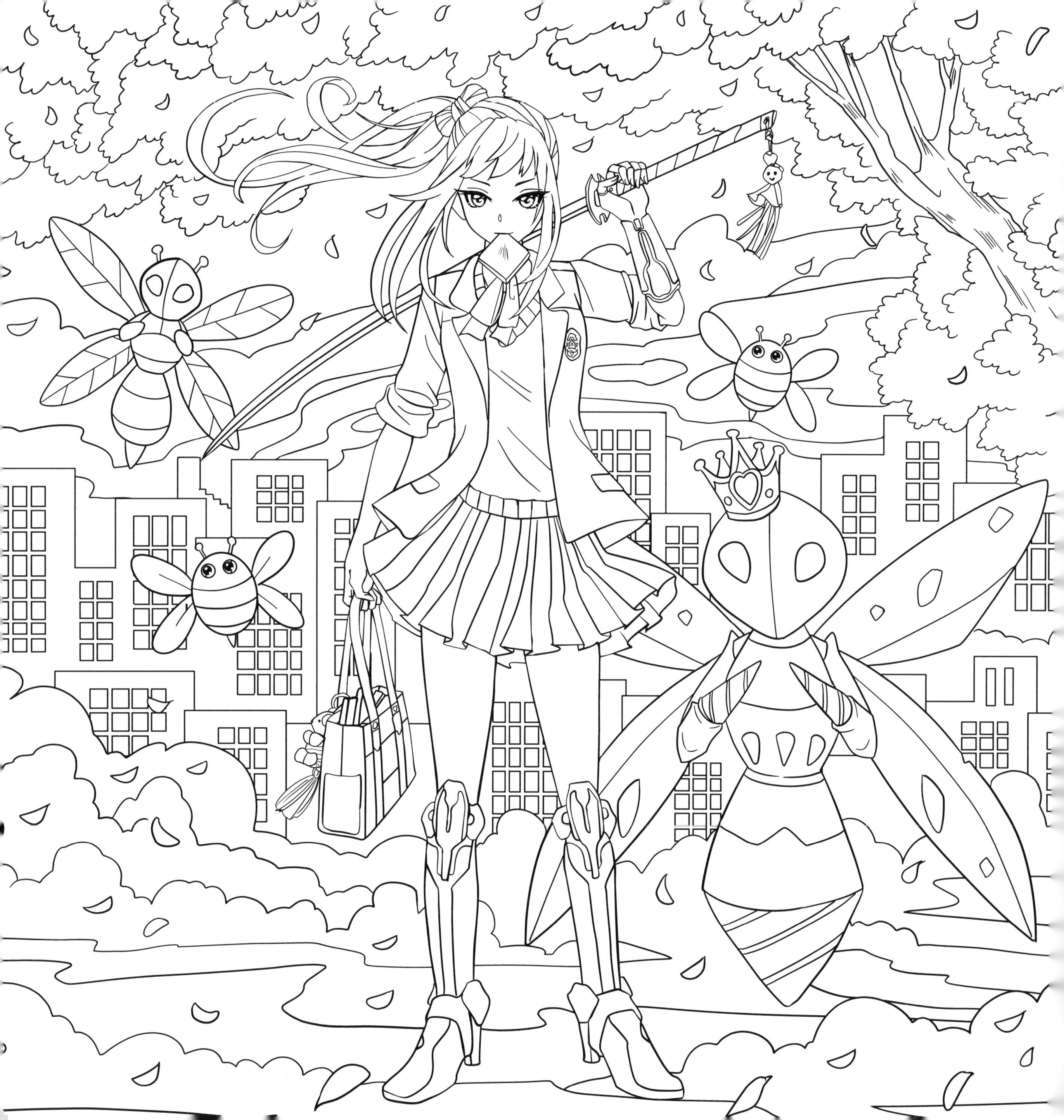

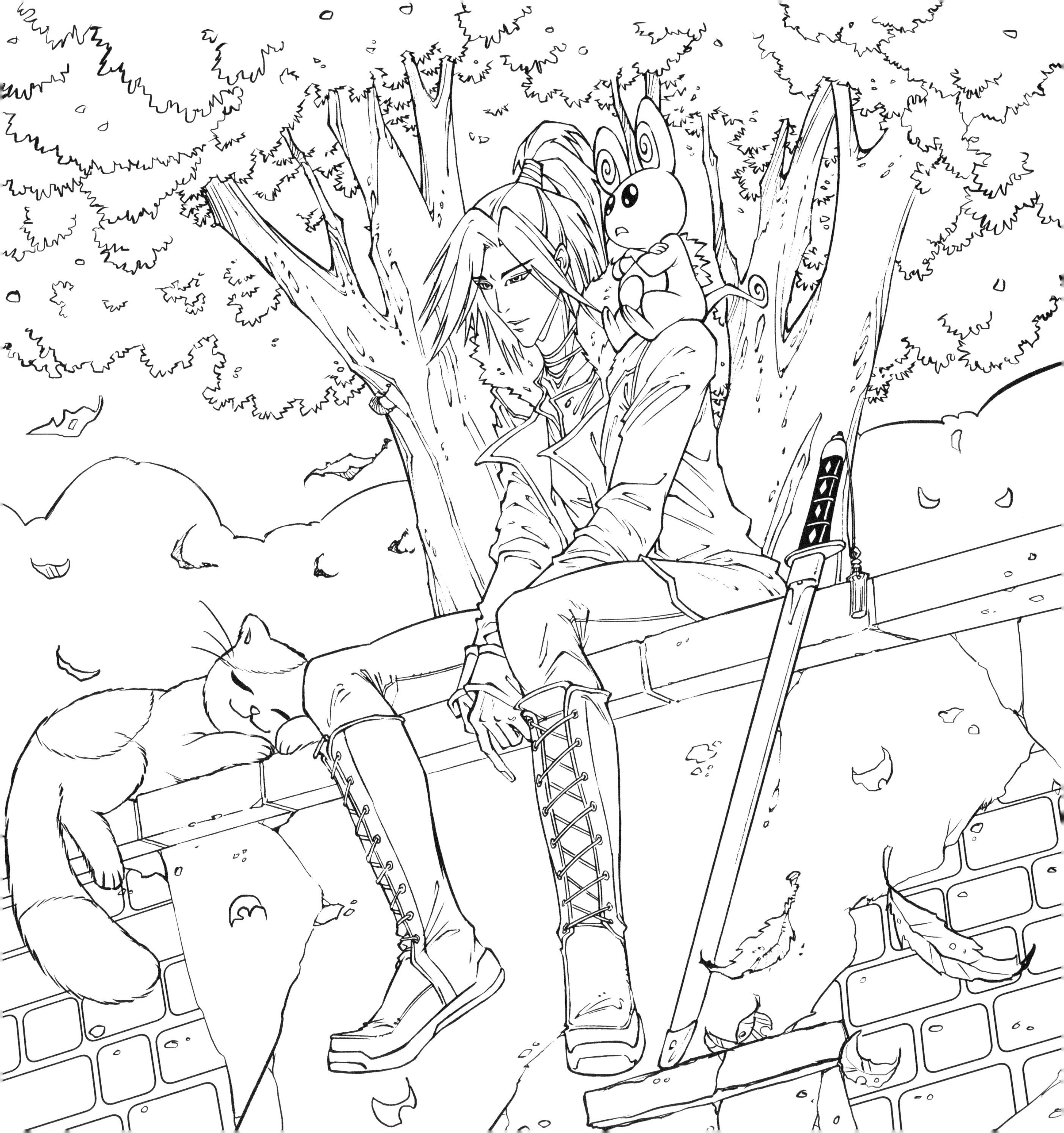

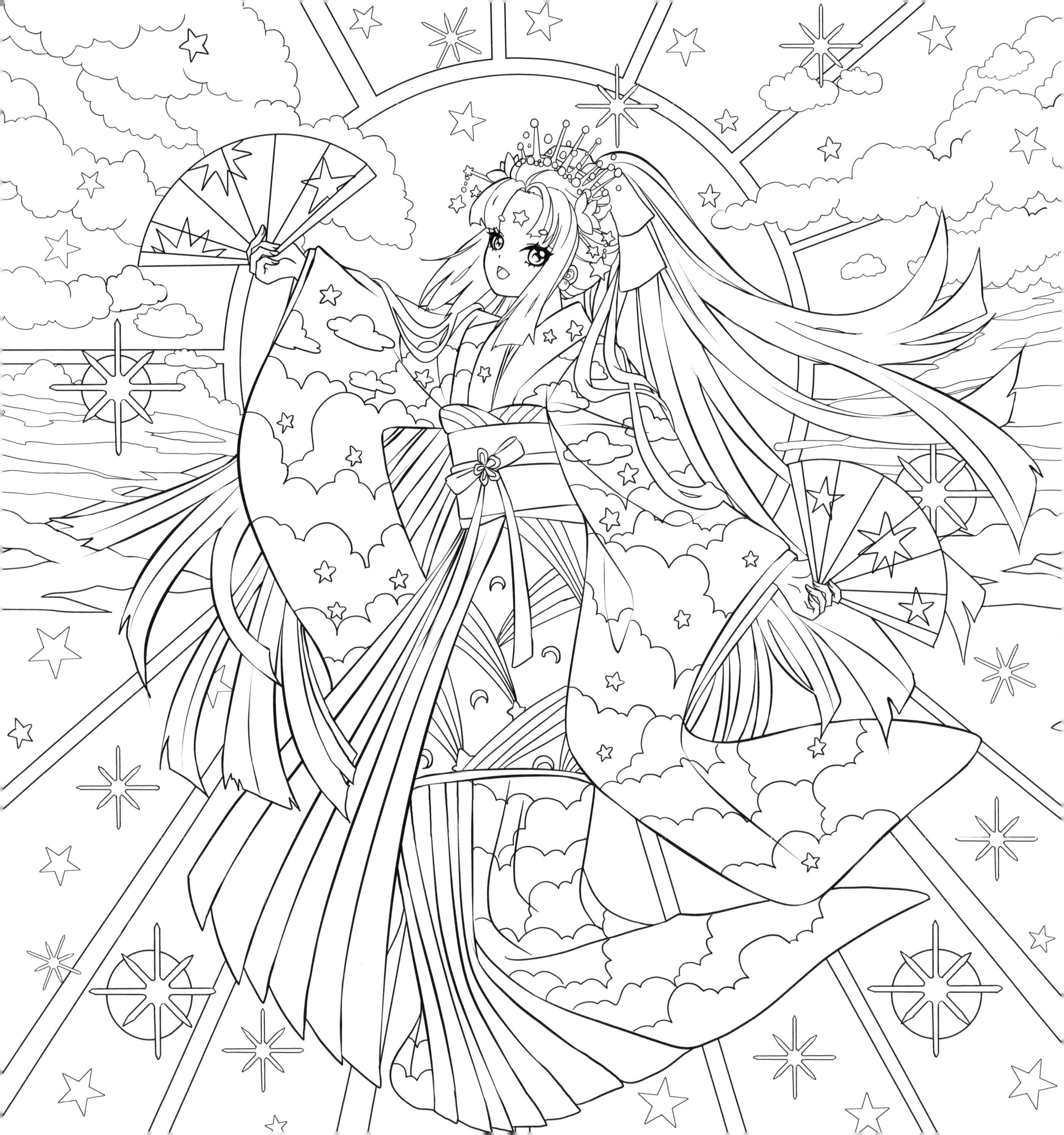

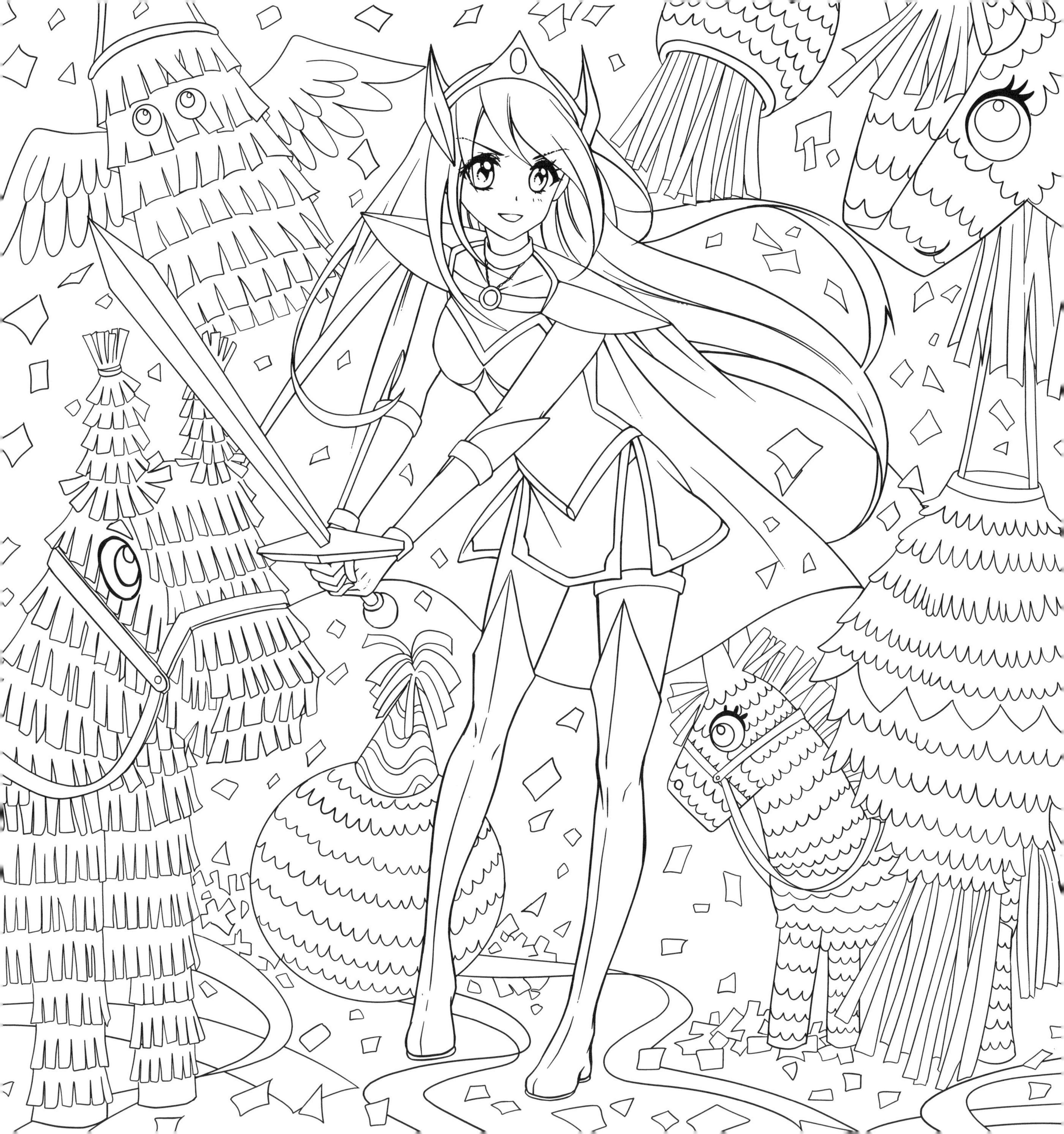

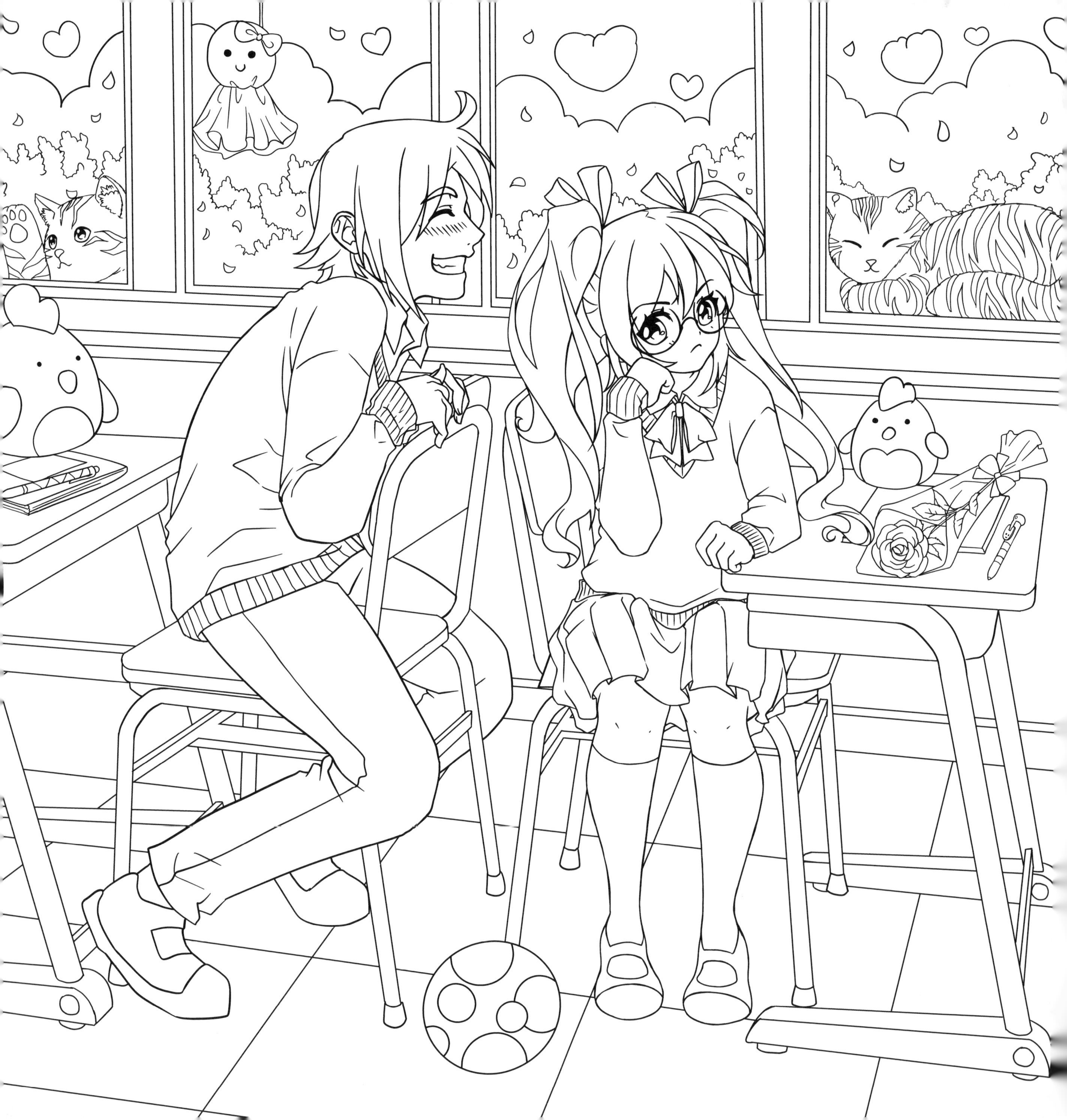

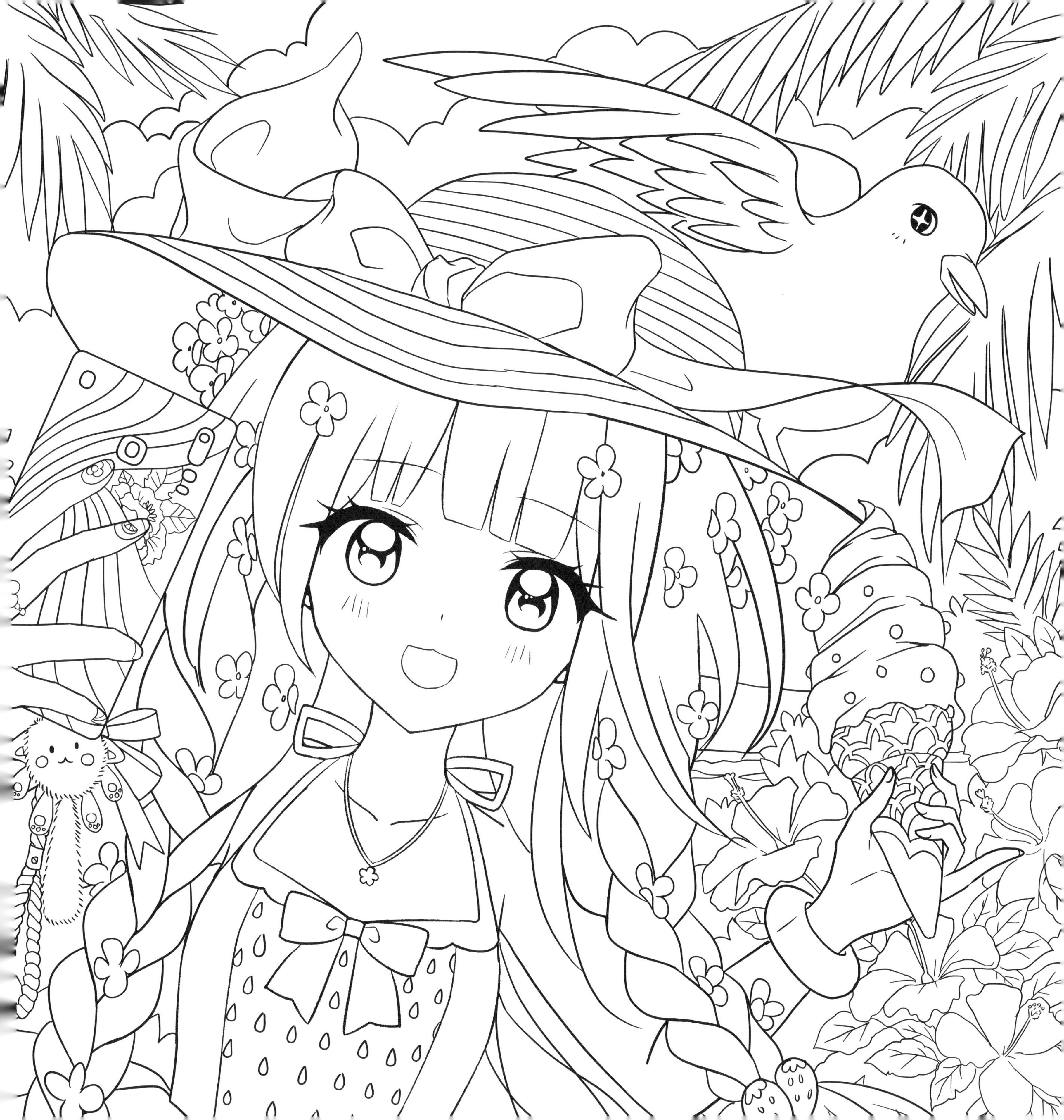

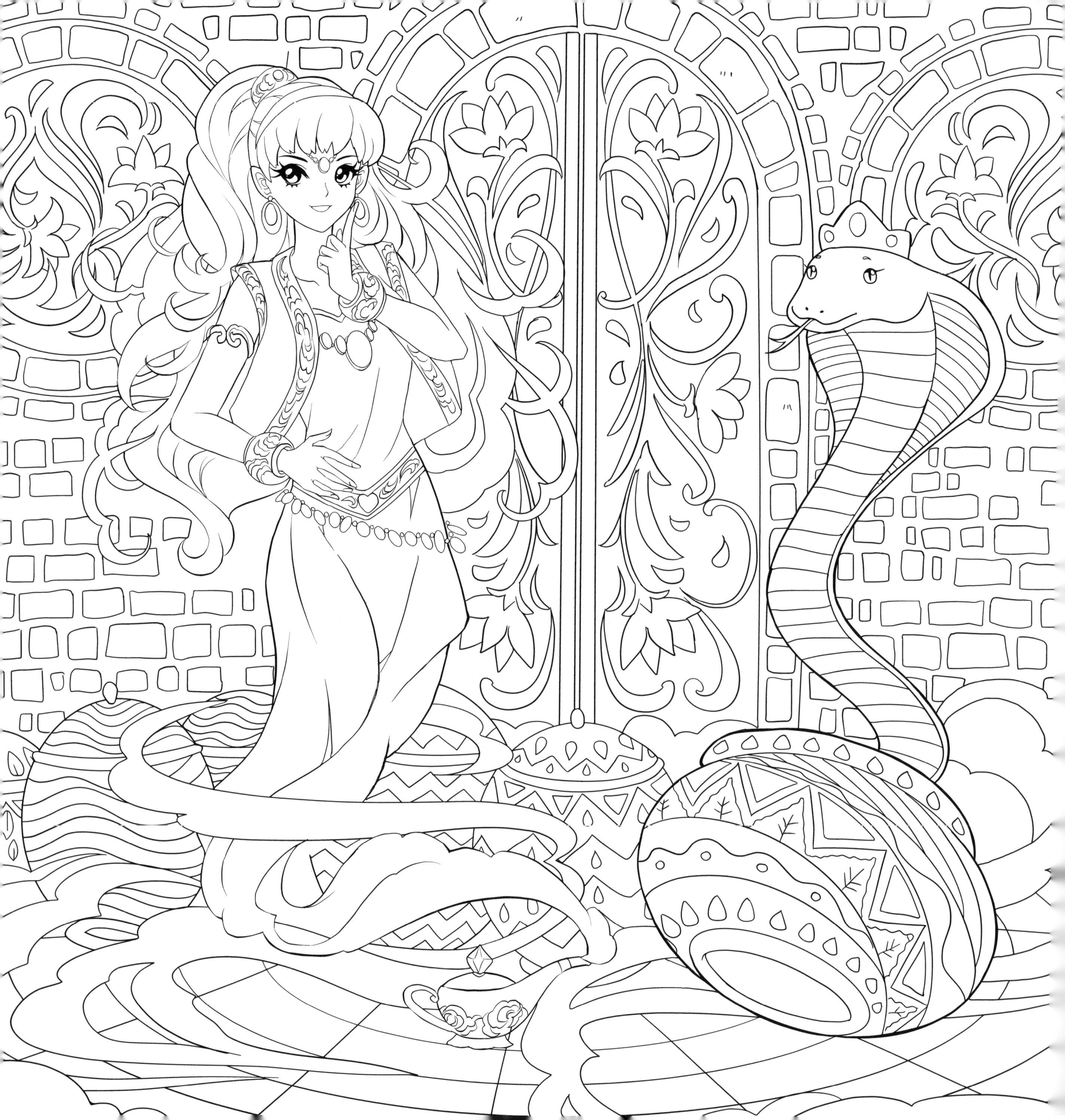

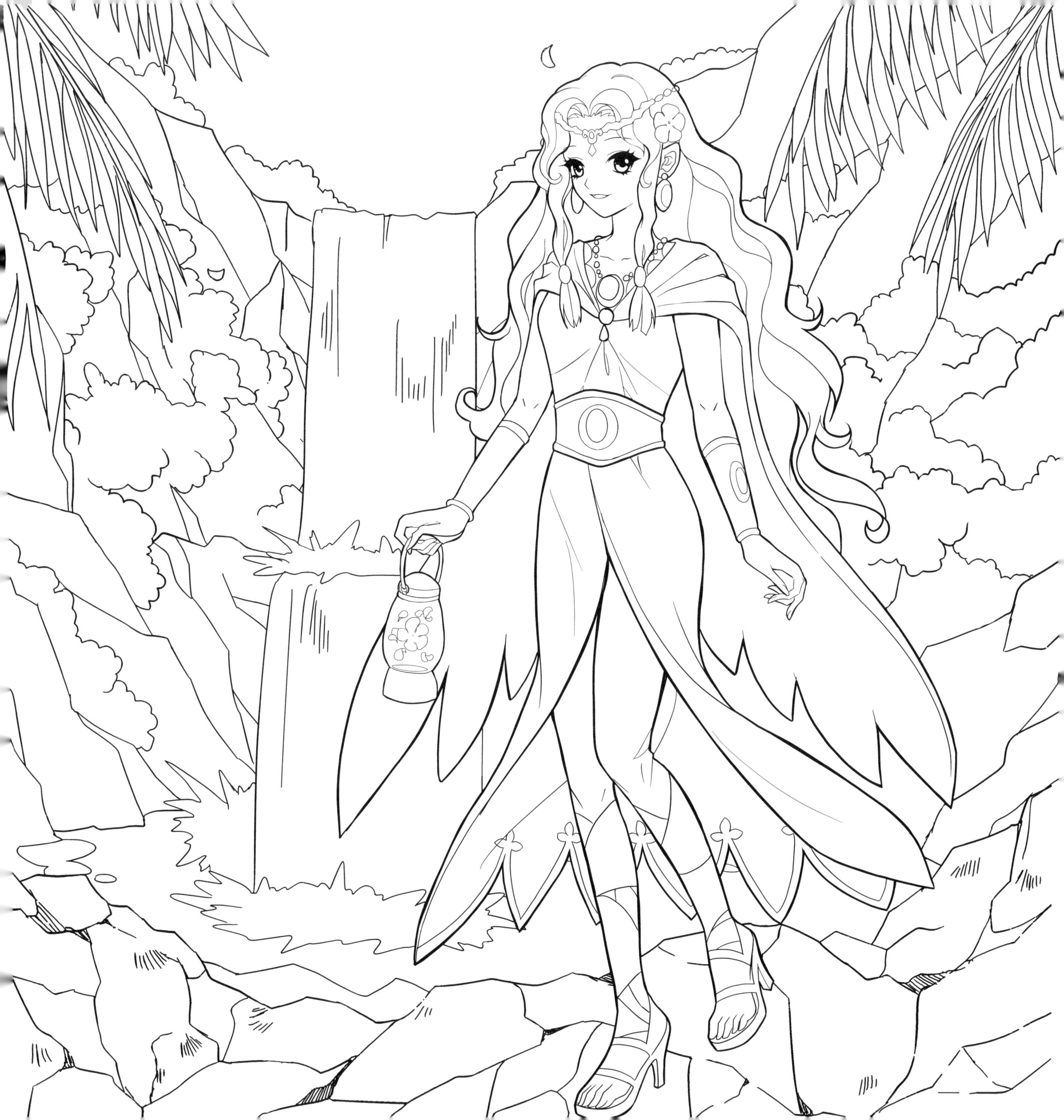

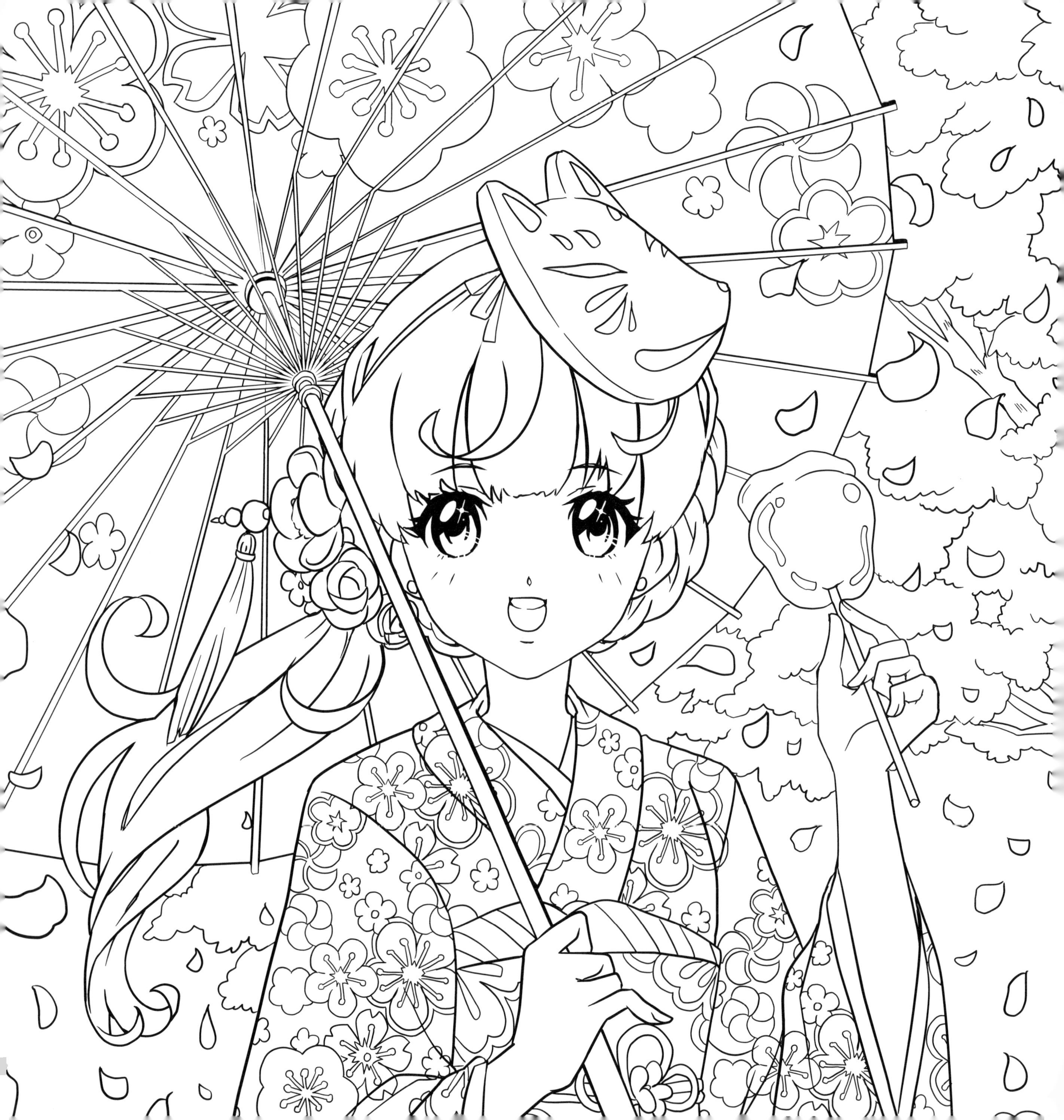

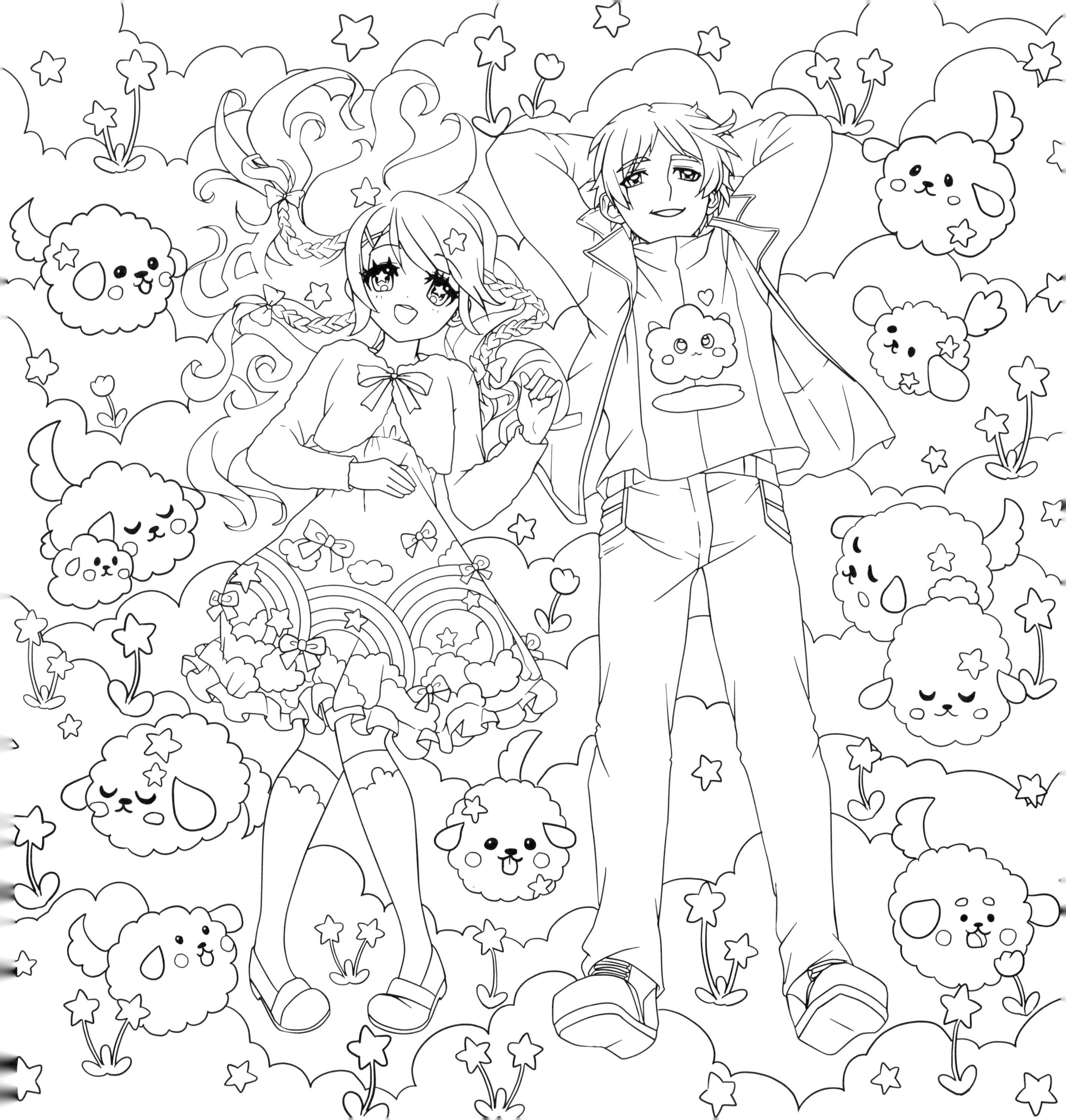

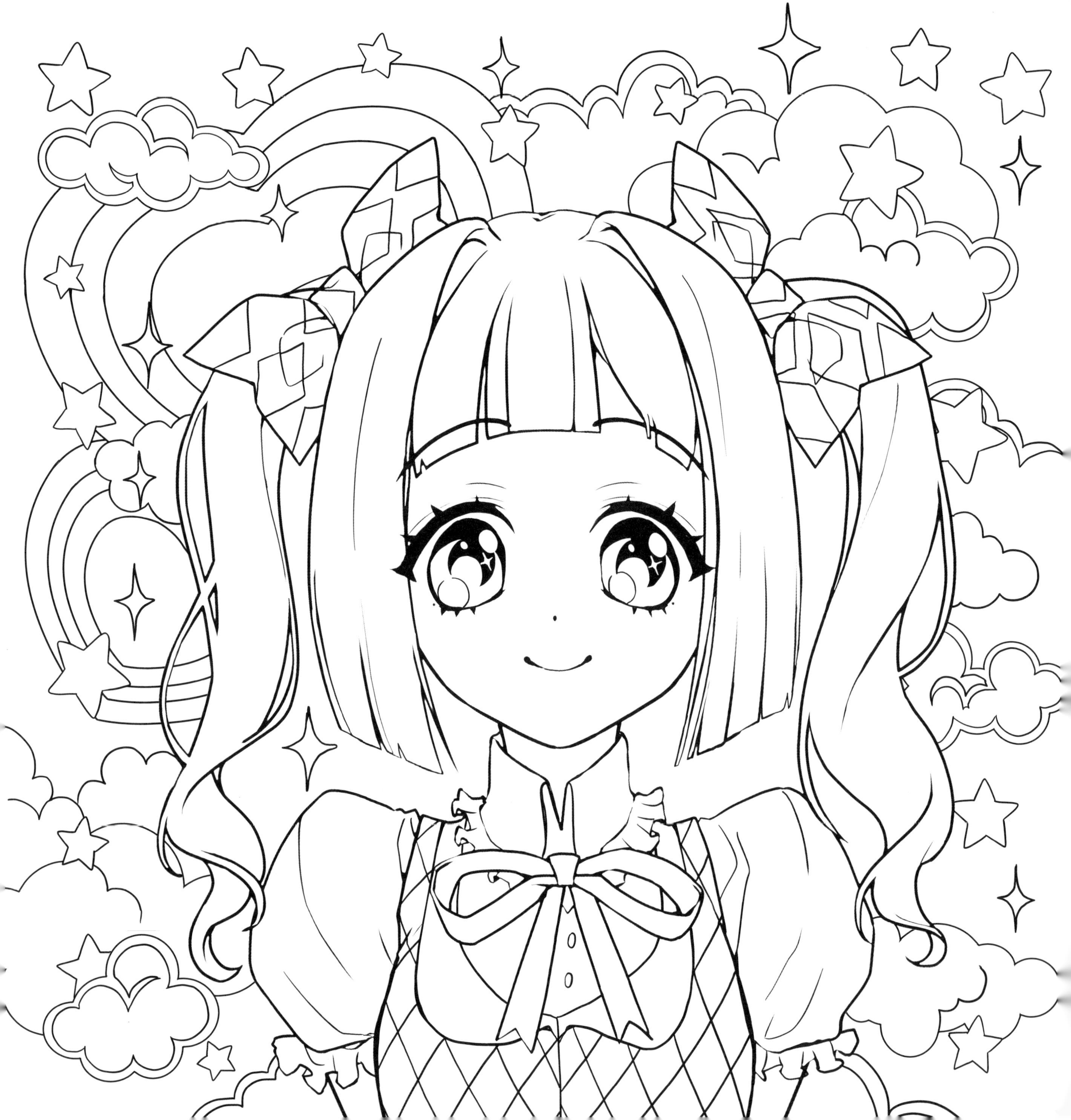

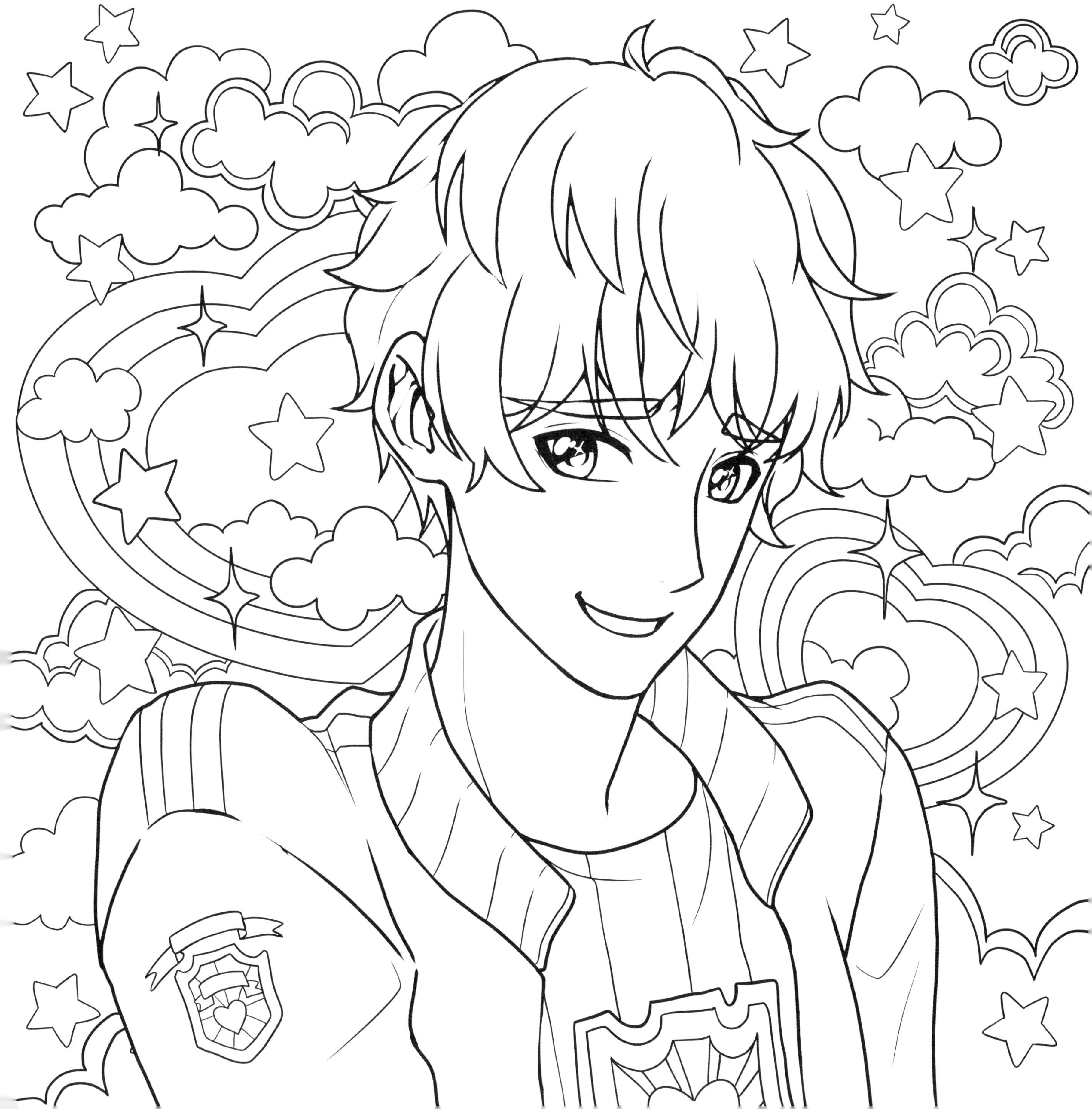

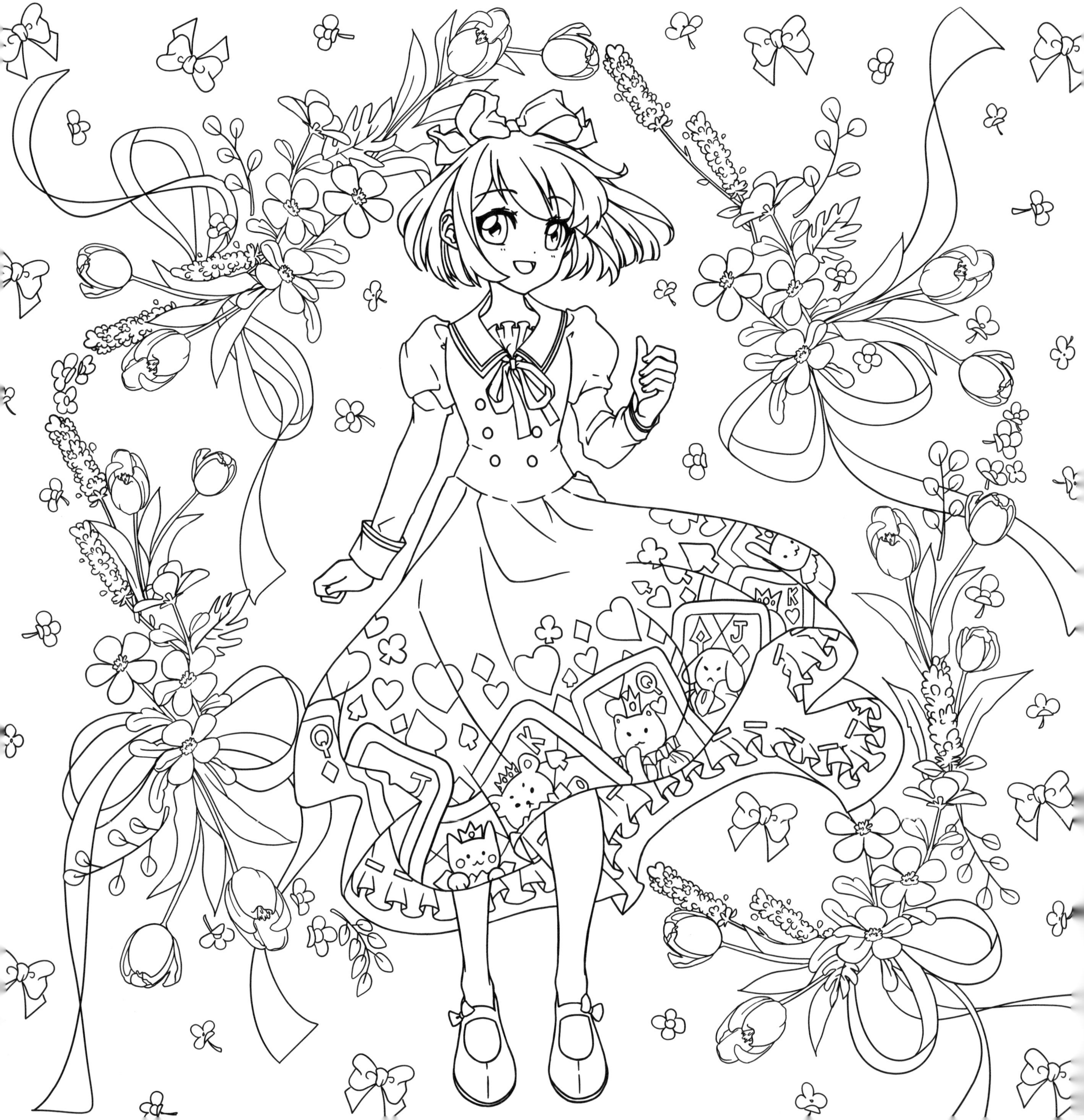

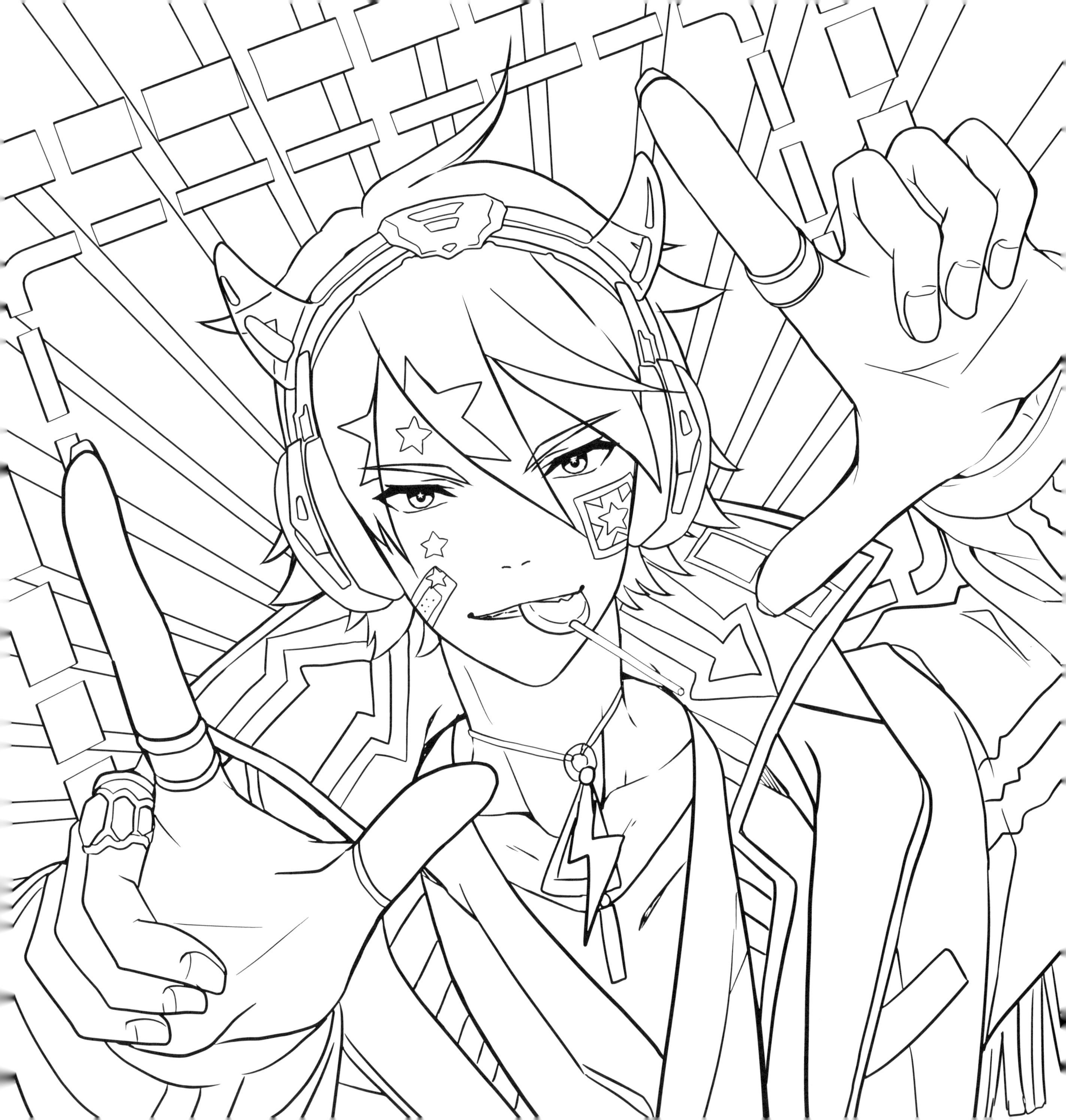

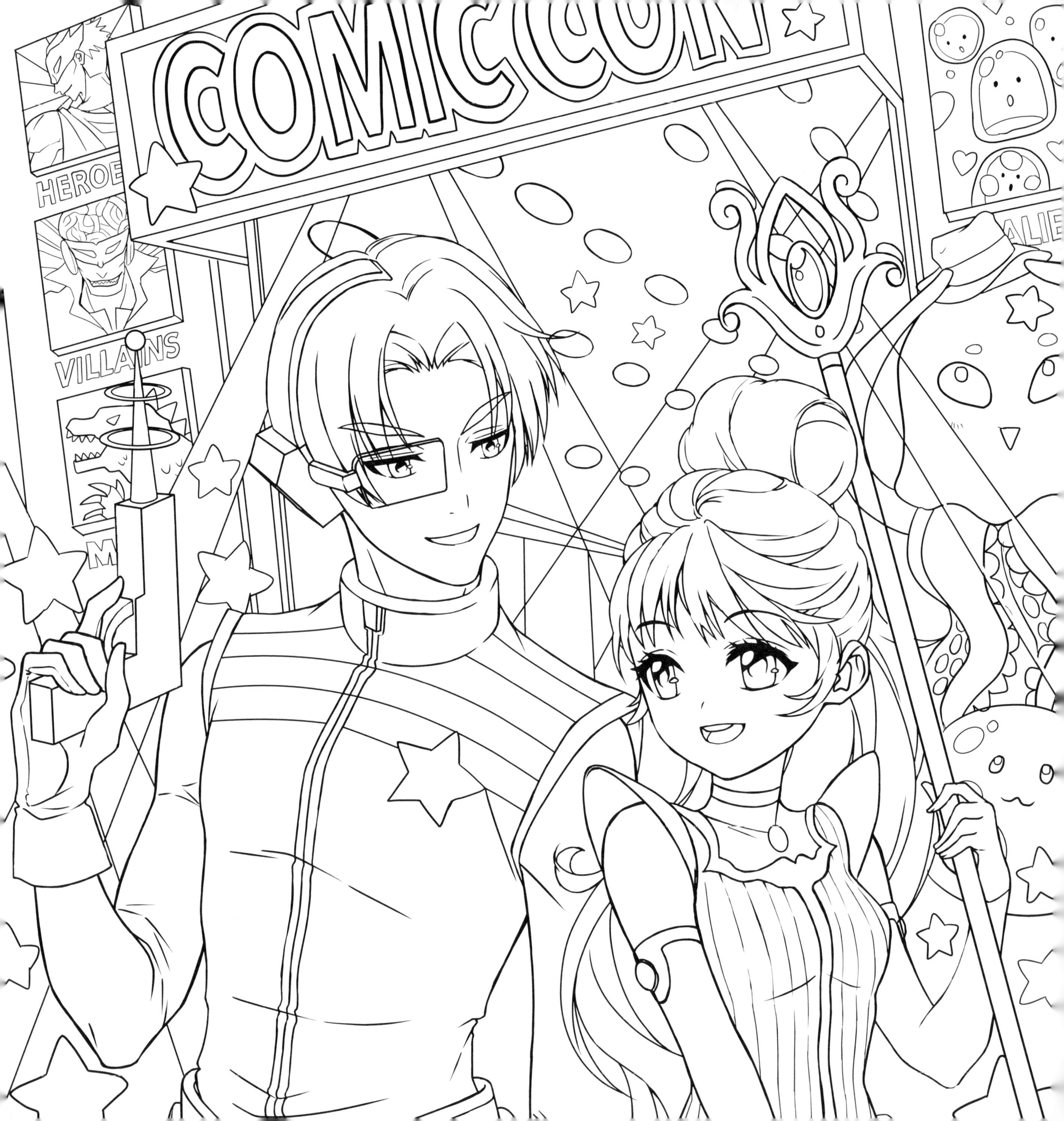
COMIC CON
HEROE
VILLAINS
M
ALIE

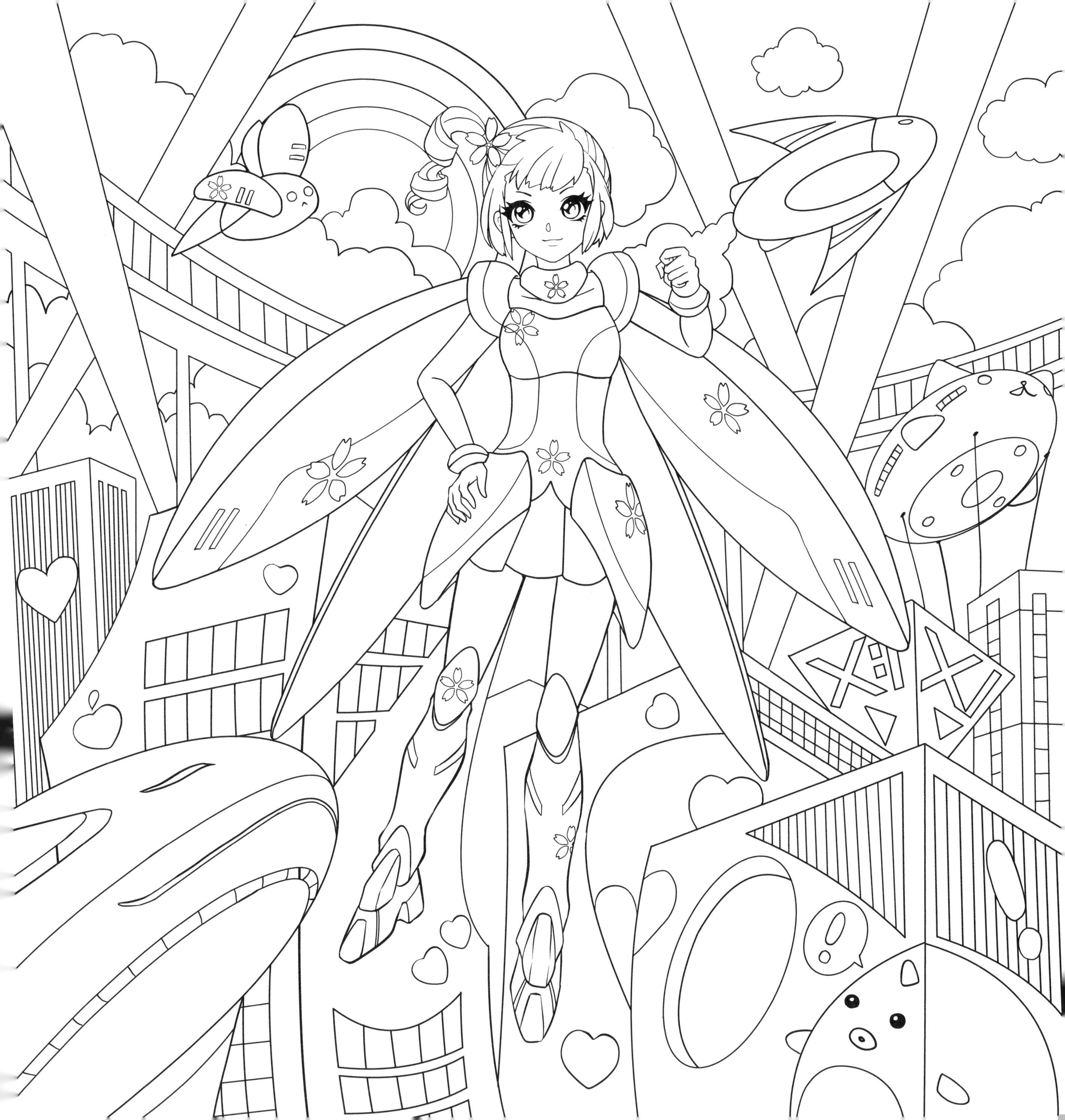

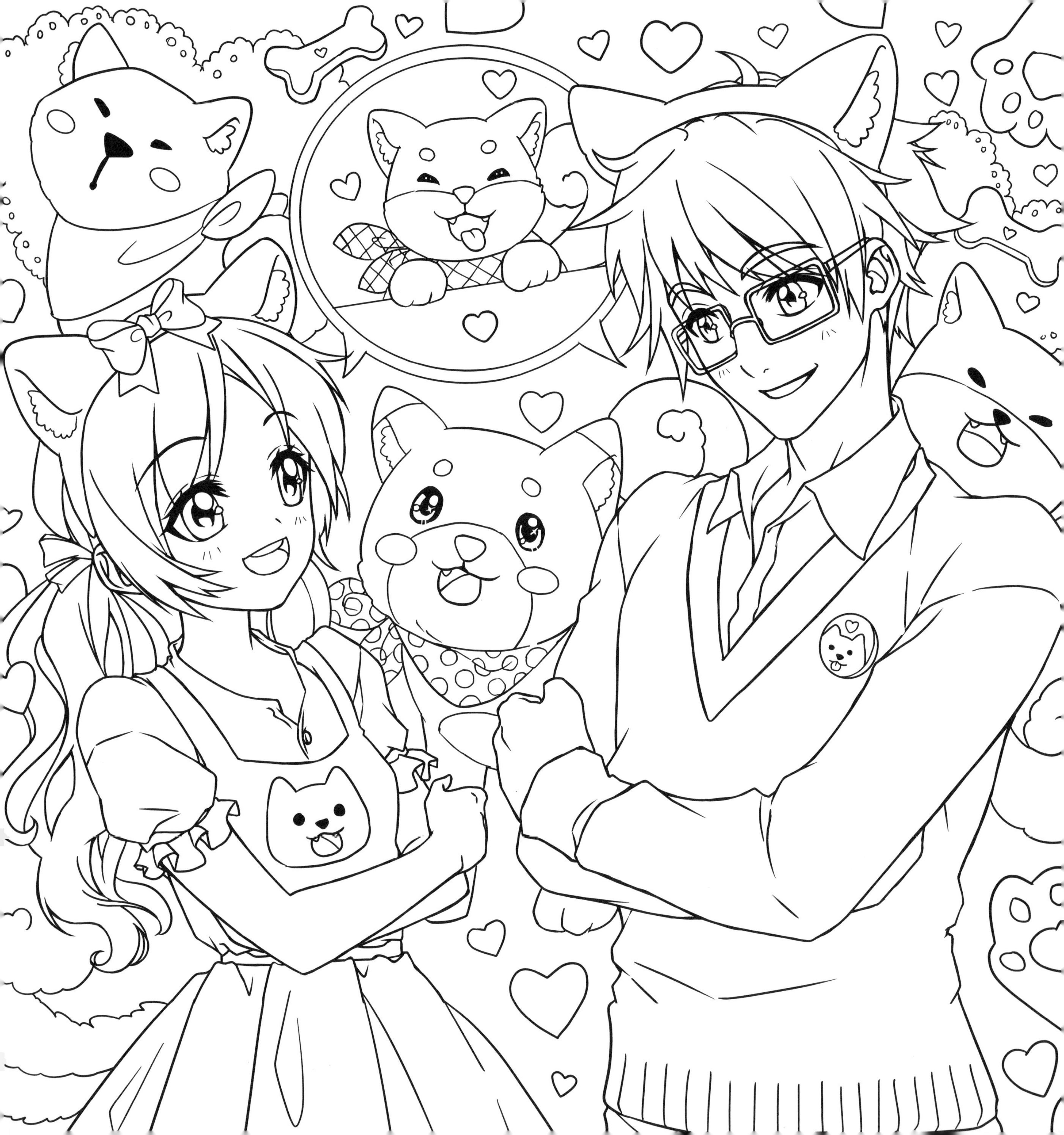

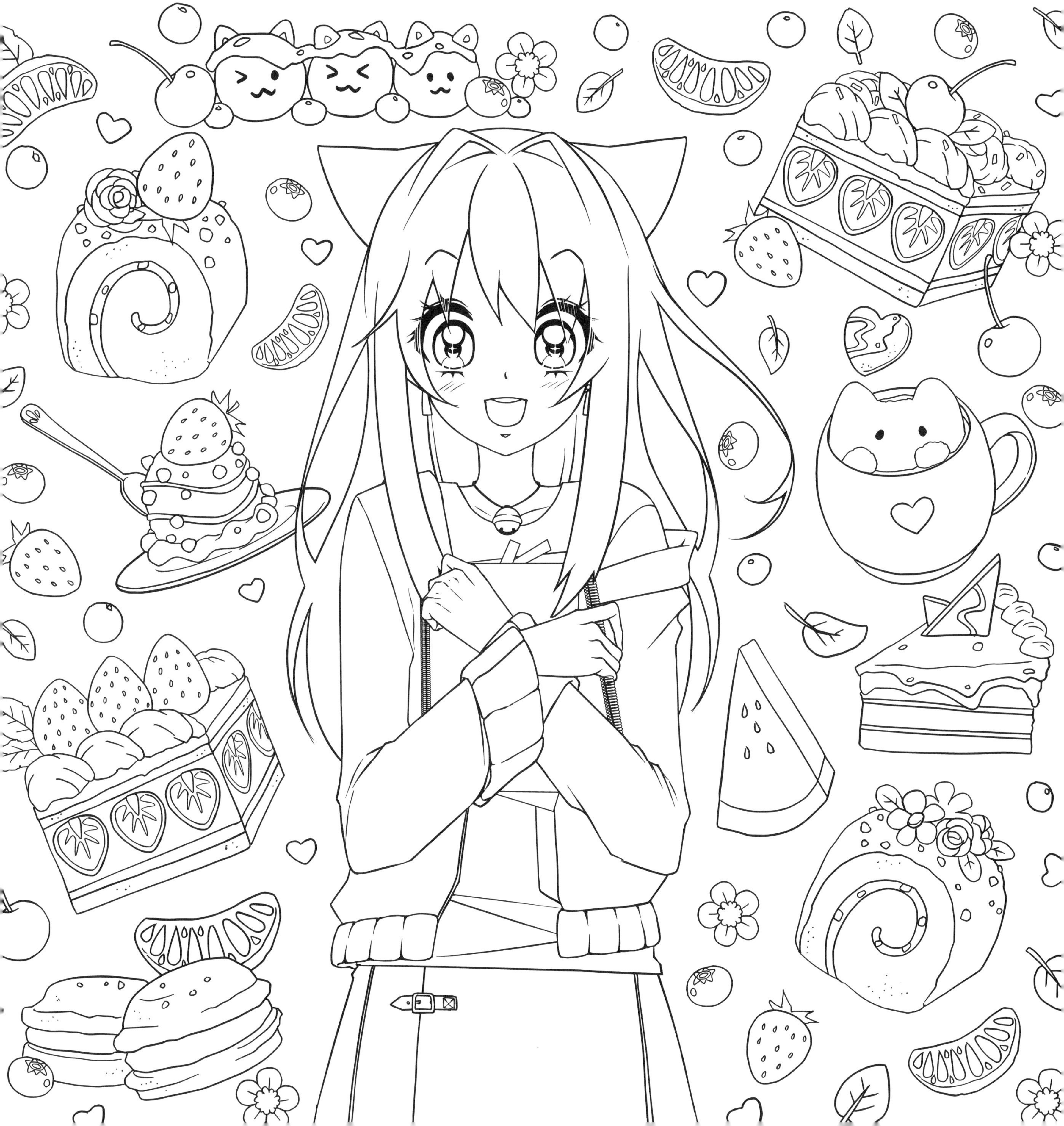

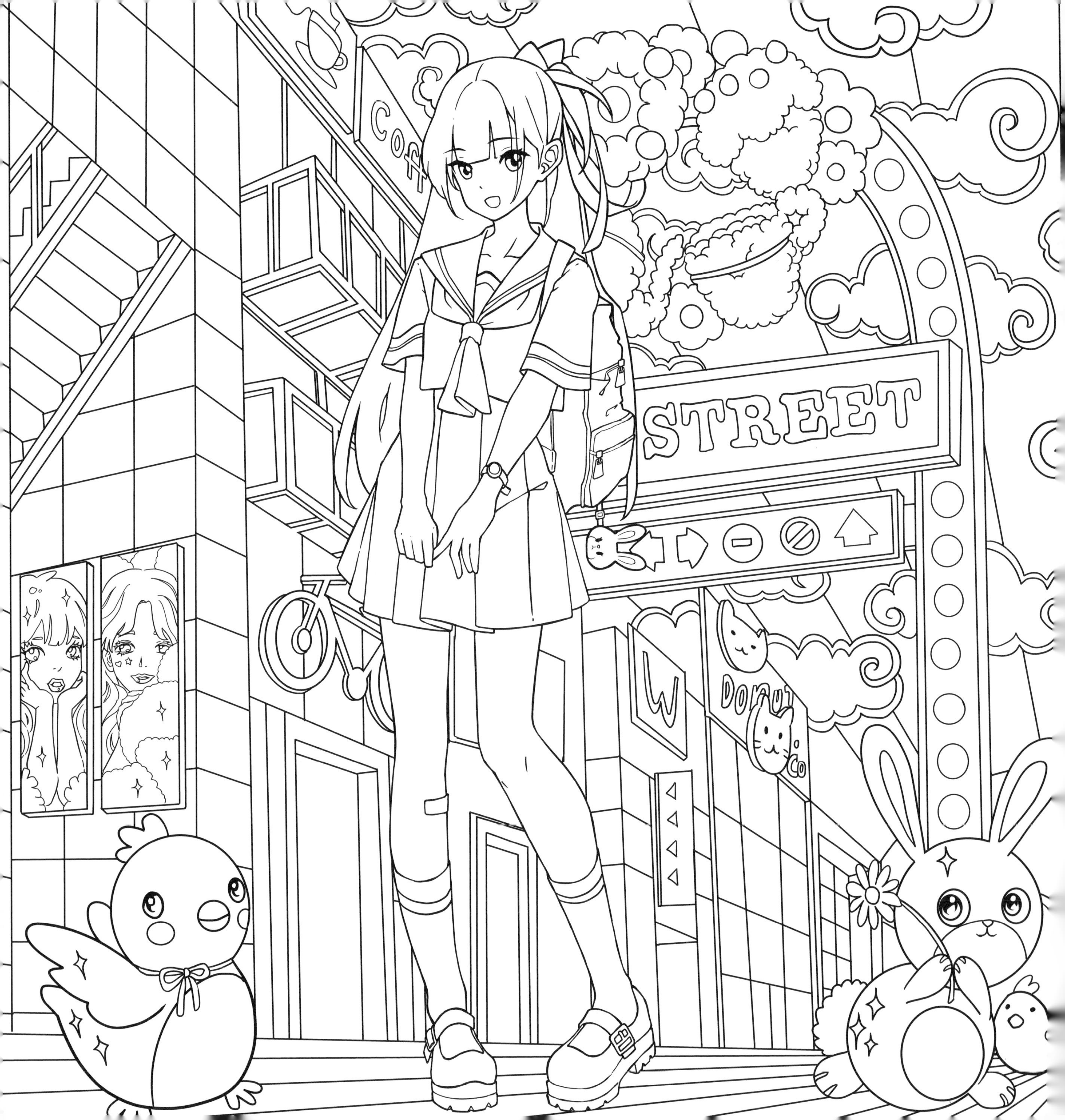
Coff
STREET
W

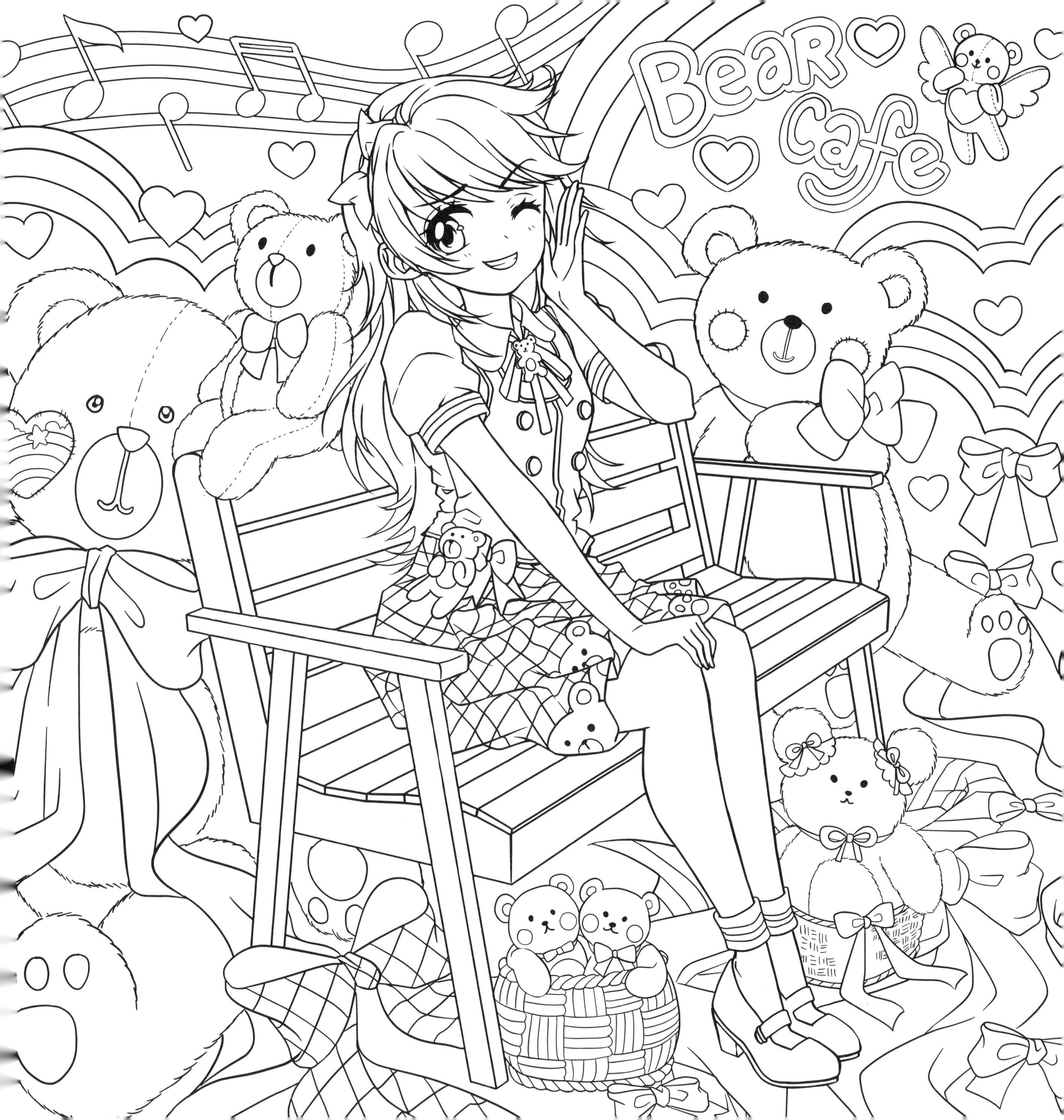
Bear
Cafe

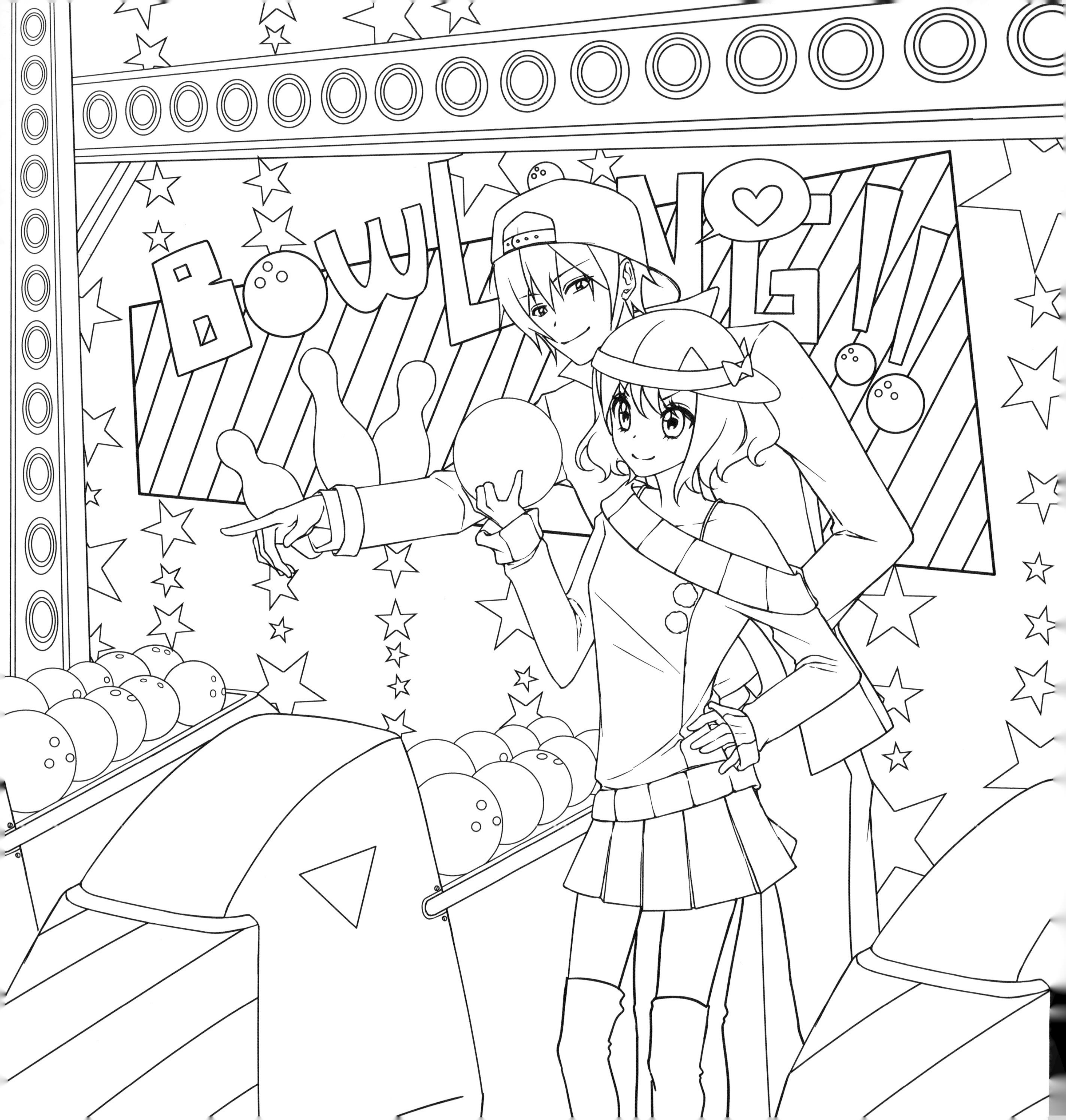

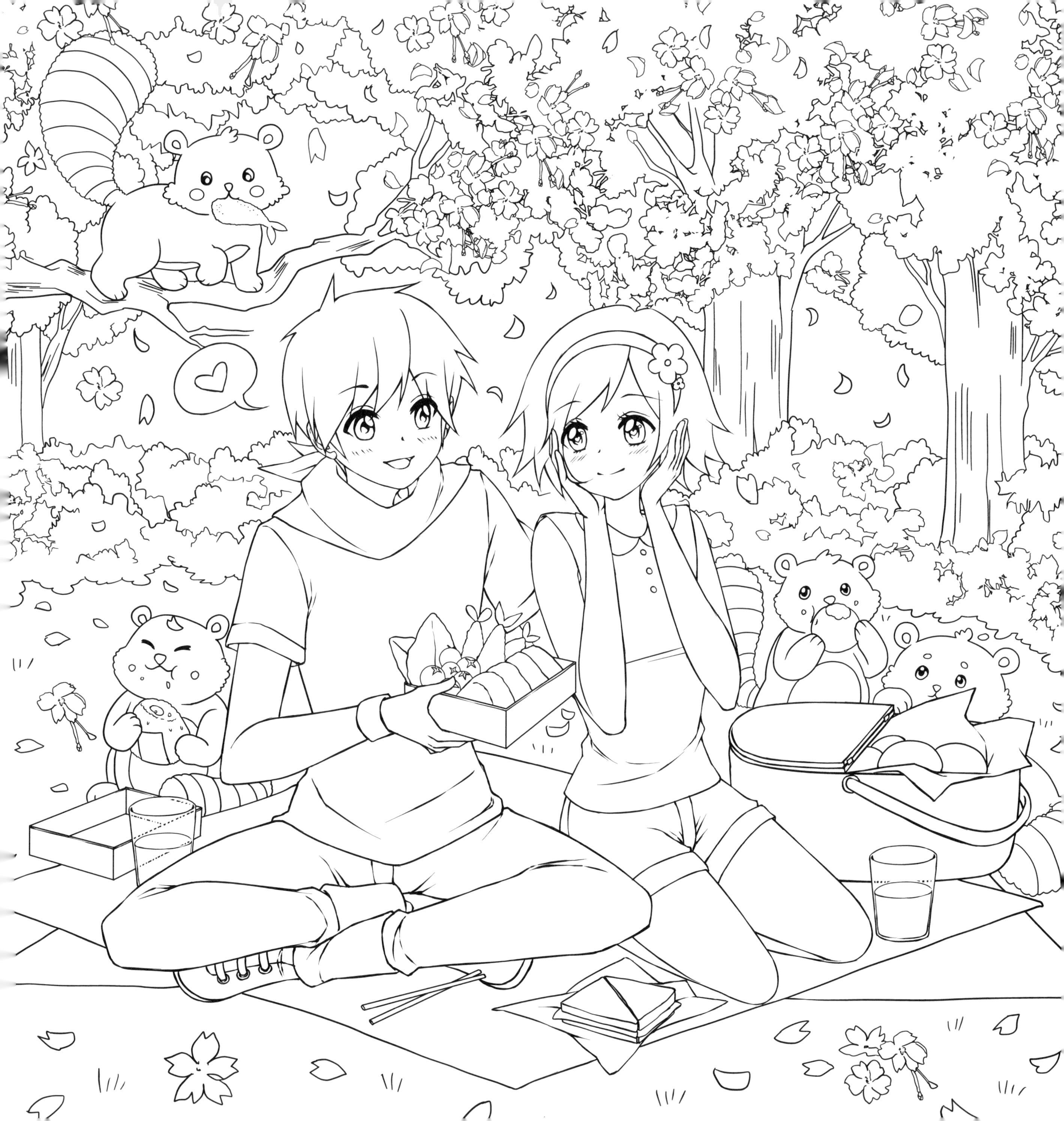

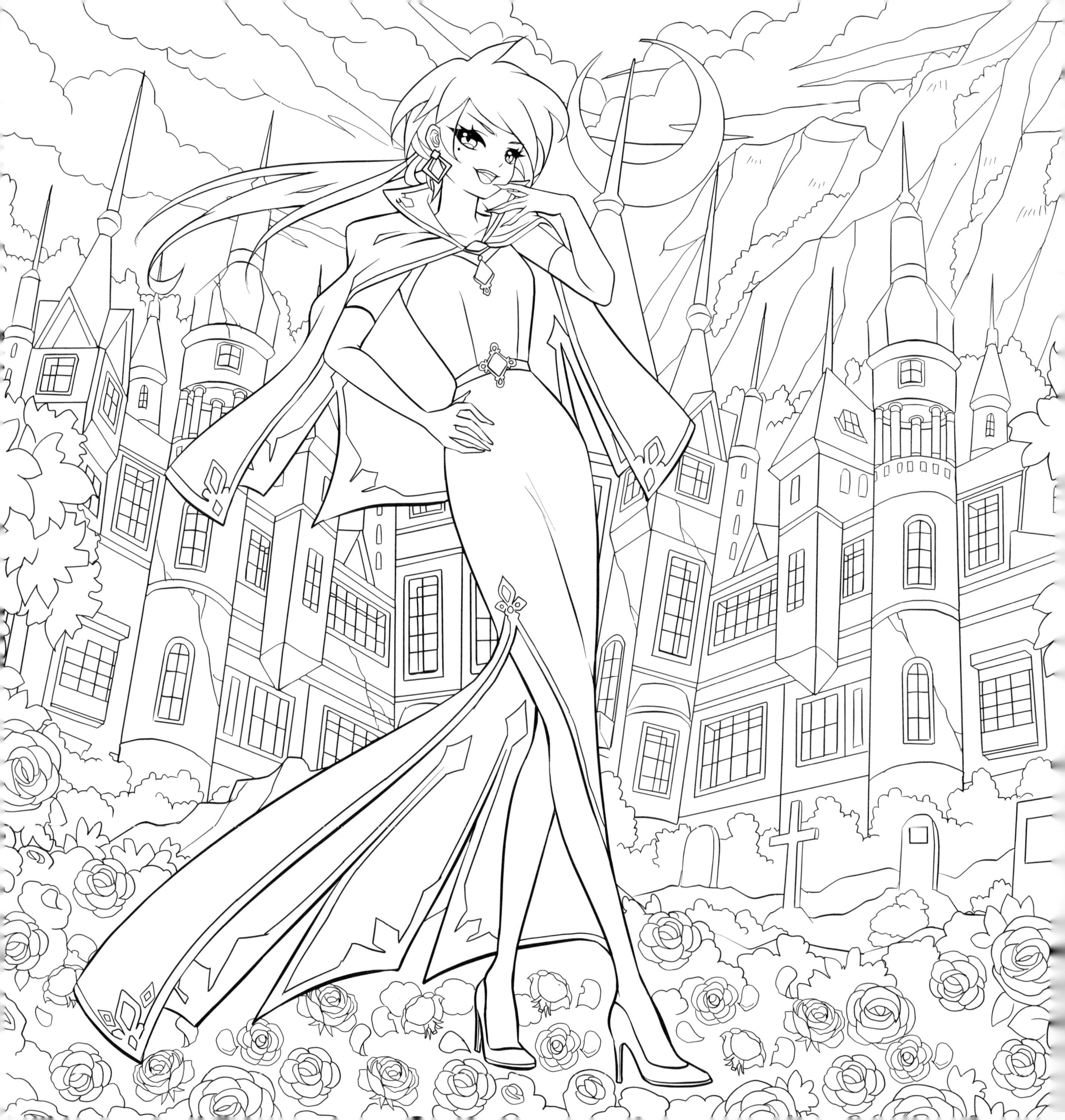

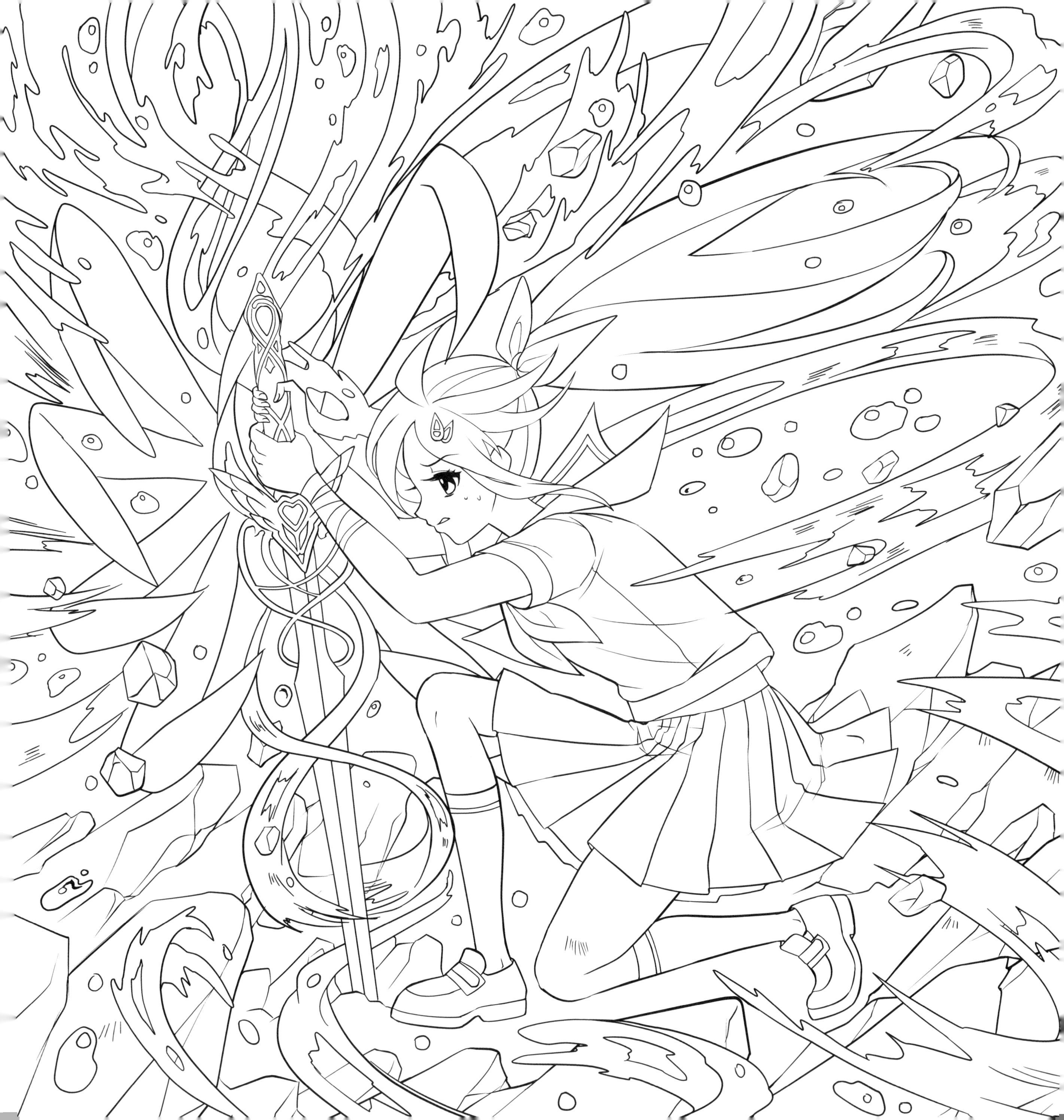

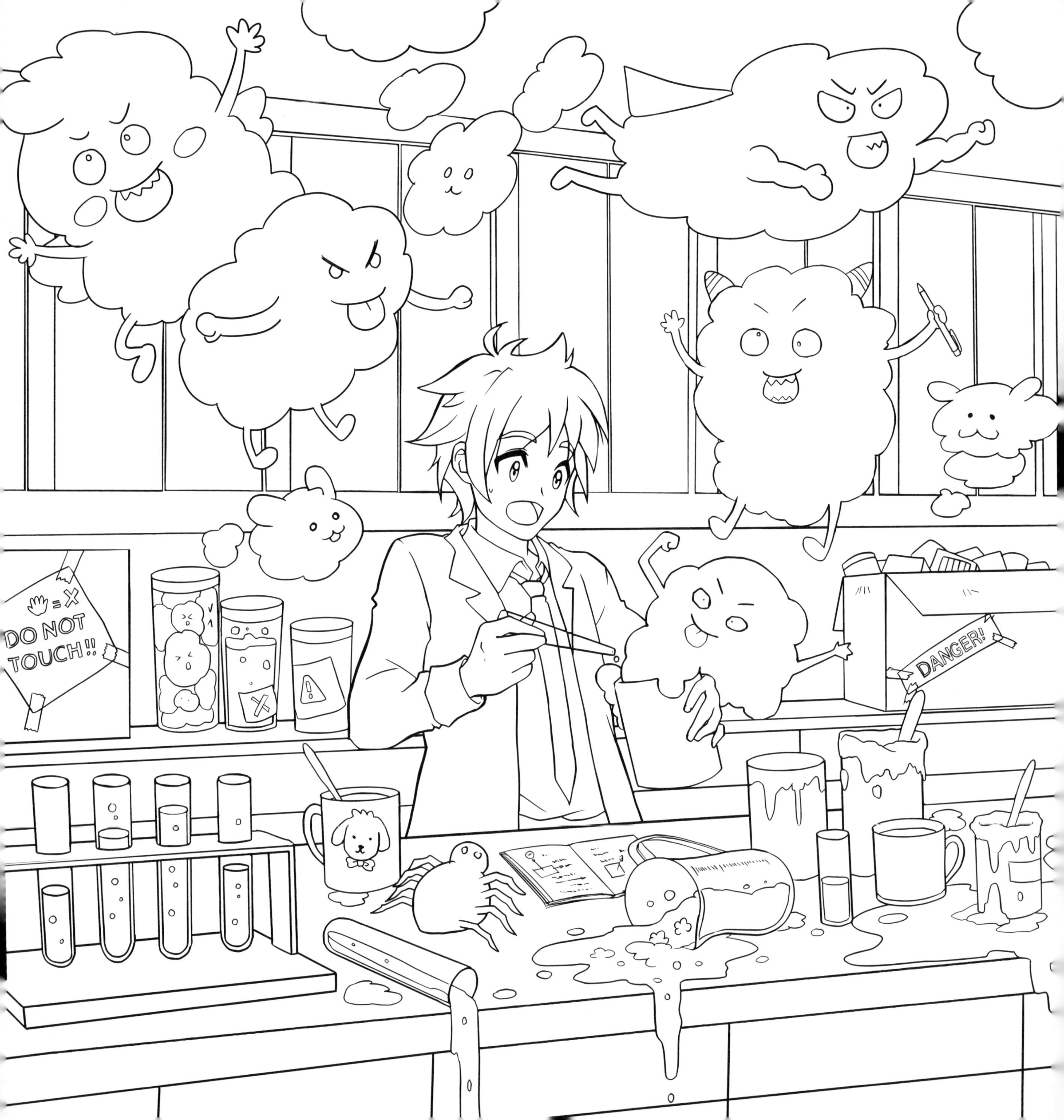
DO NOT TOUCH!!
DANGER!

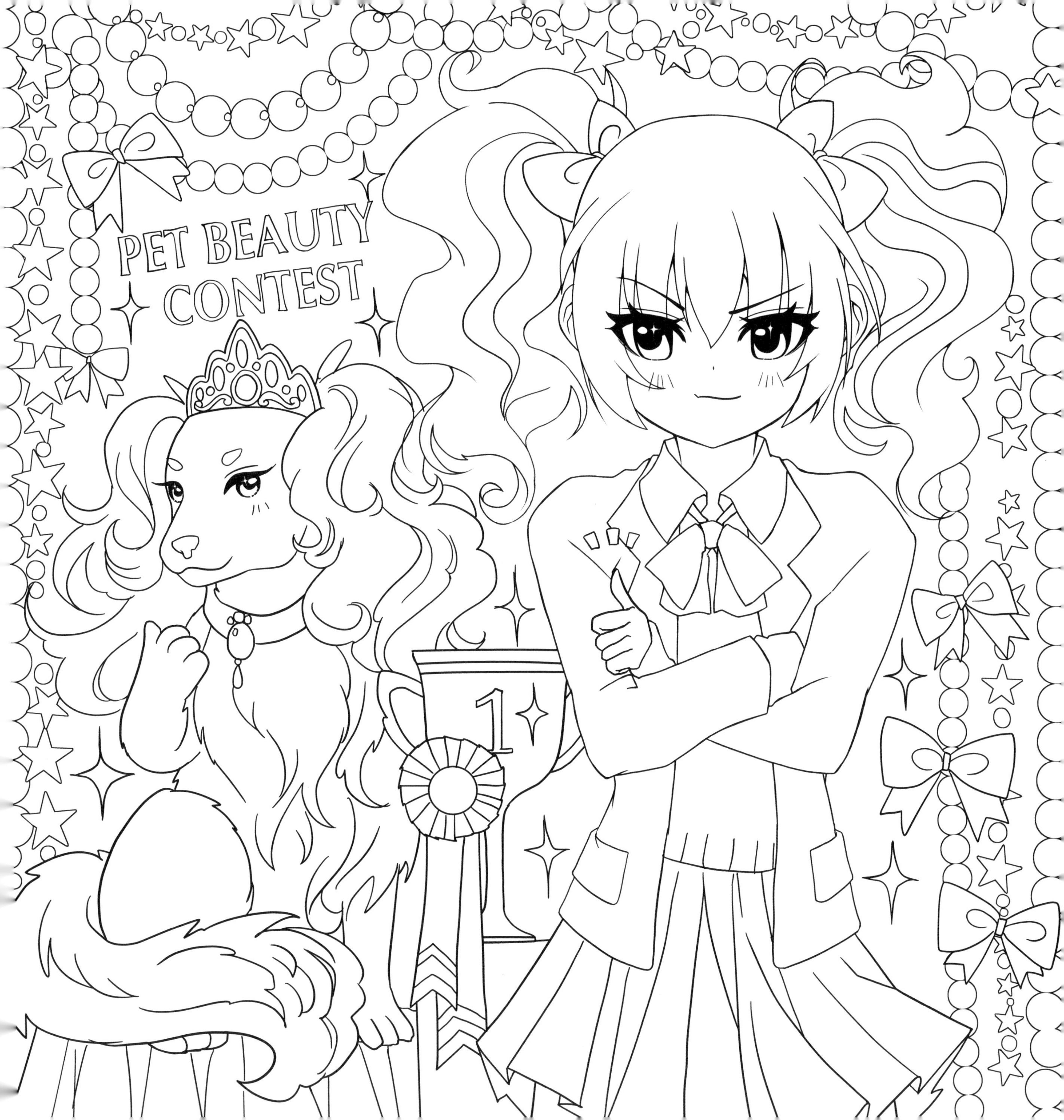
PET BEAUTY
CONTEST
1

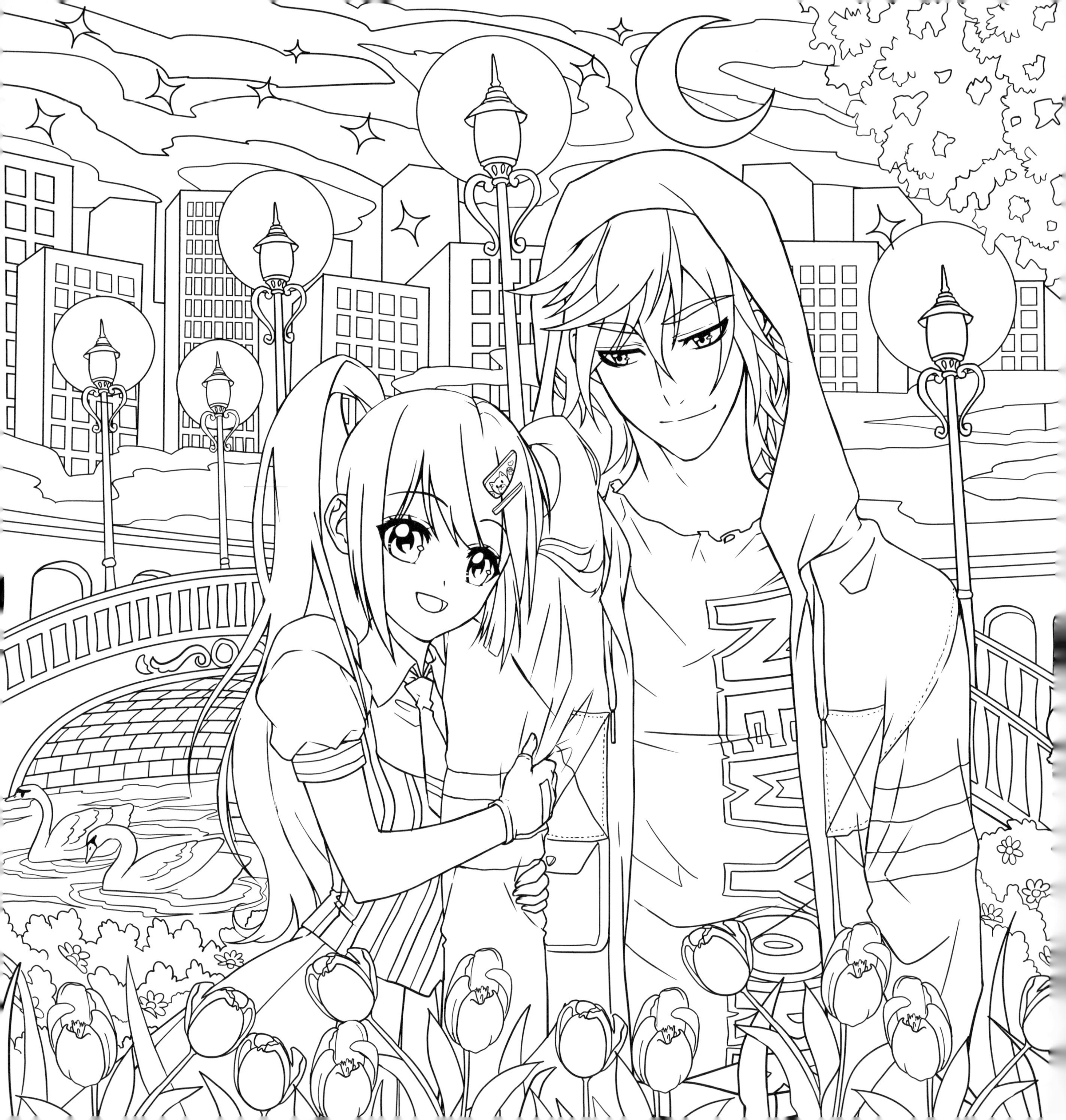

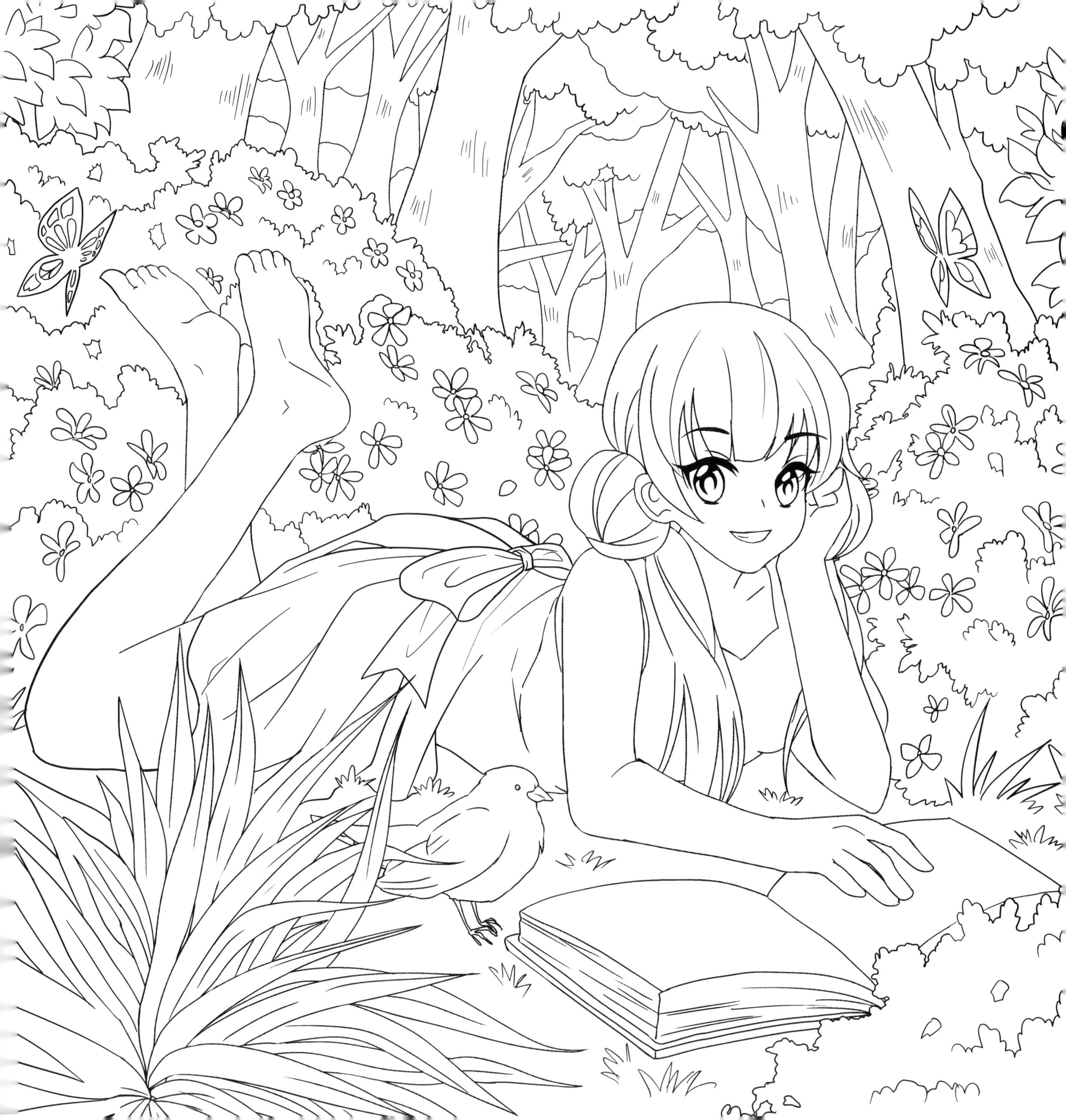

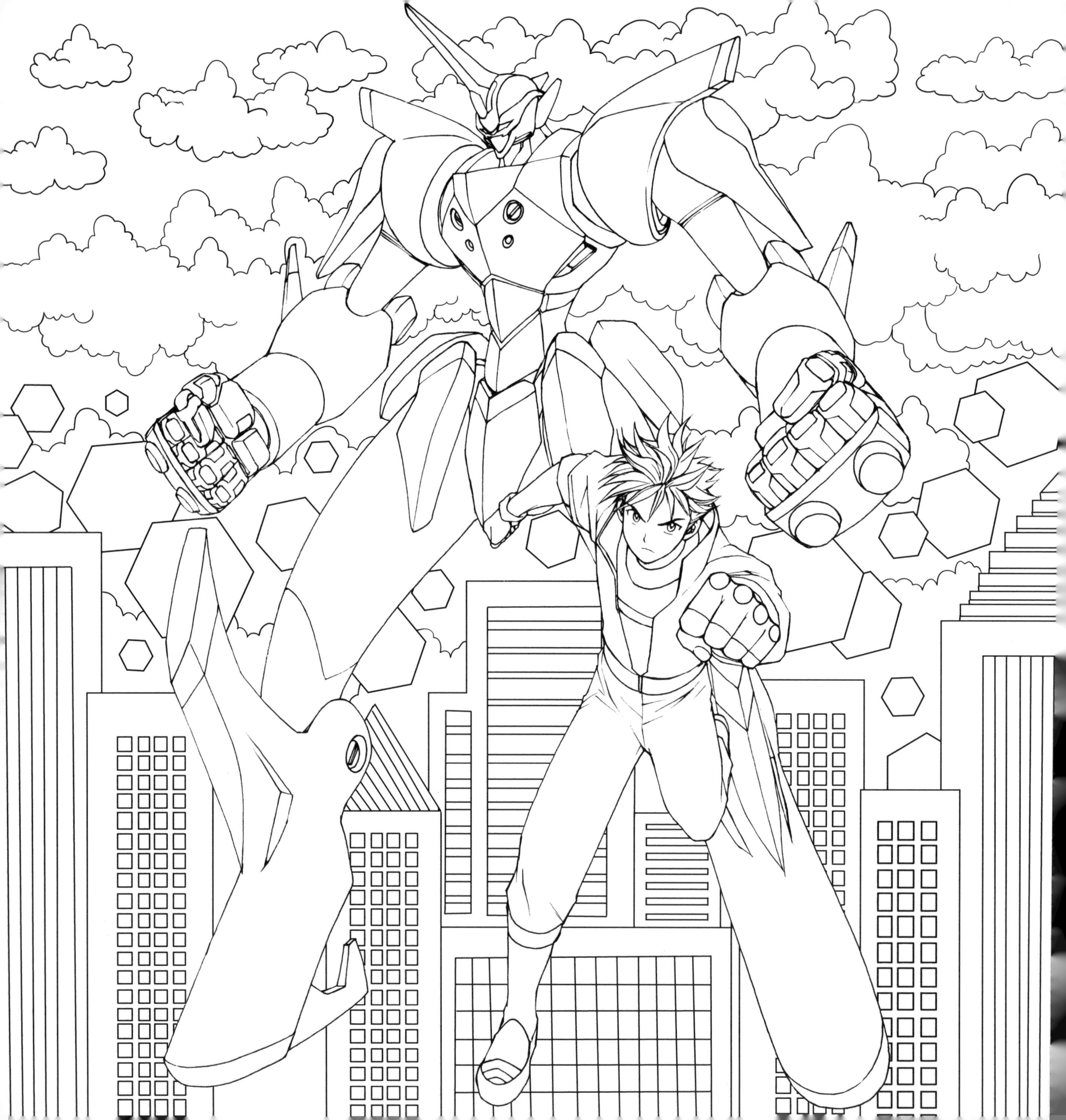

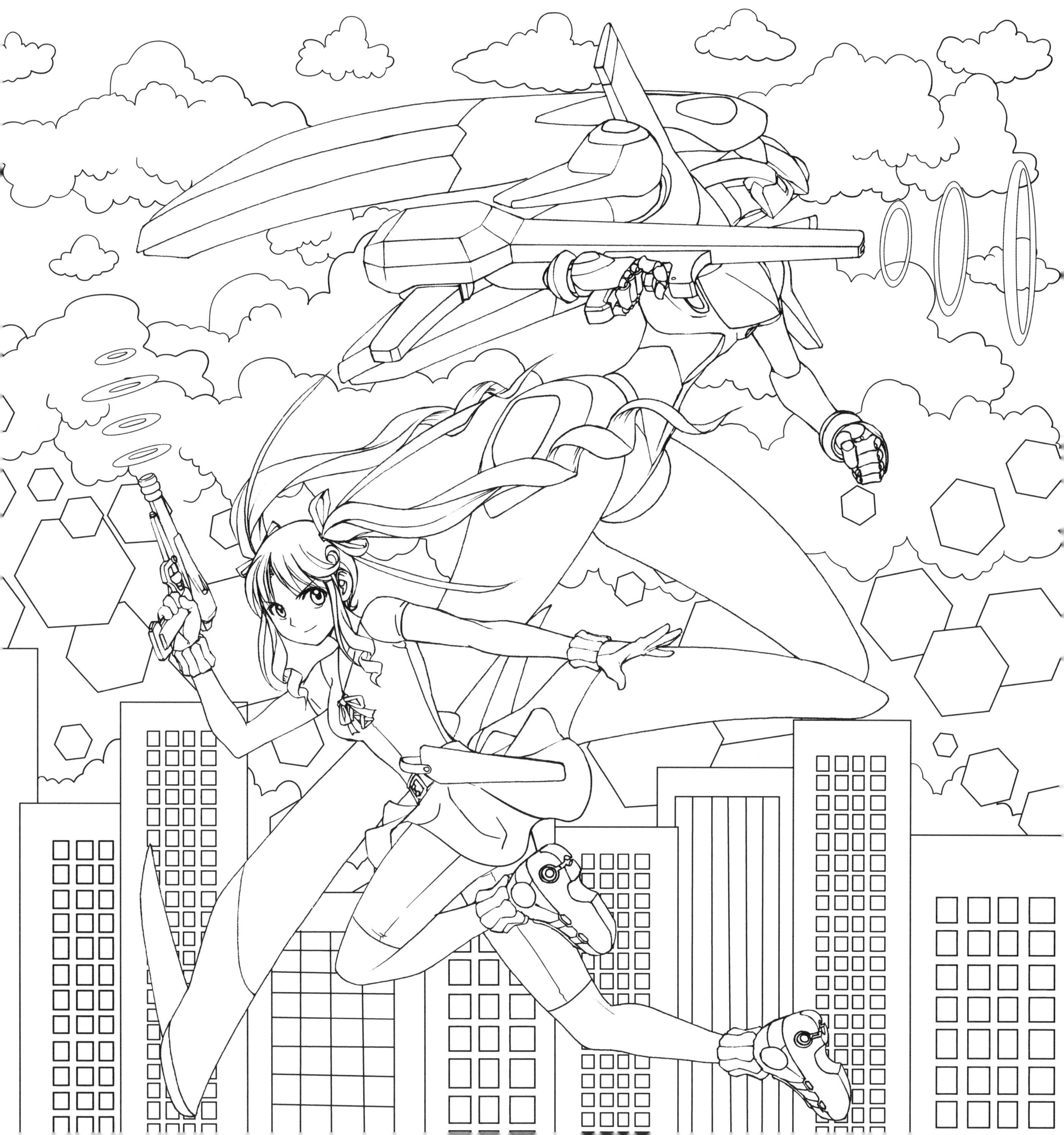

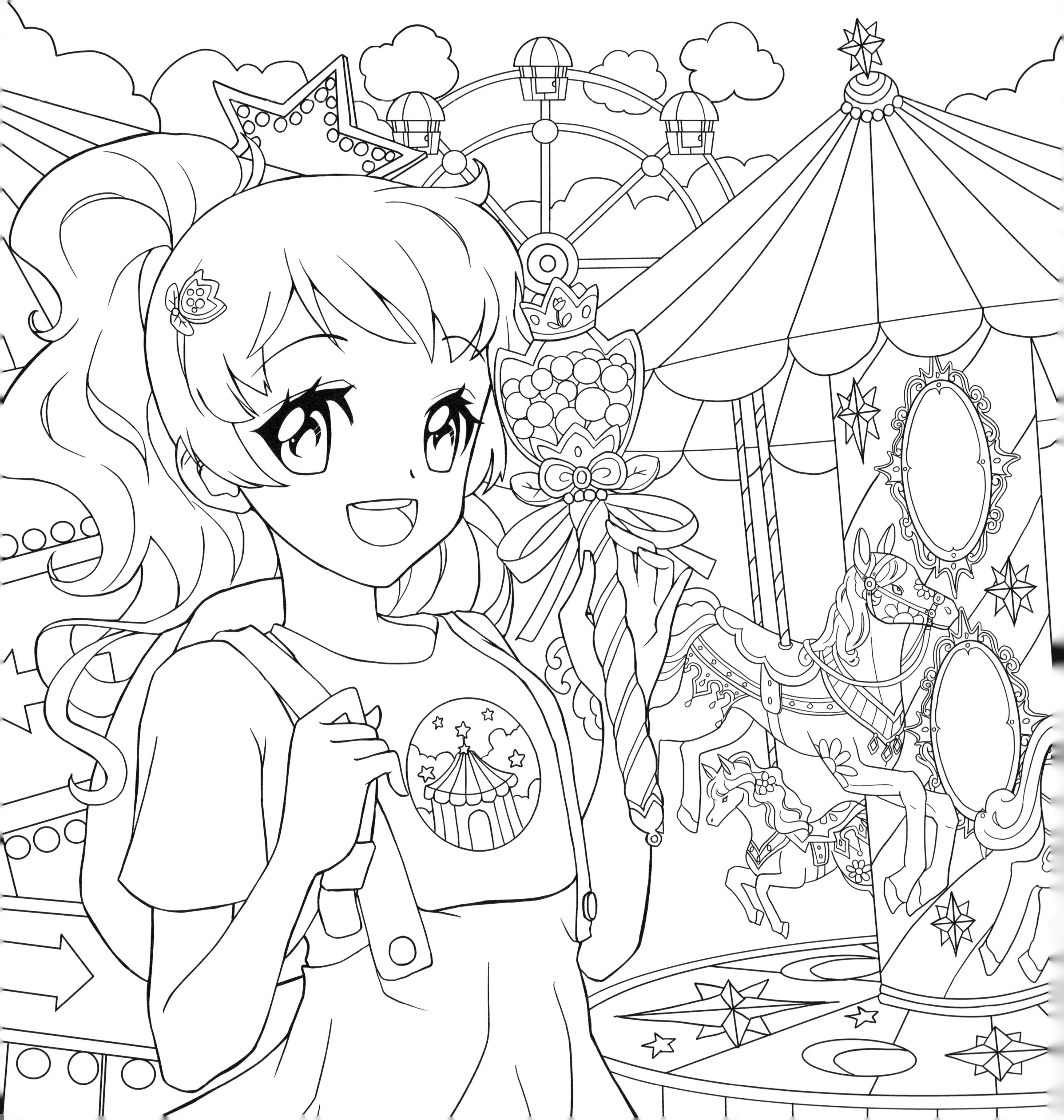

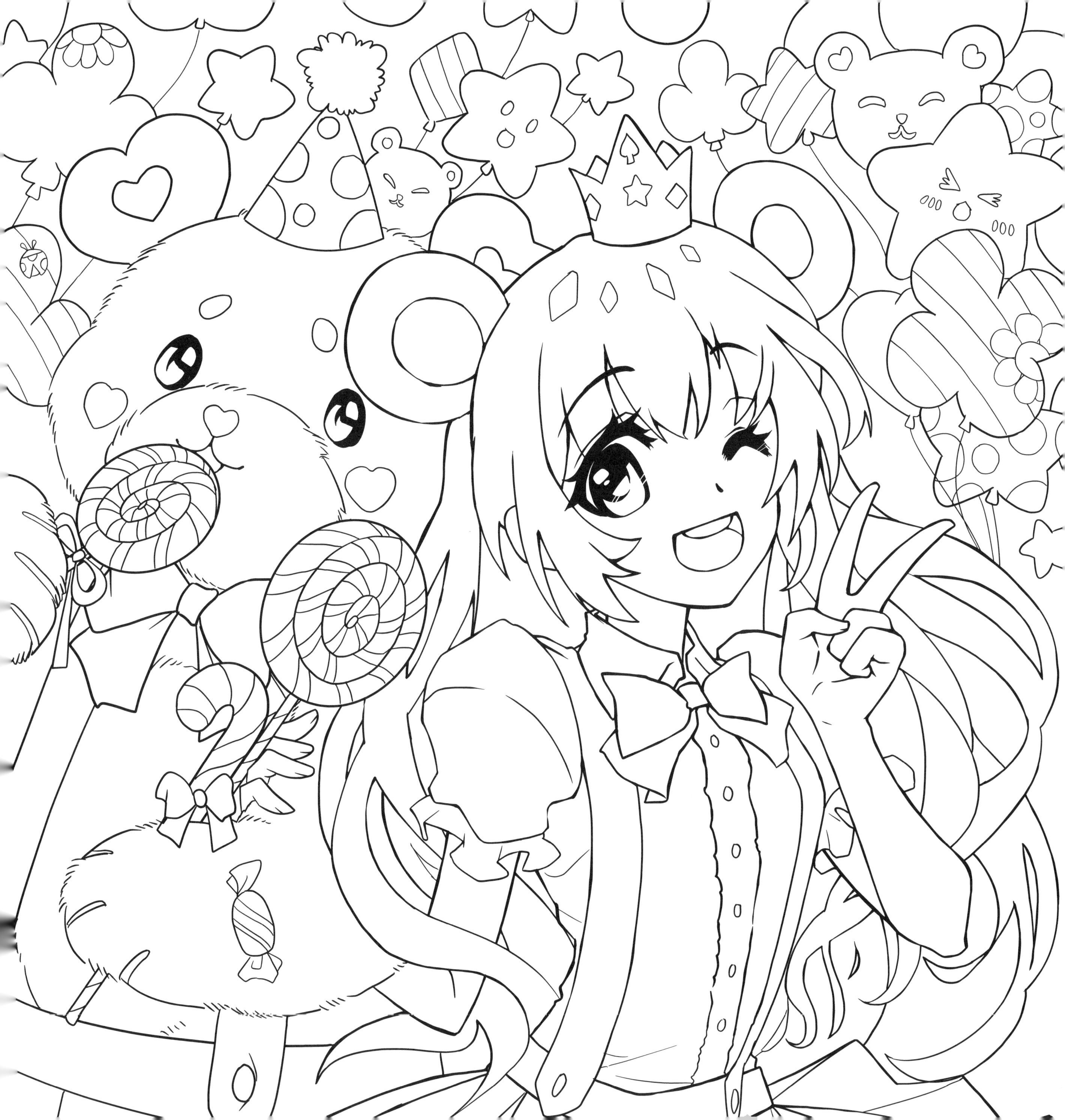

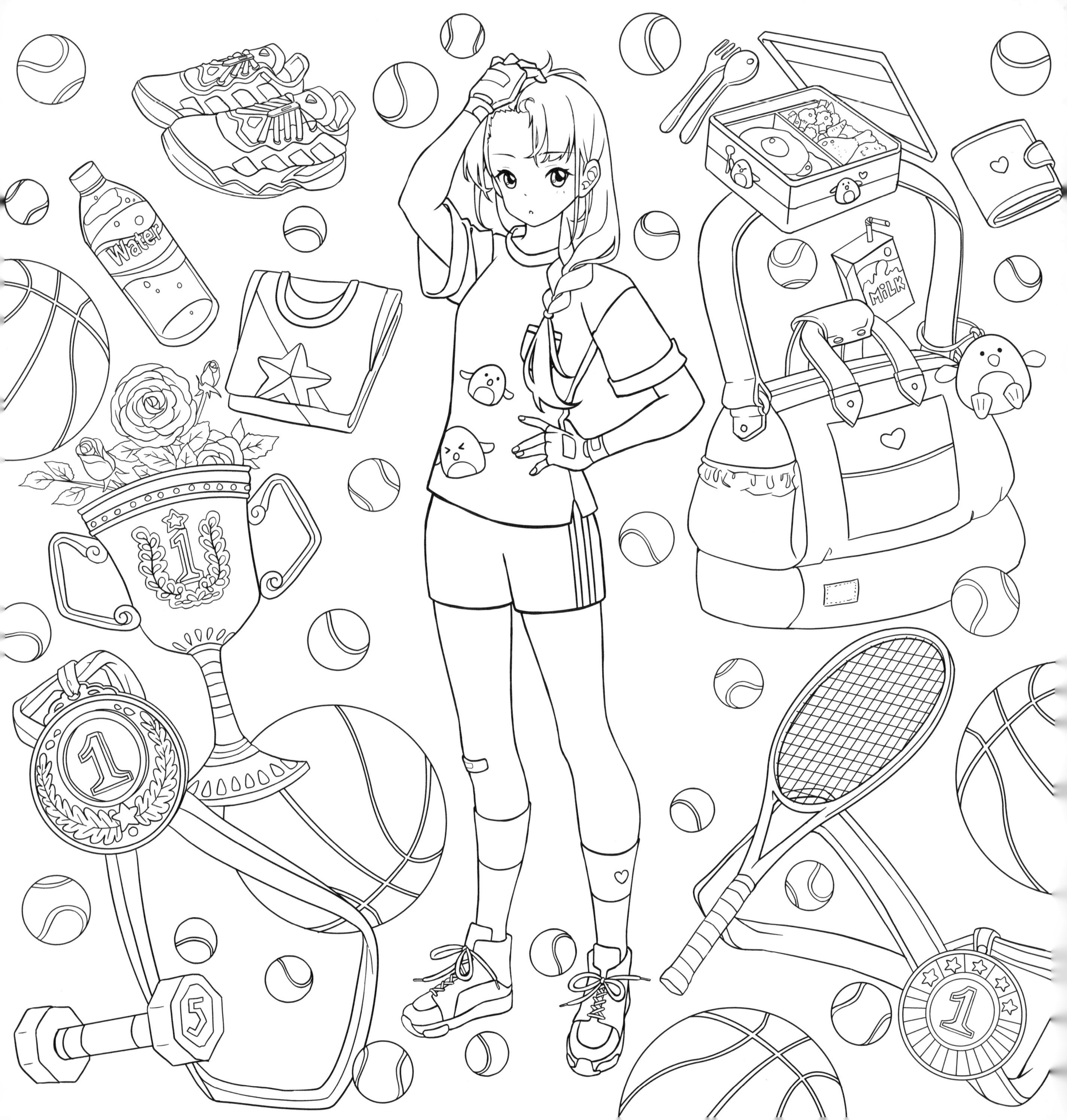
Water
MILK
1
1
5
1

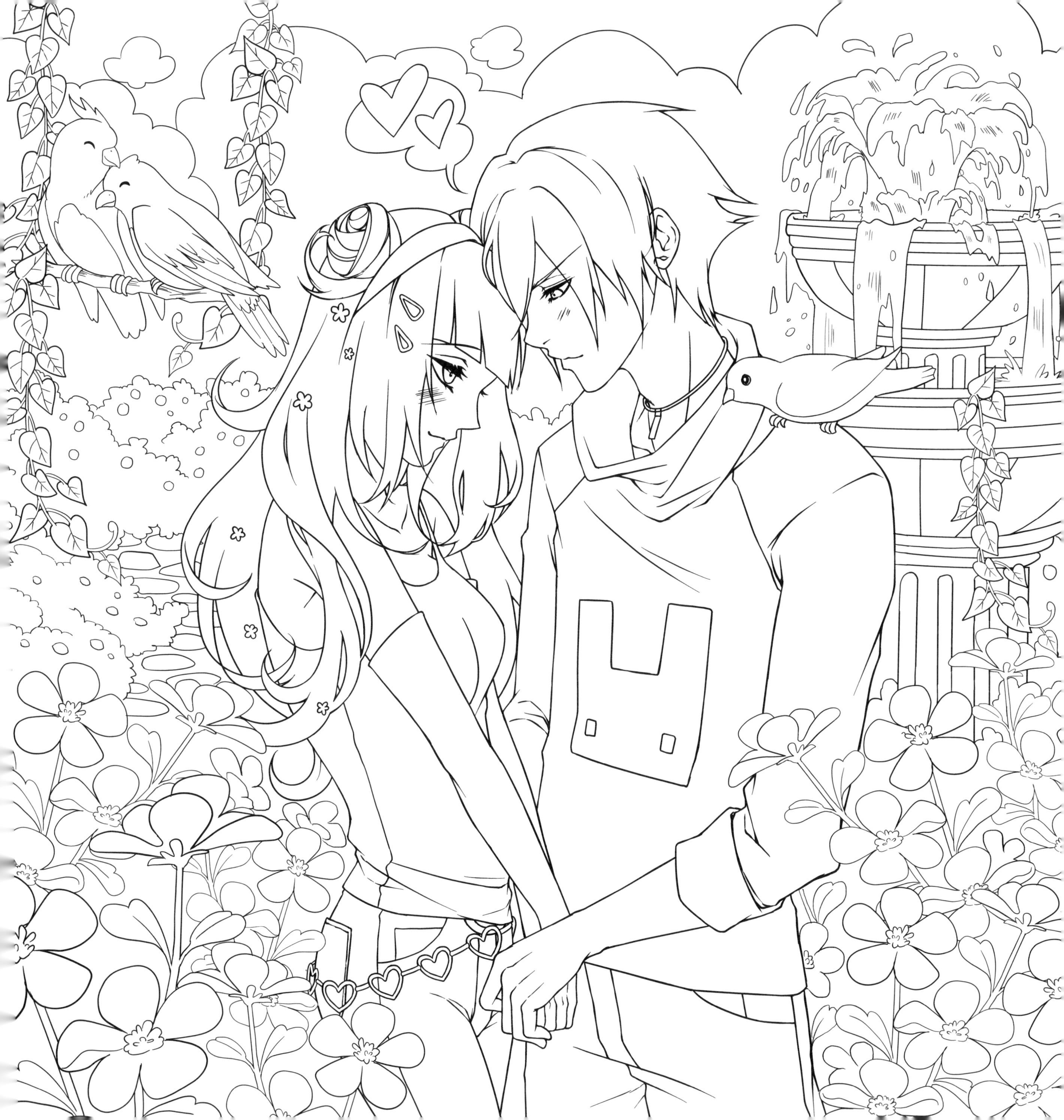

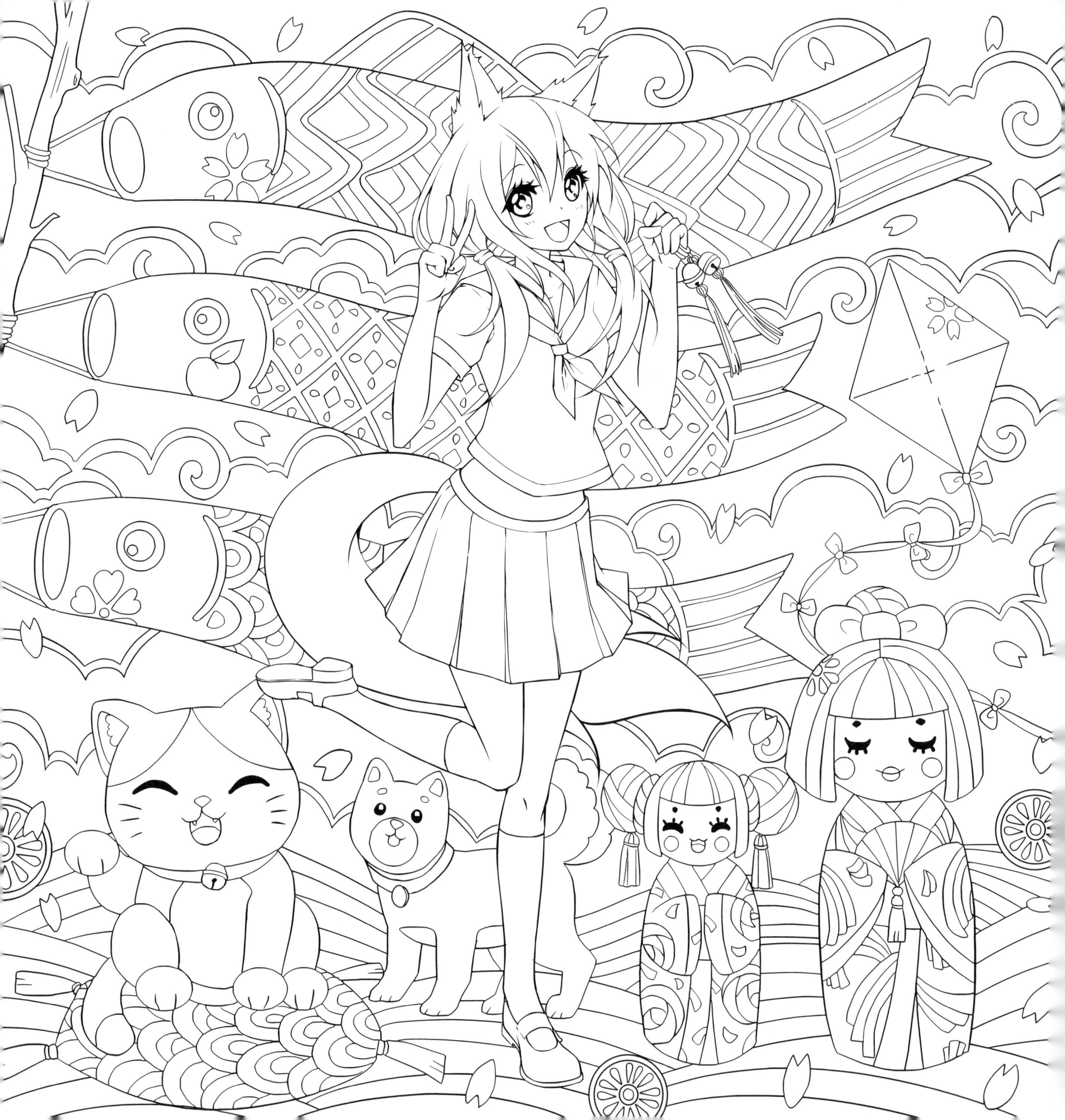

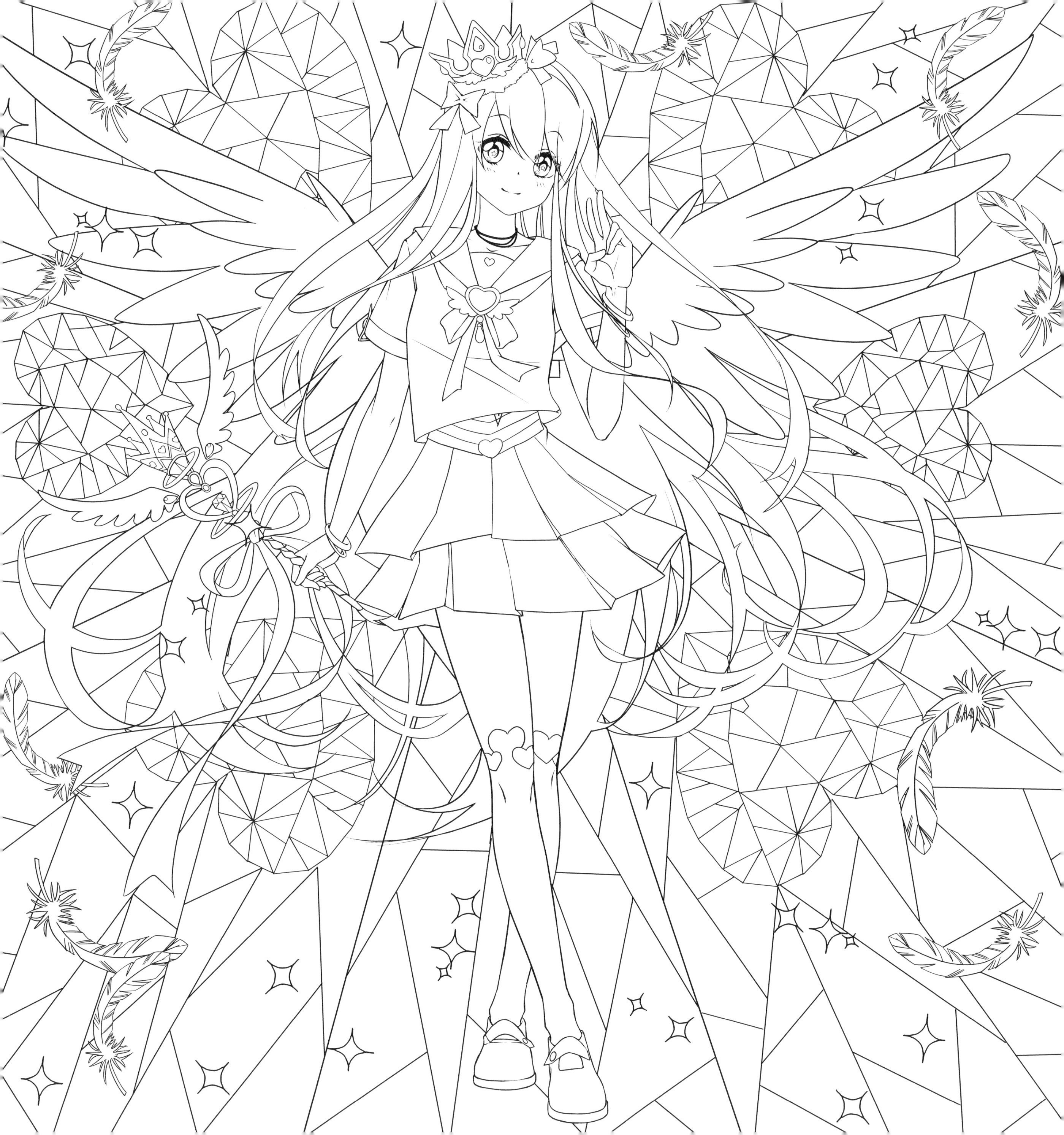

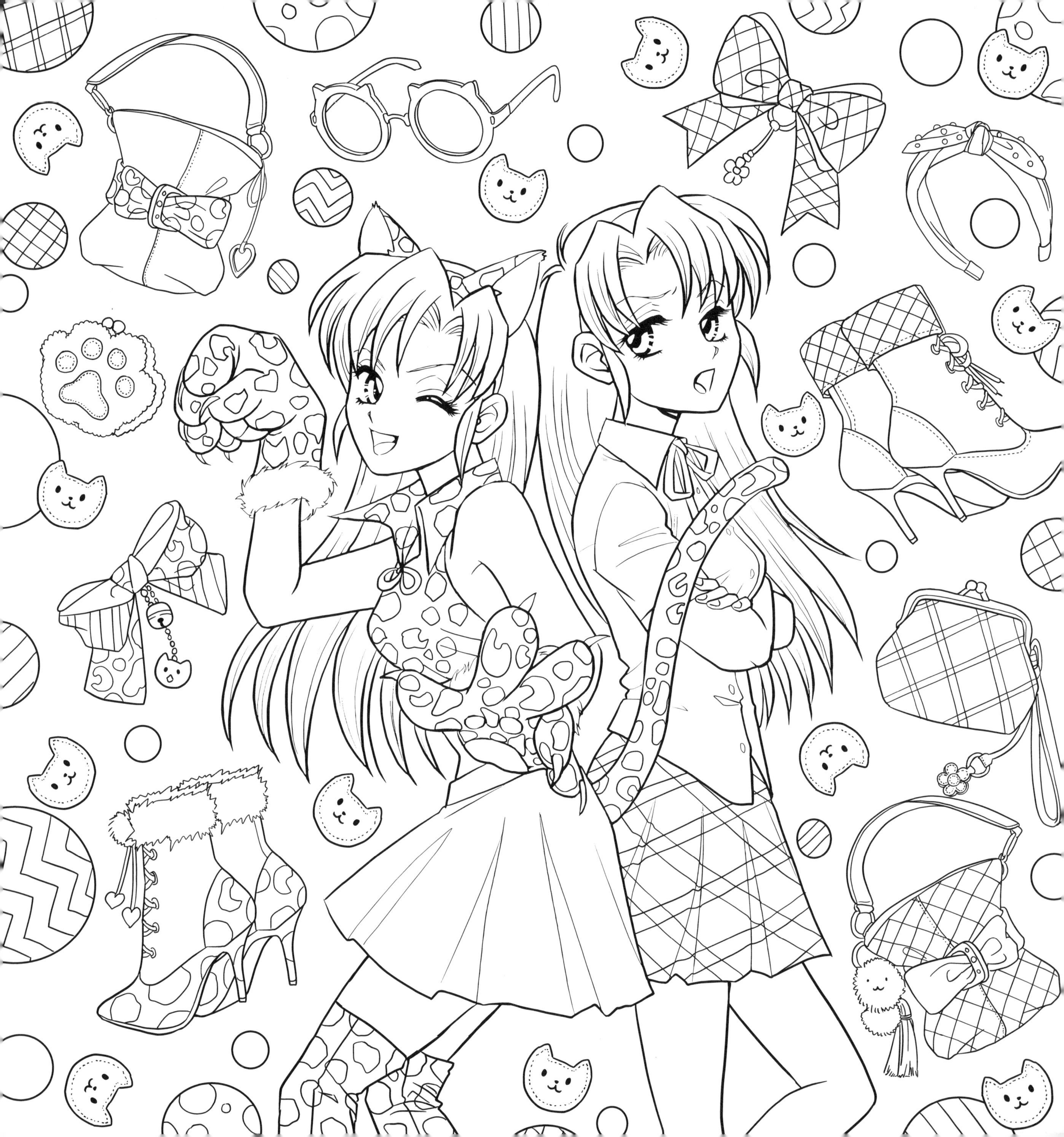

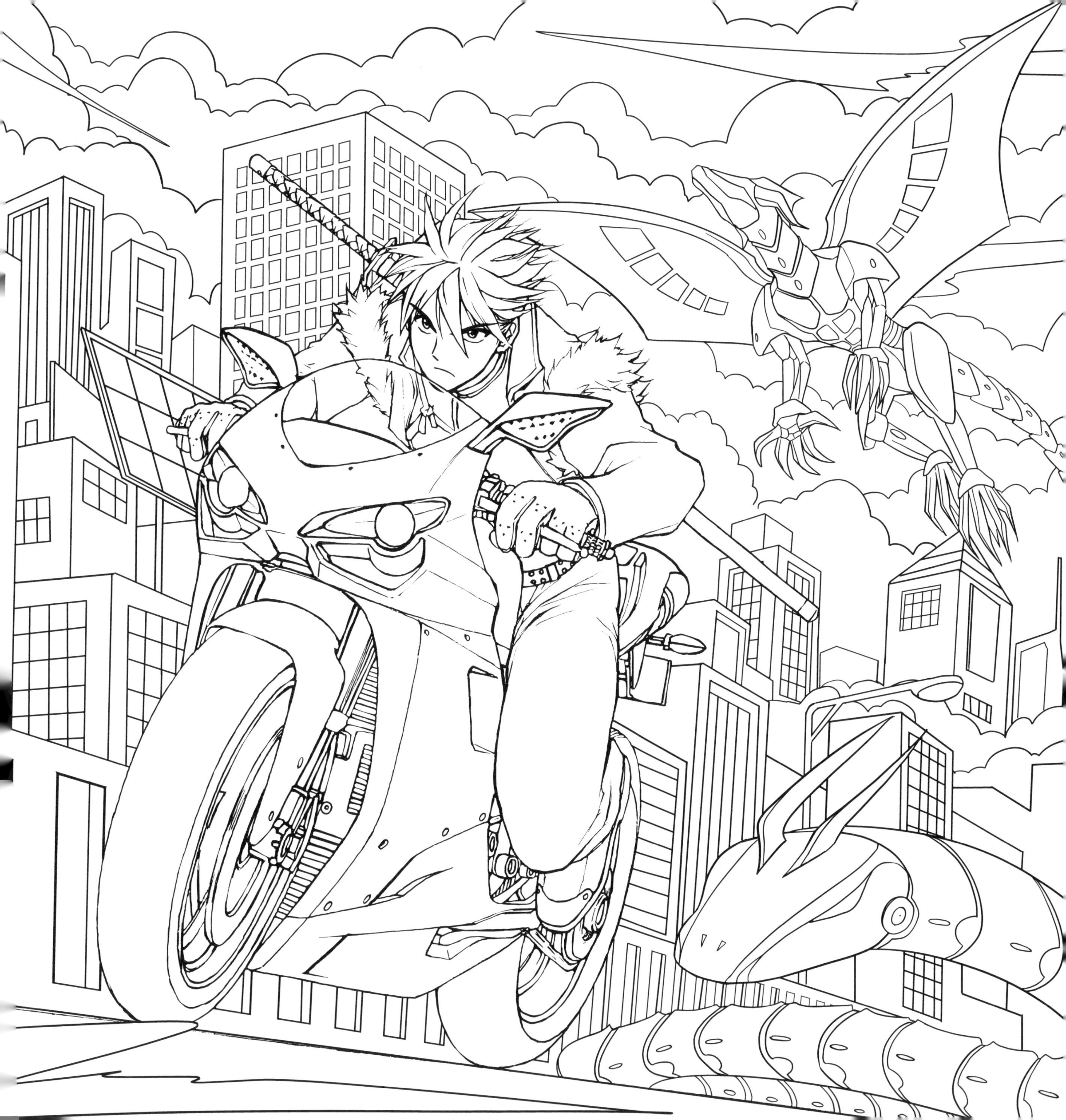

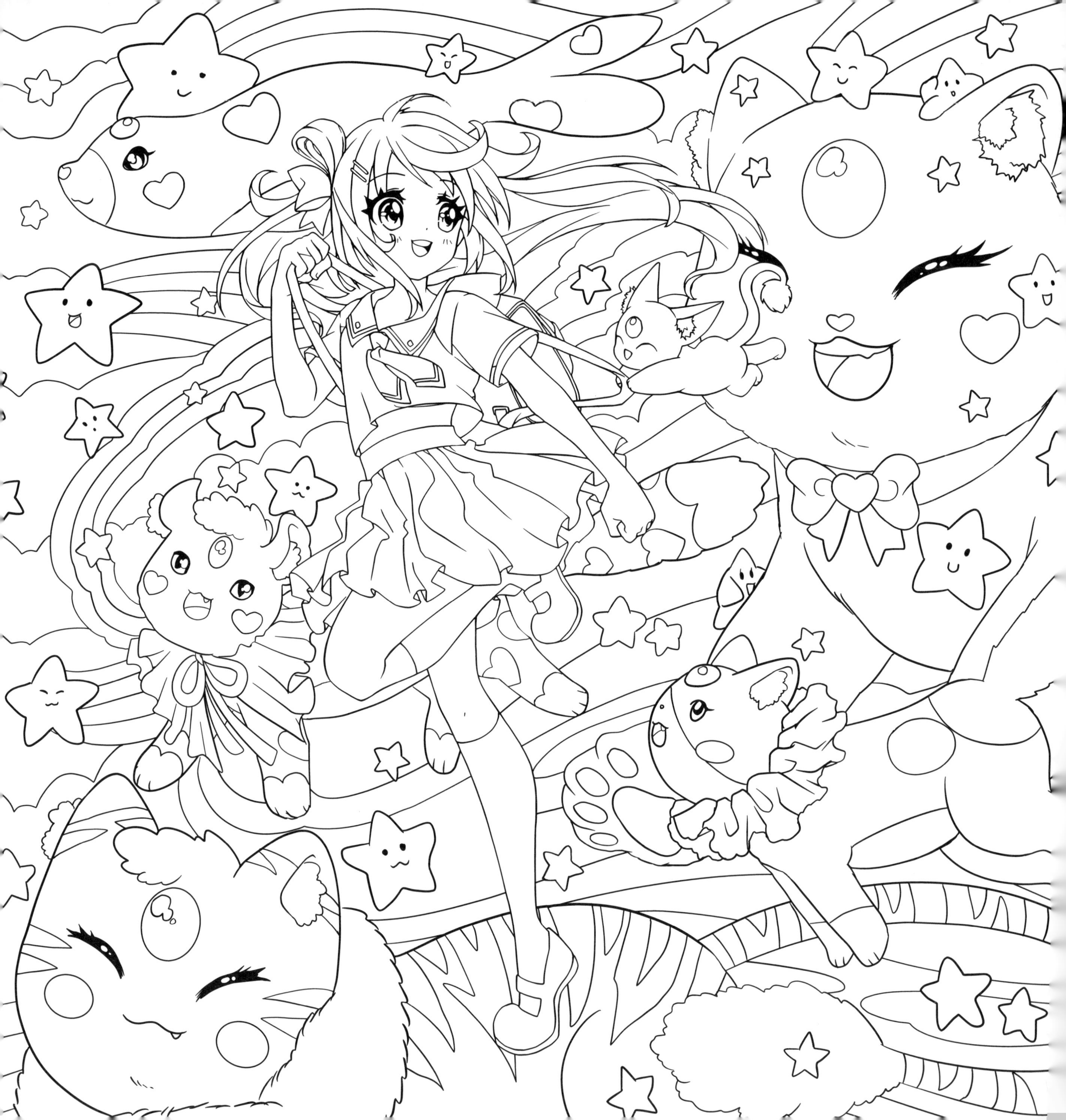

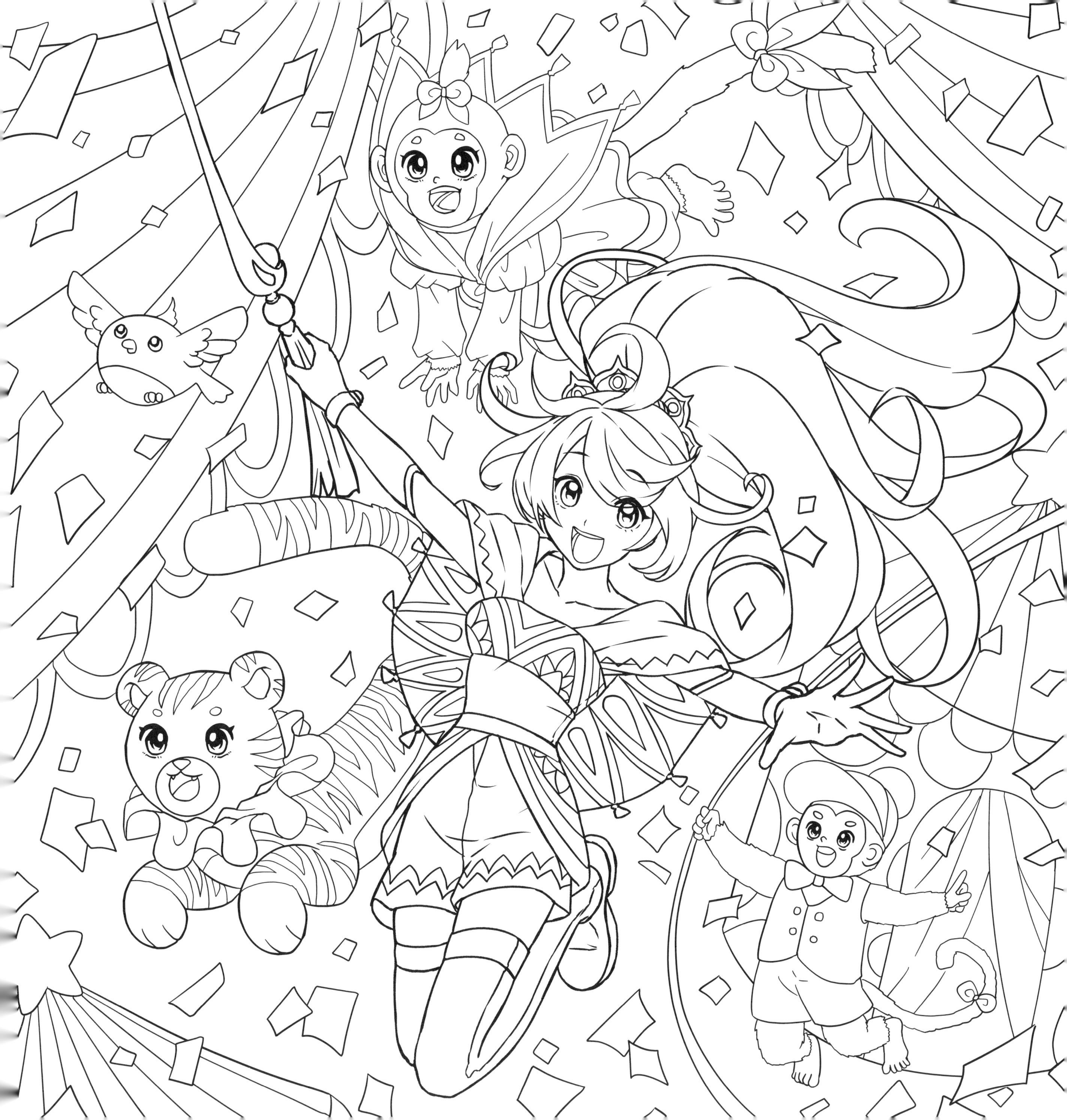

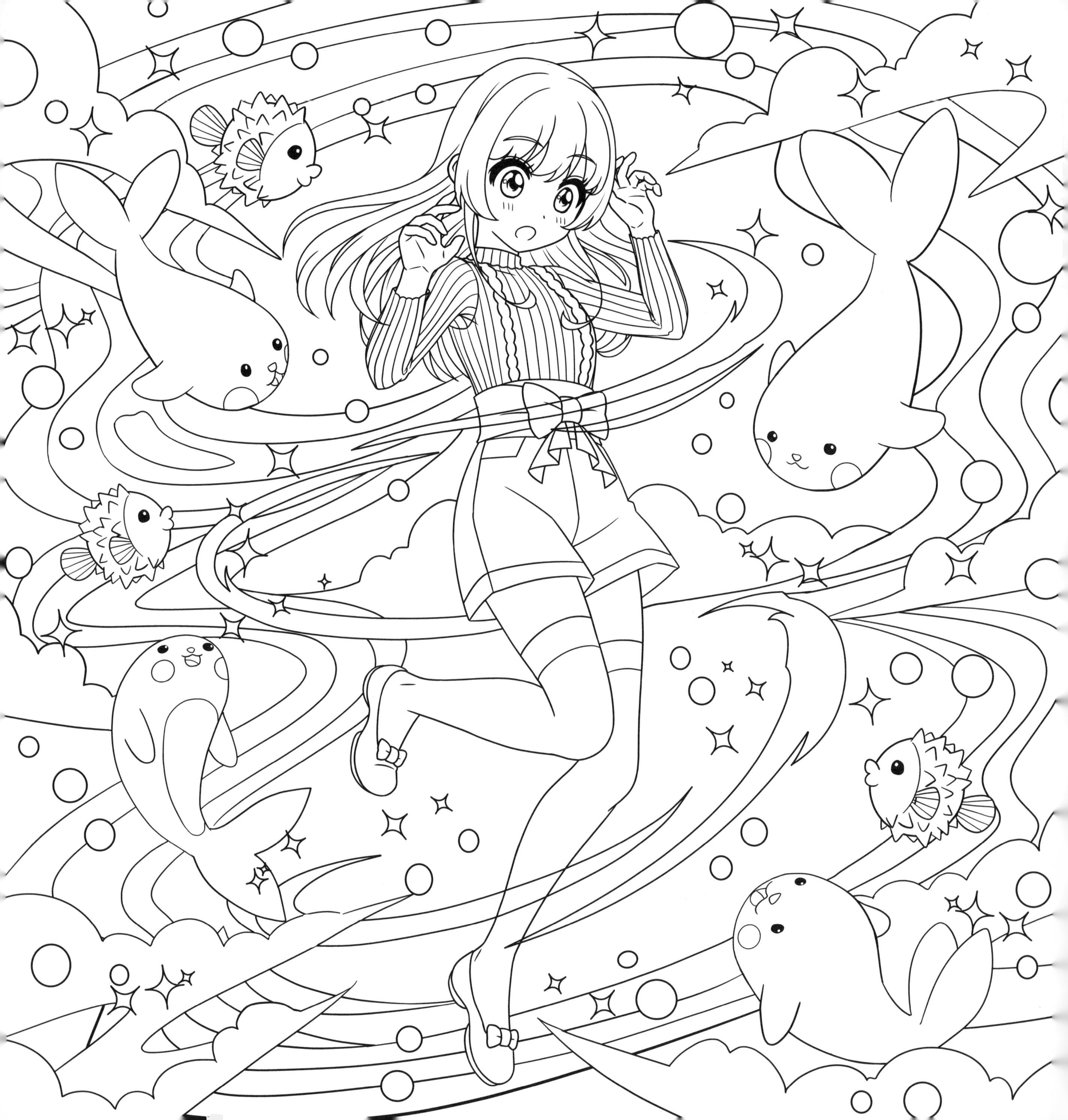

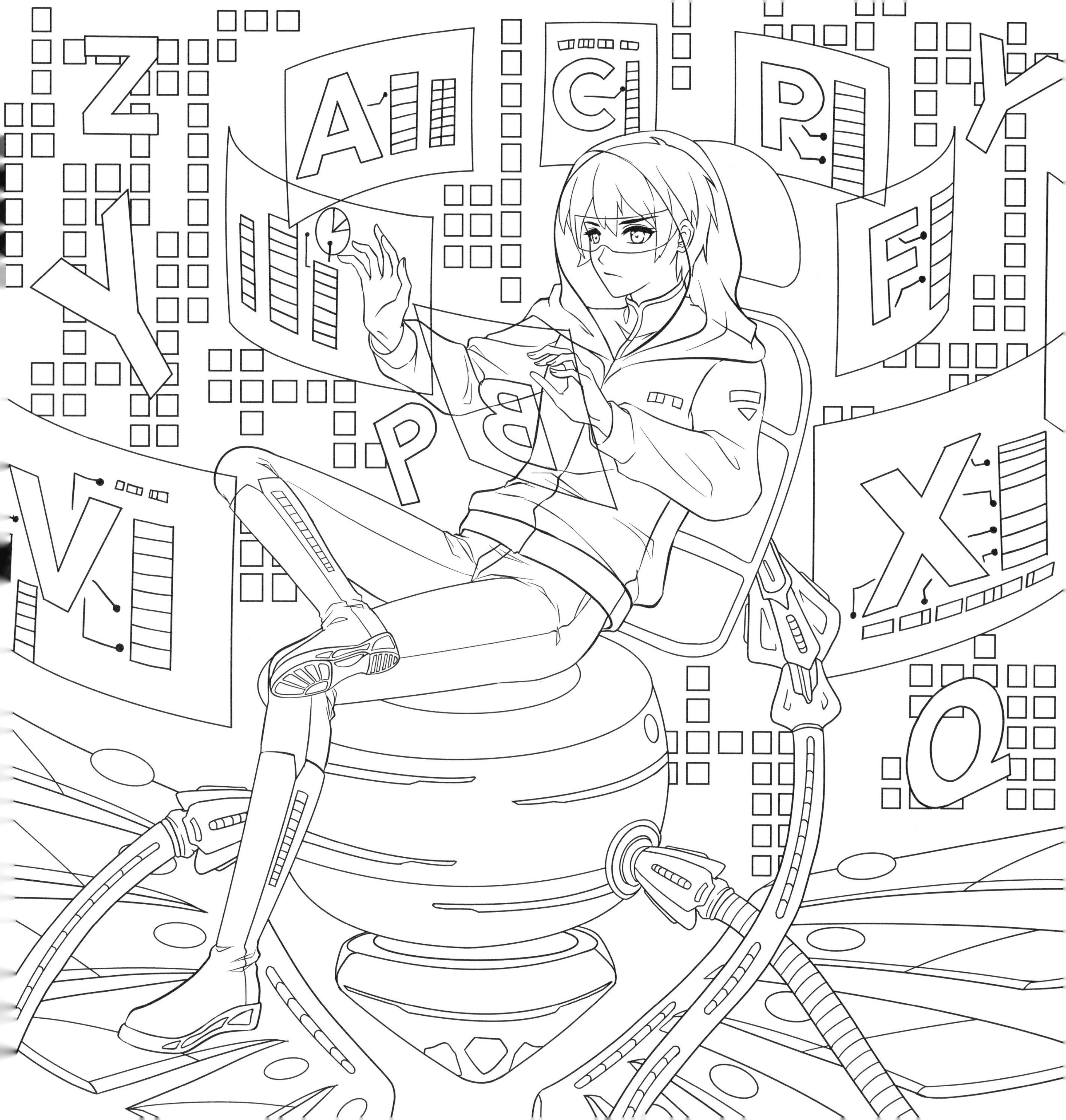
Z
Y
A
C
R
Y
F
P
B
V
X
Q

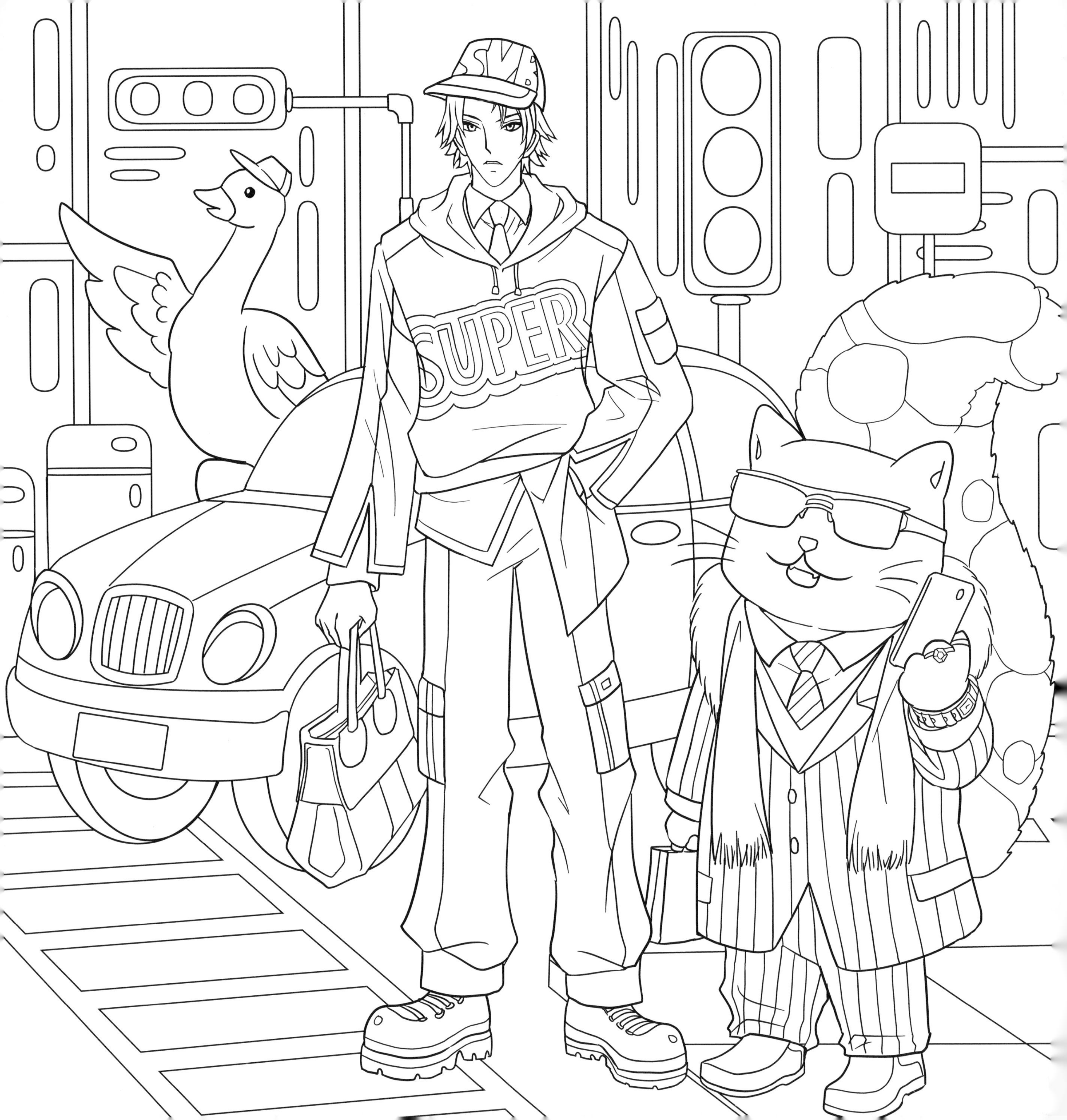
SUPER

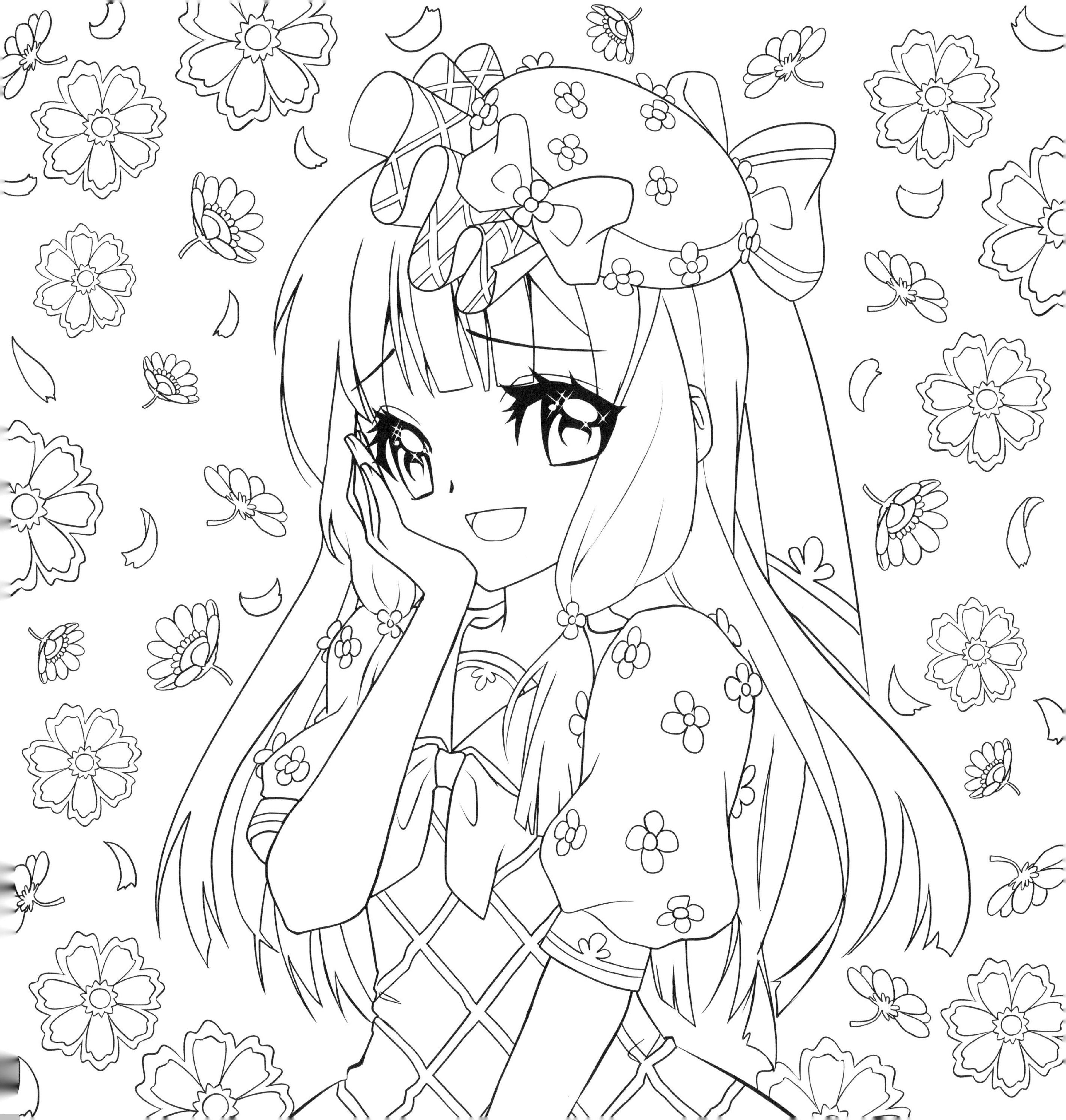

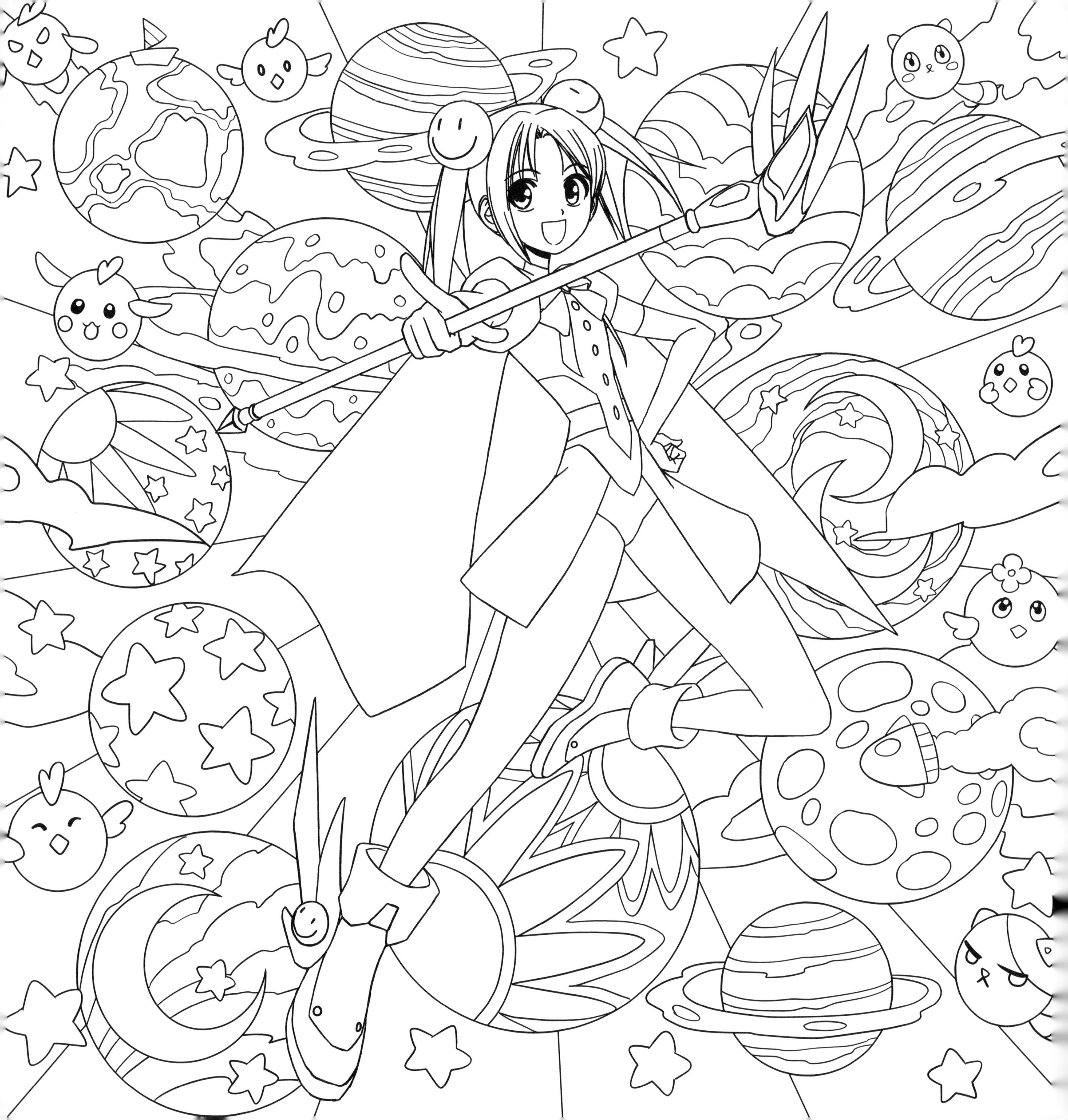

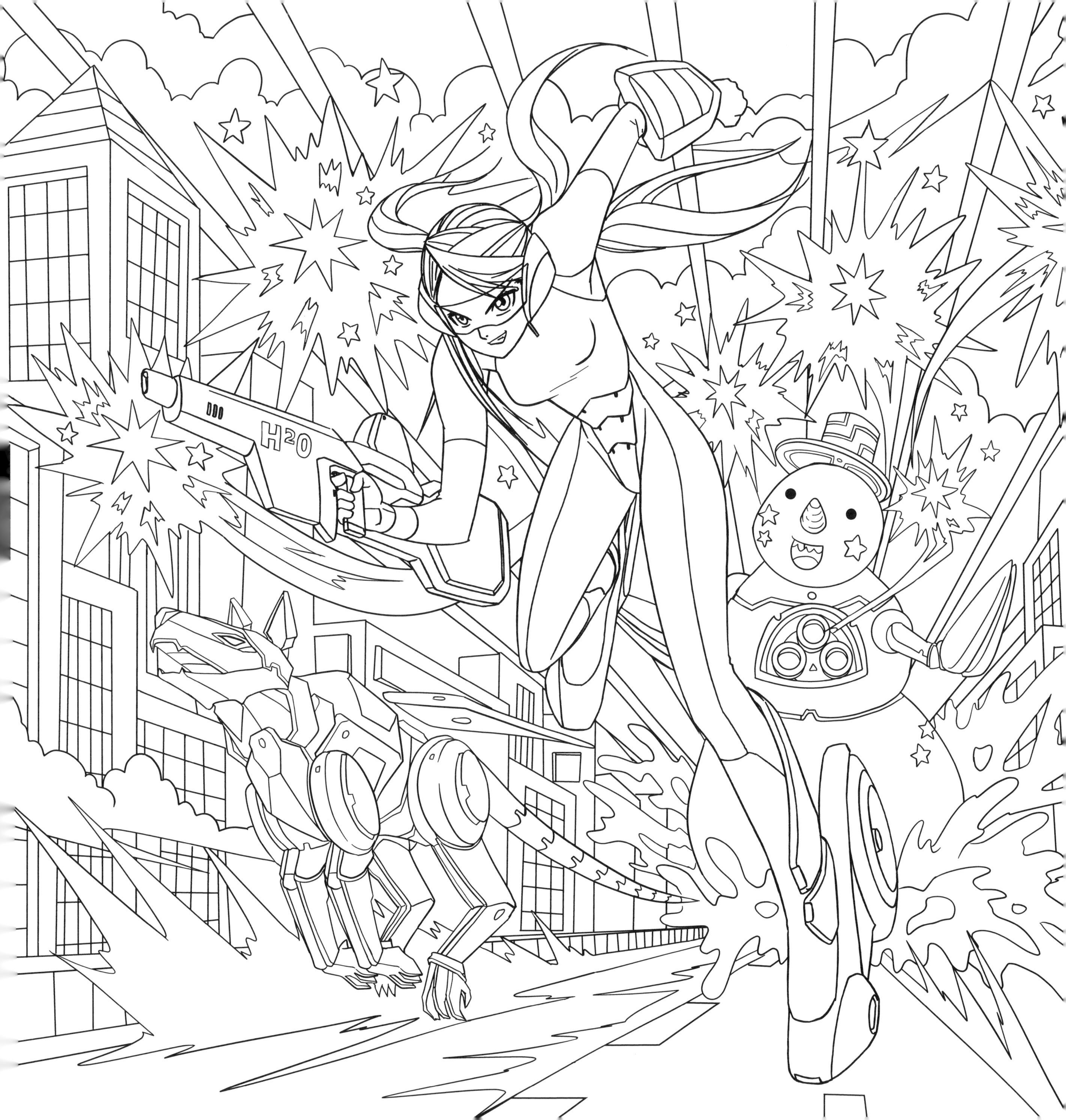
H2O

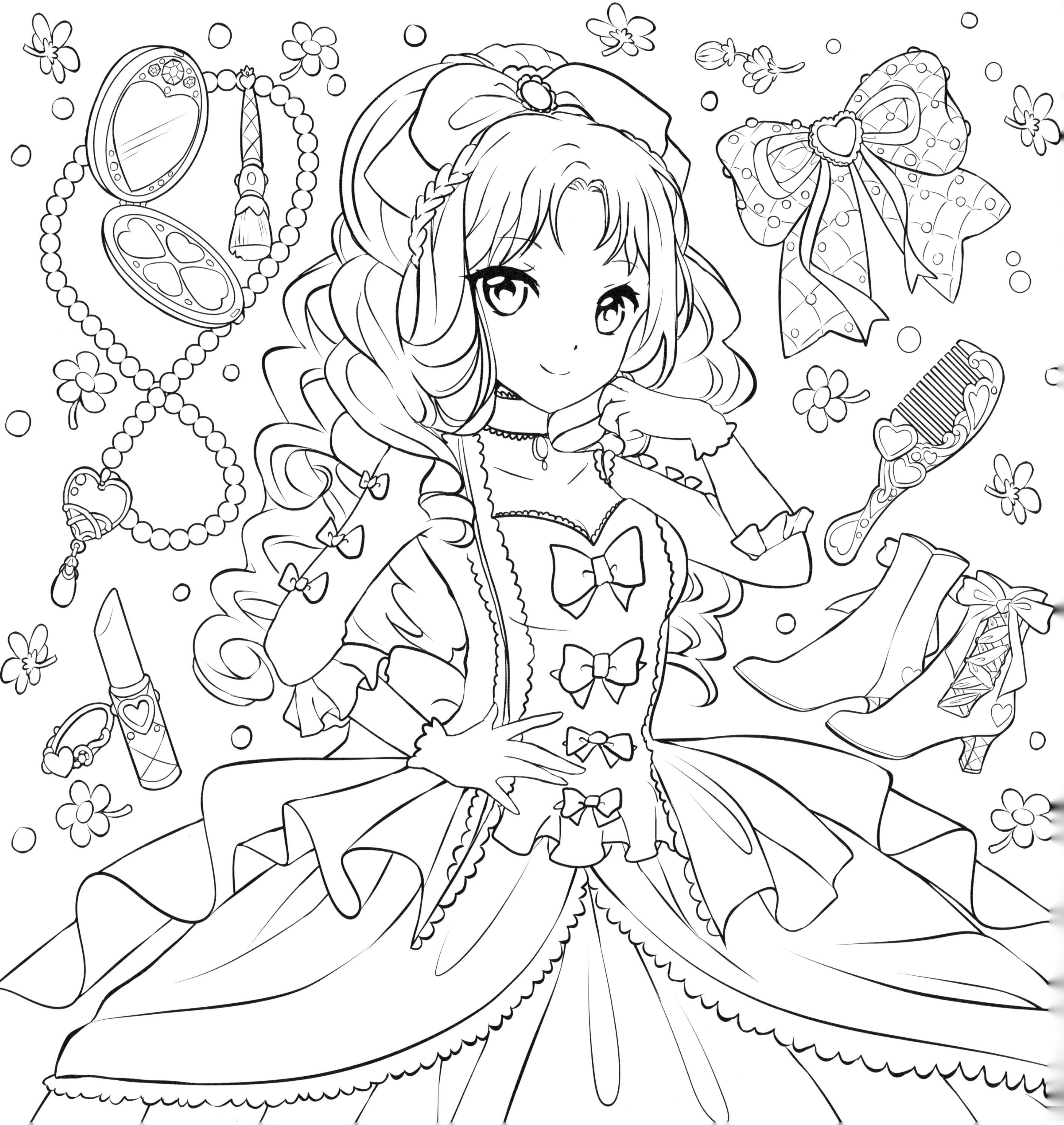

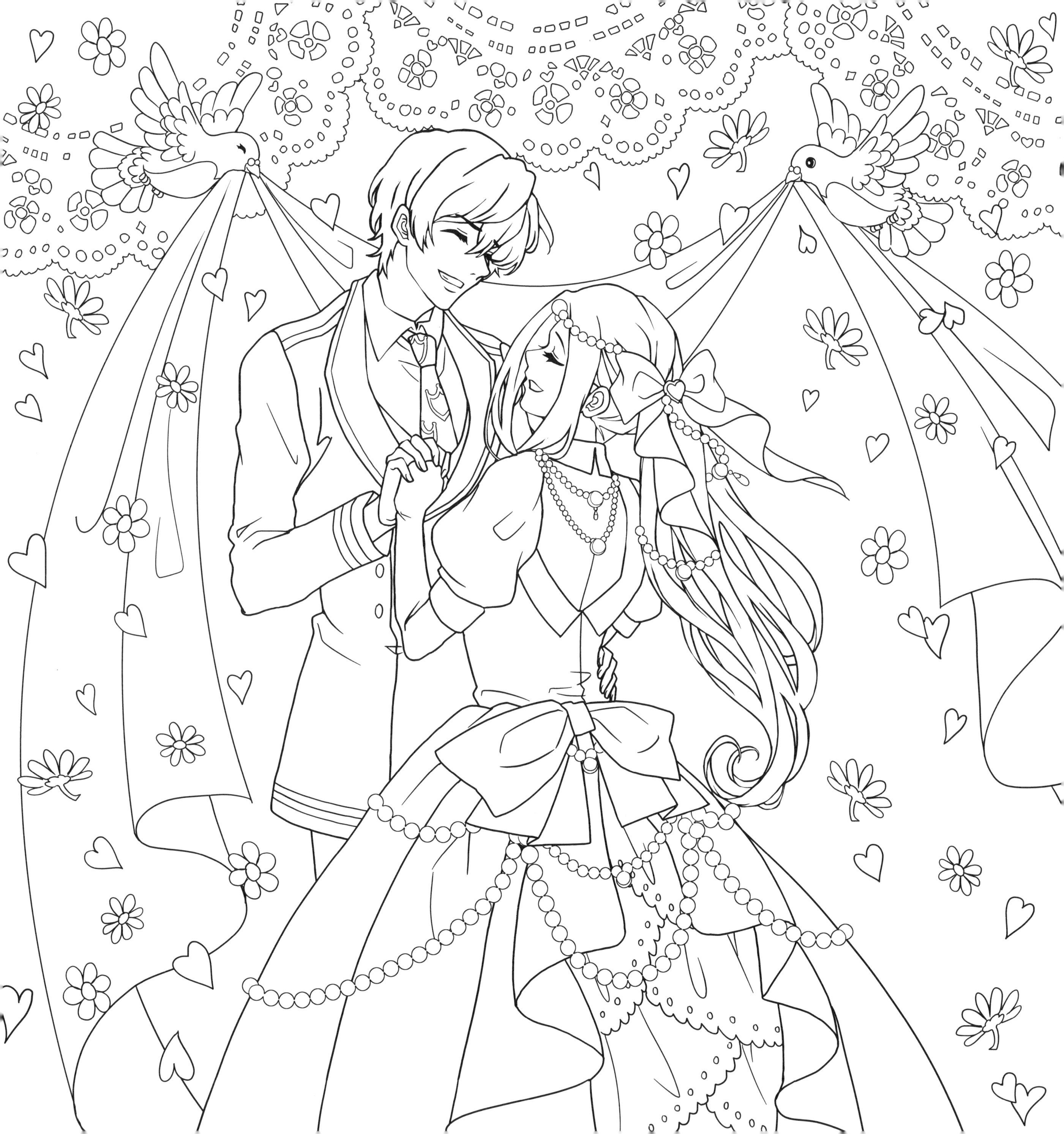

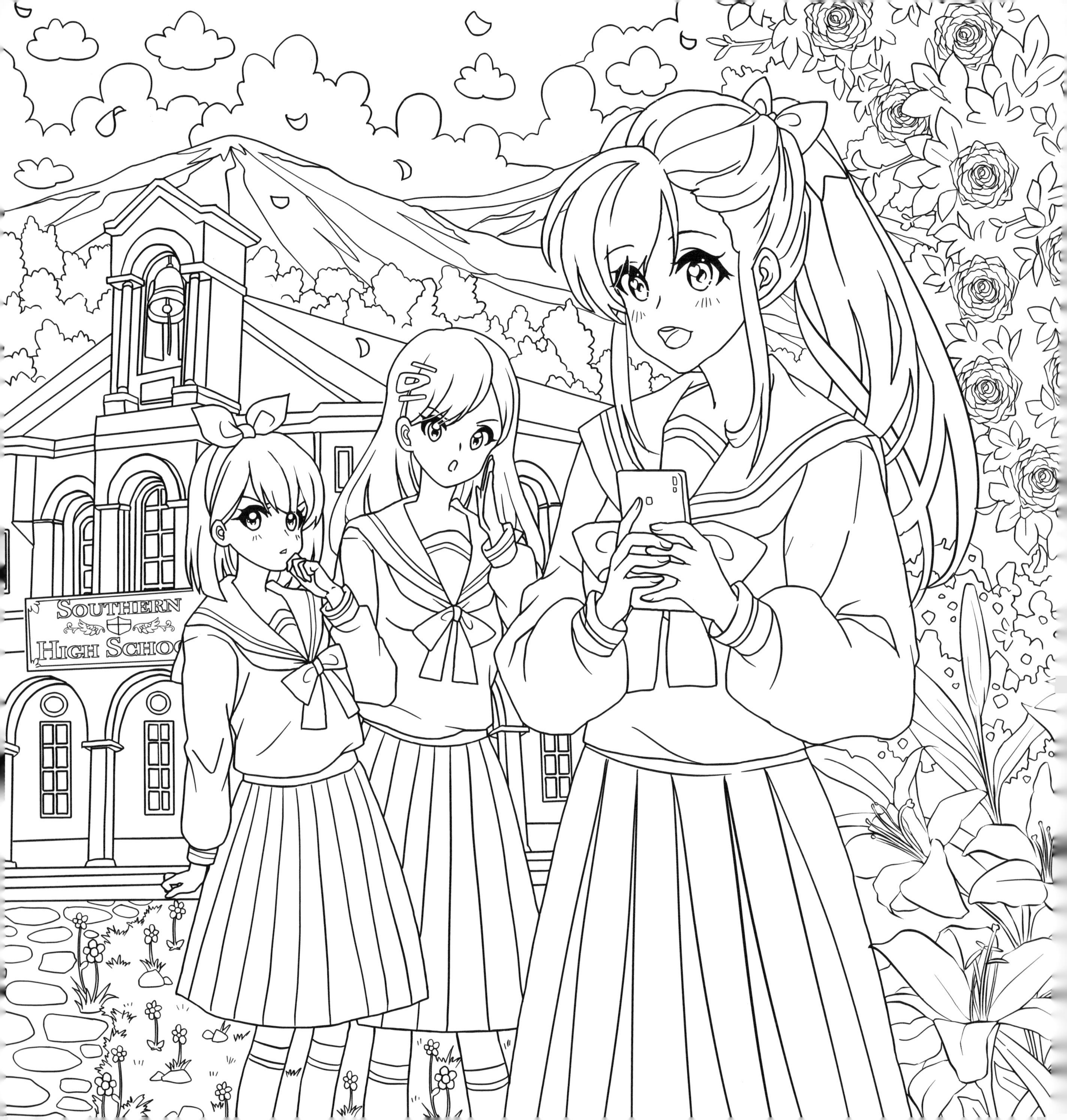
SOUTHERN
HIGH SCHOO

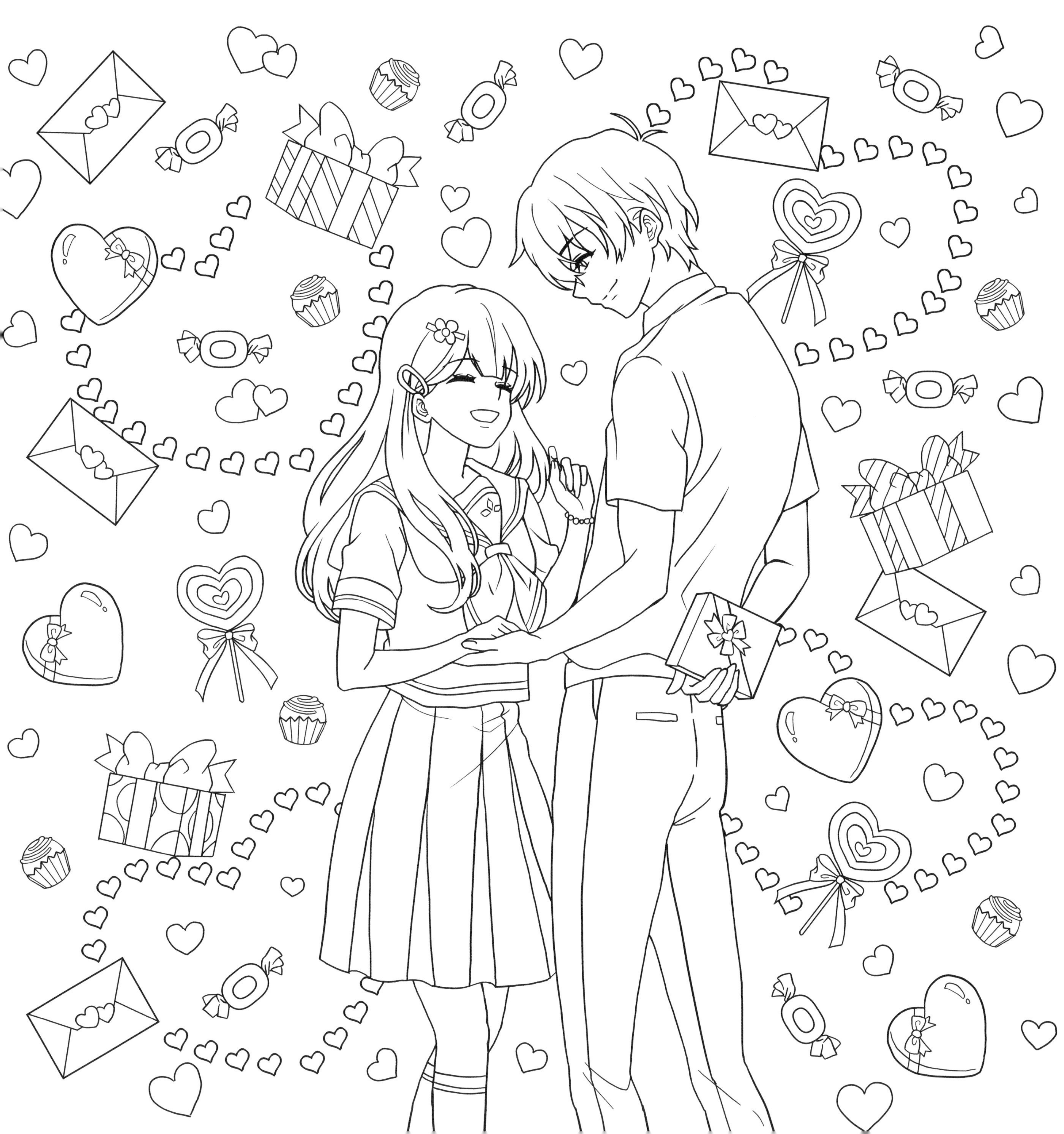

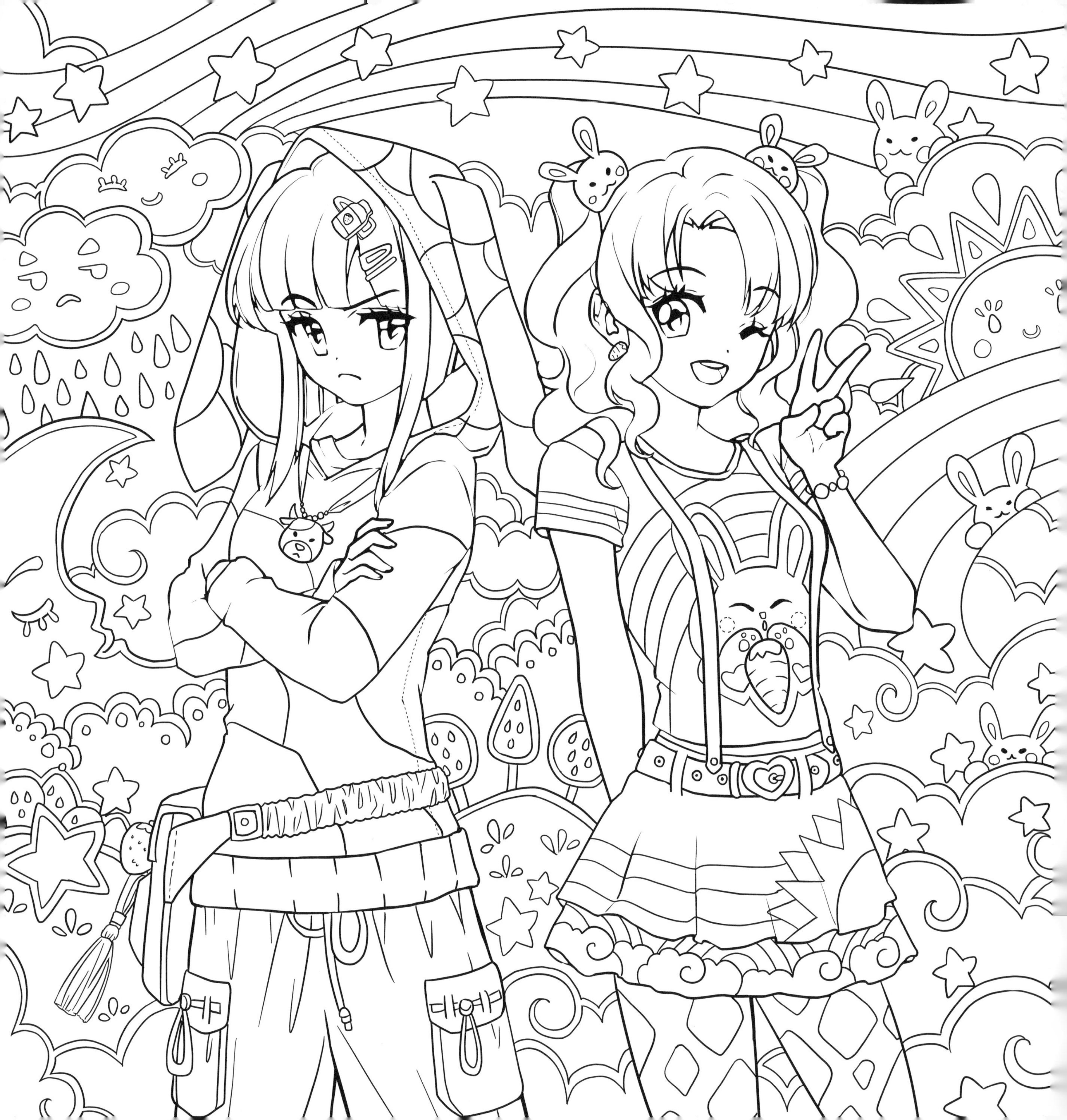

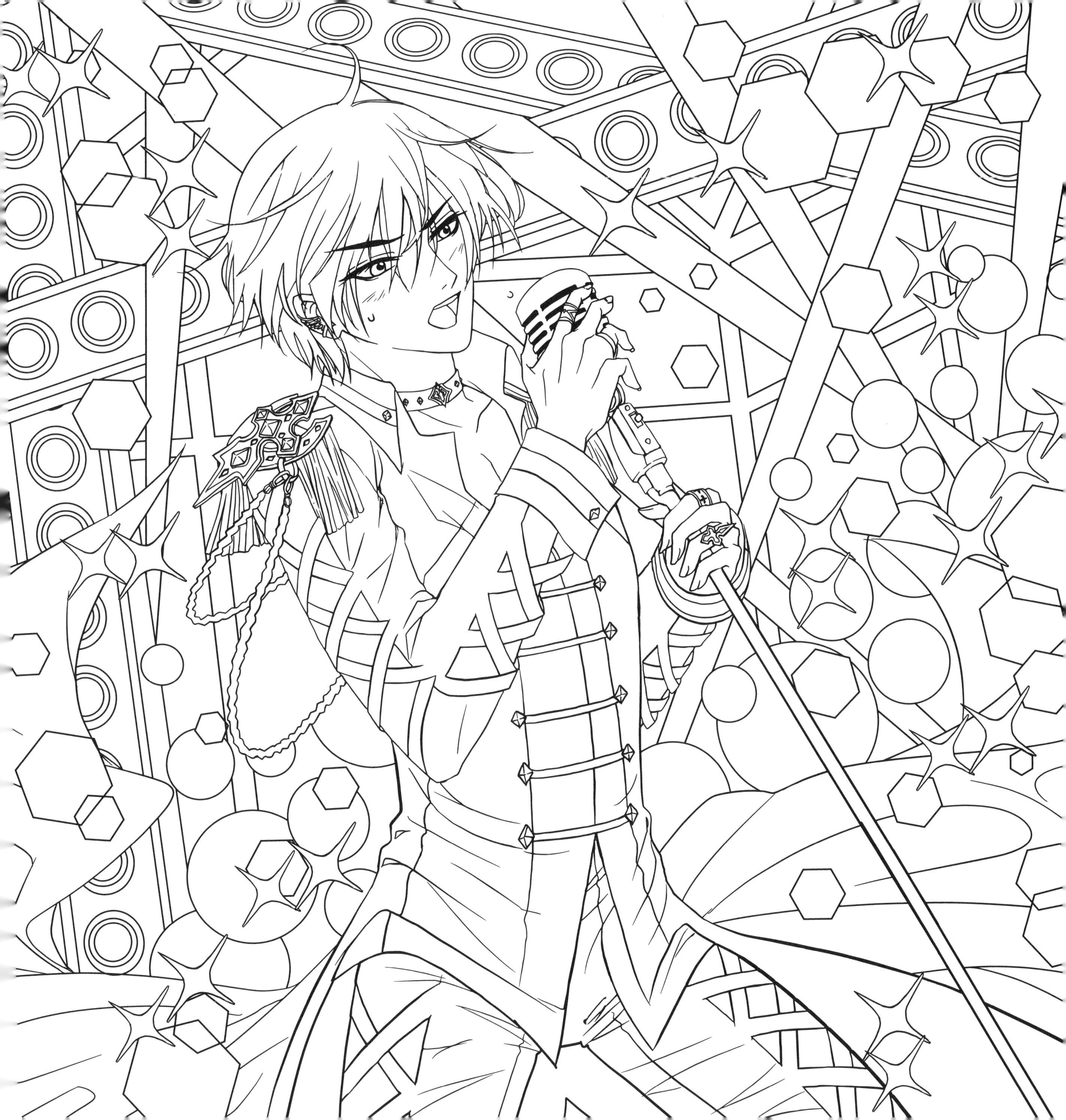

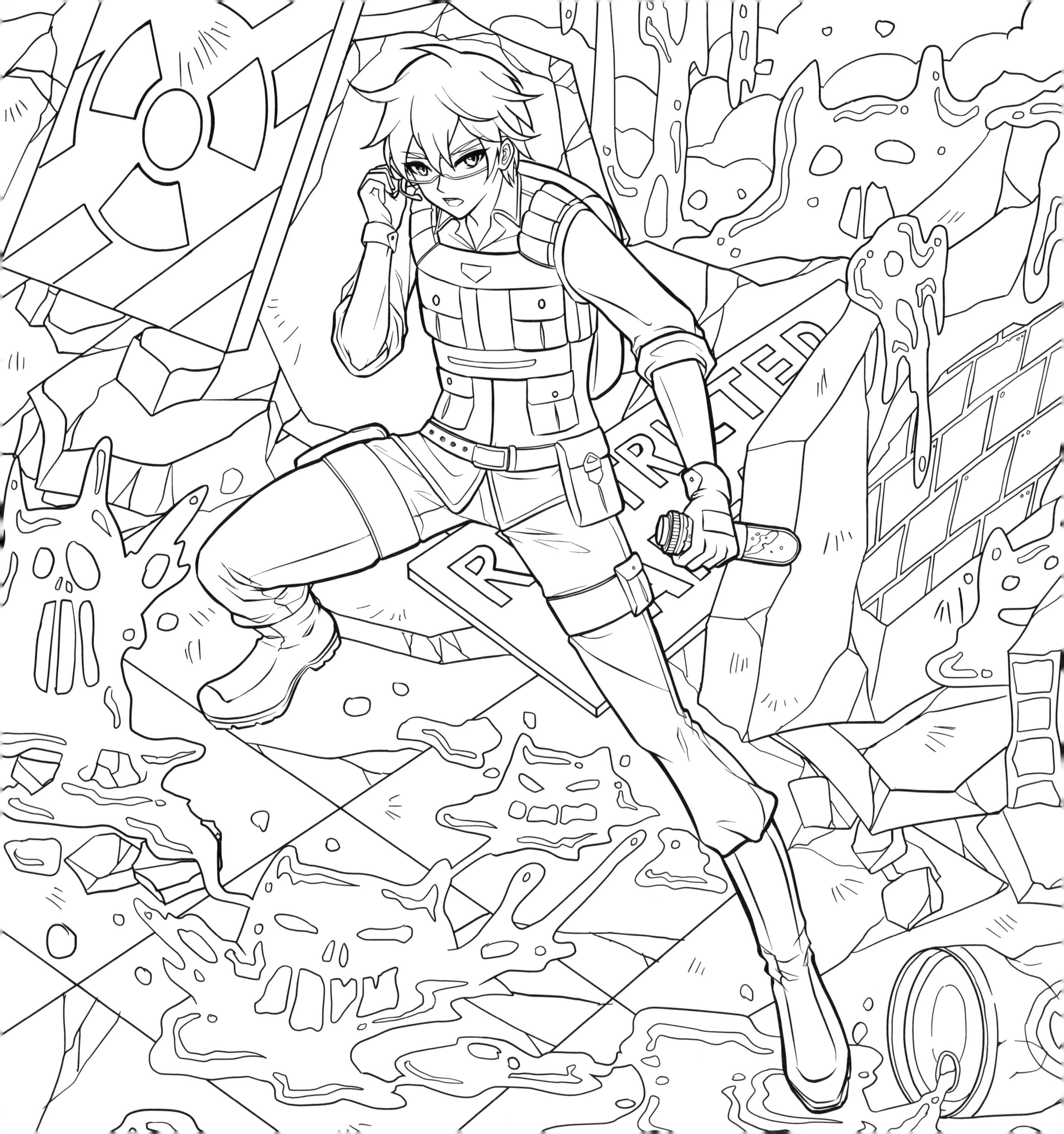

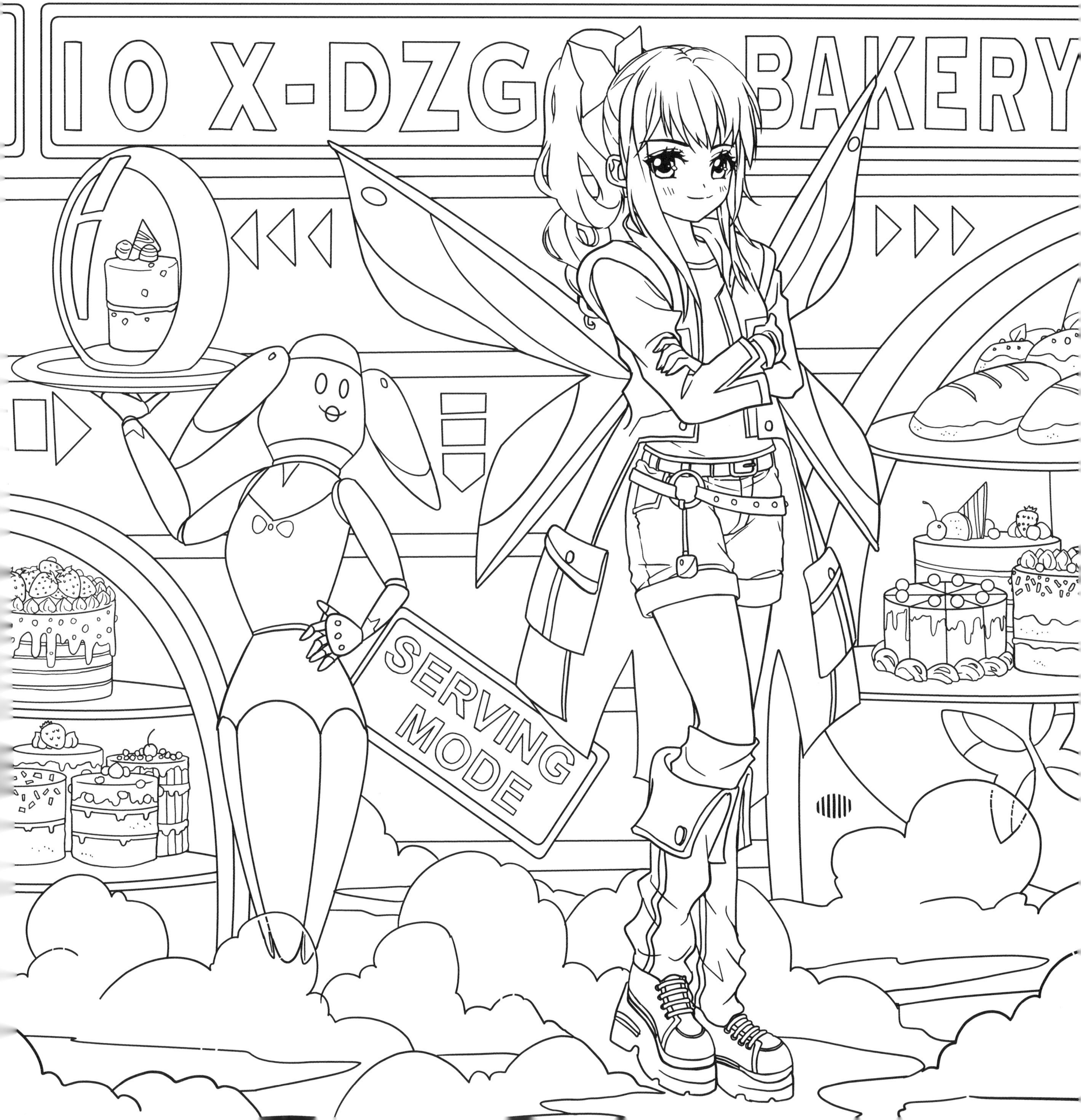
IO X-DZG BAKERY
SERVING MODE

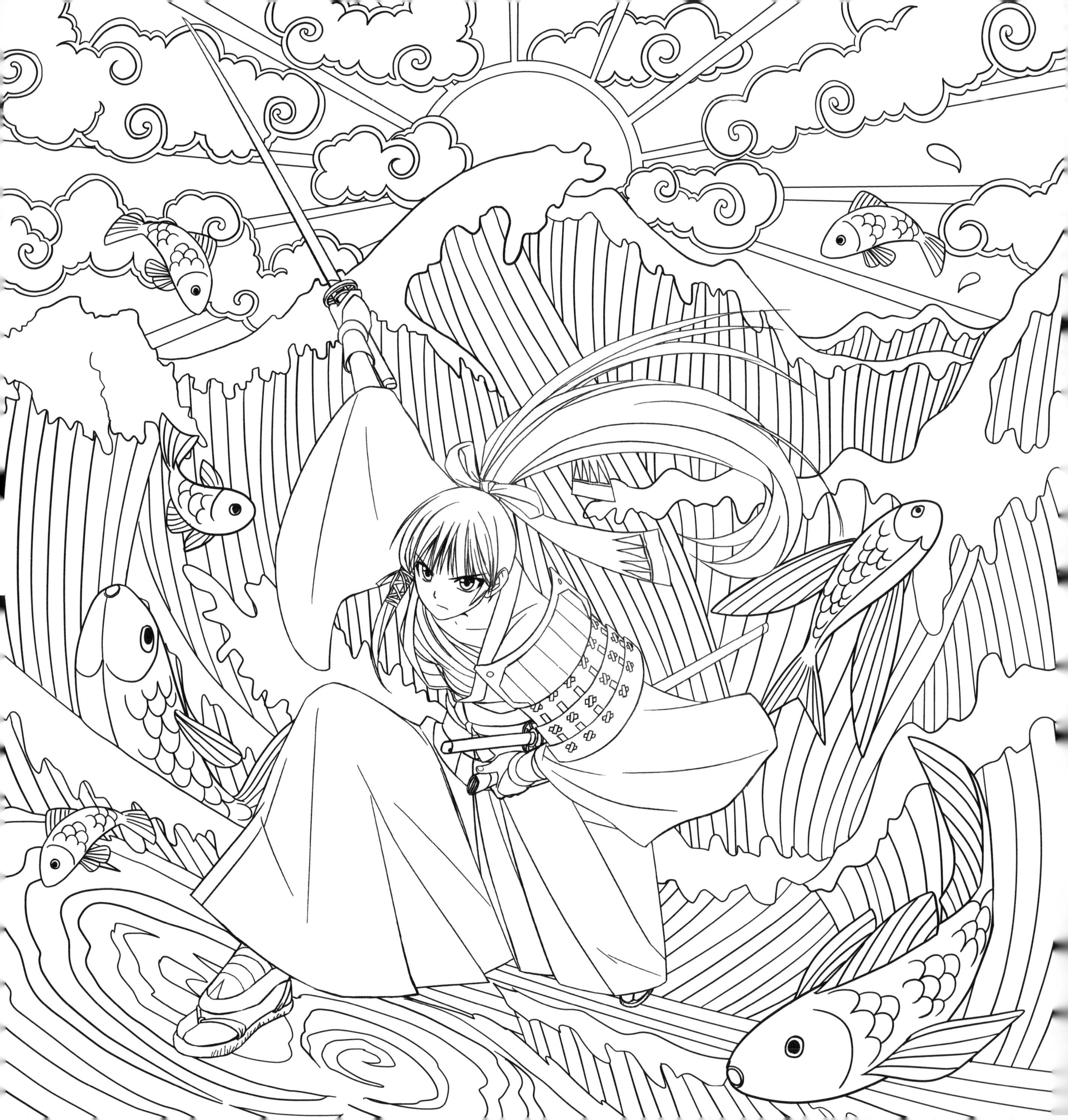

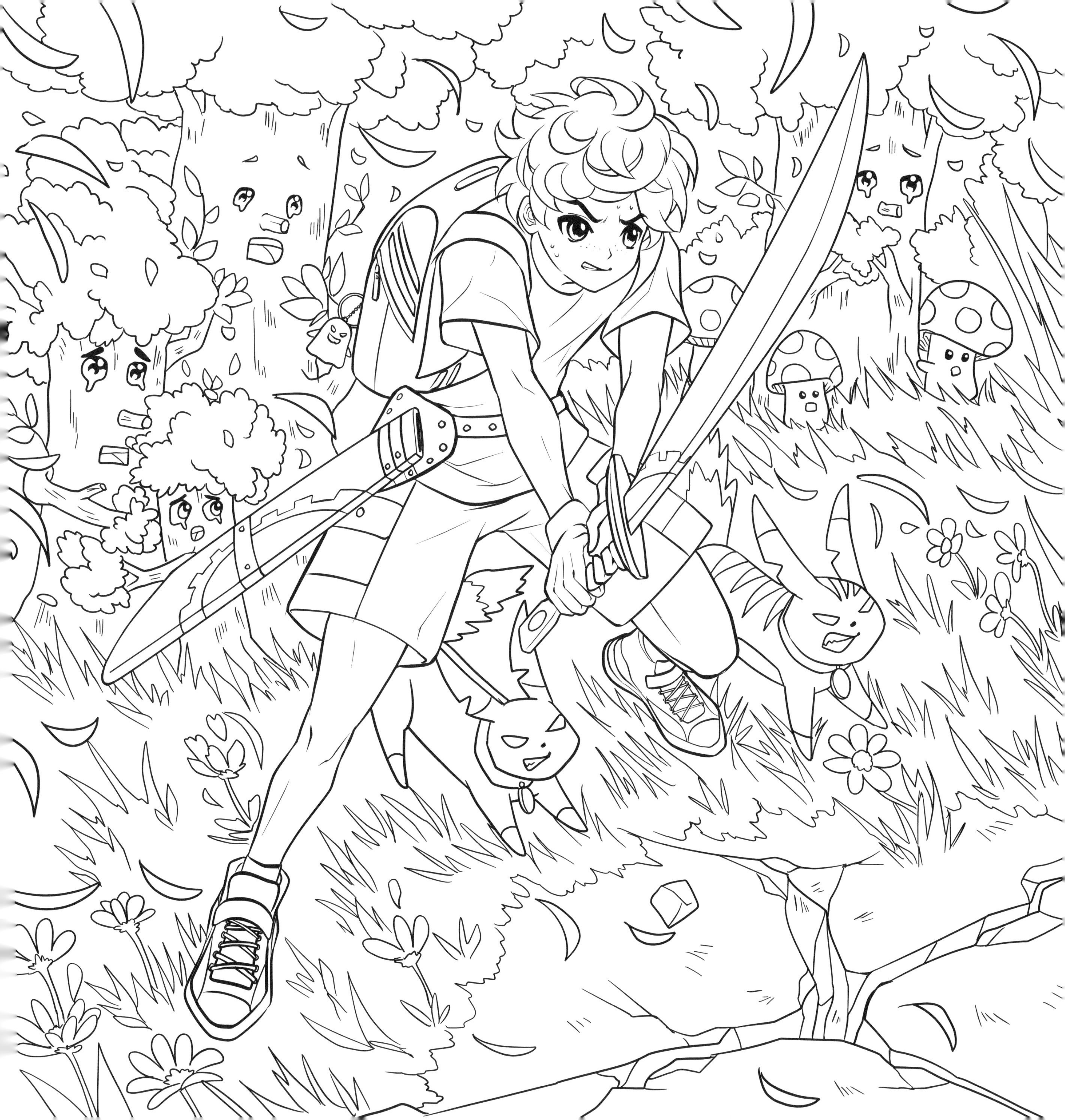

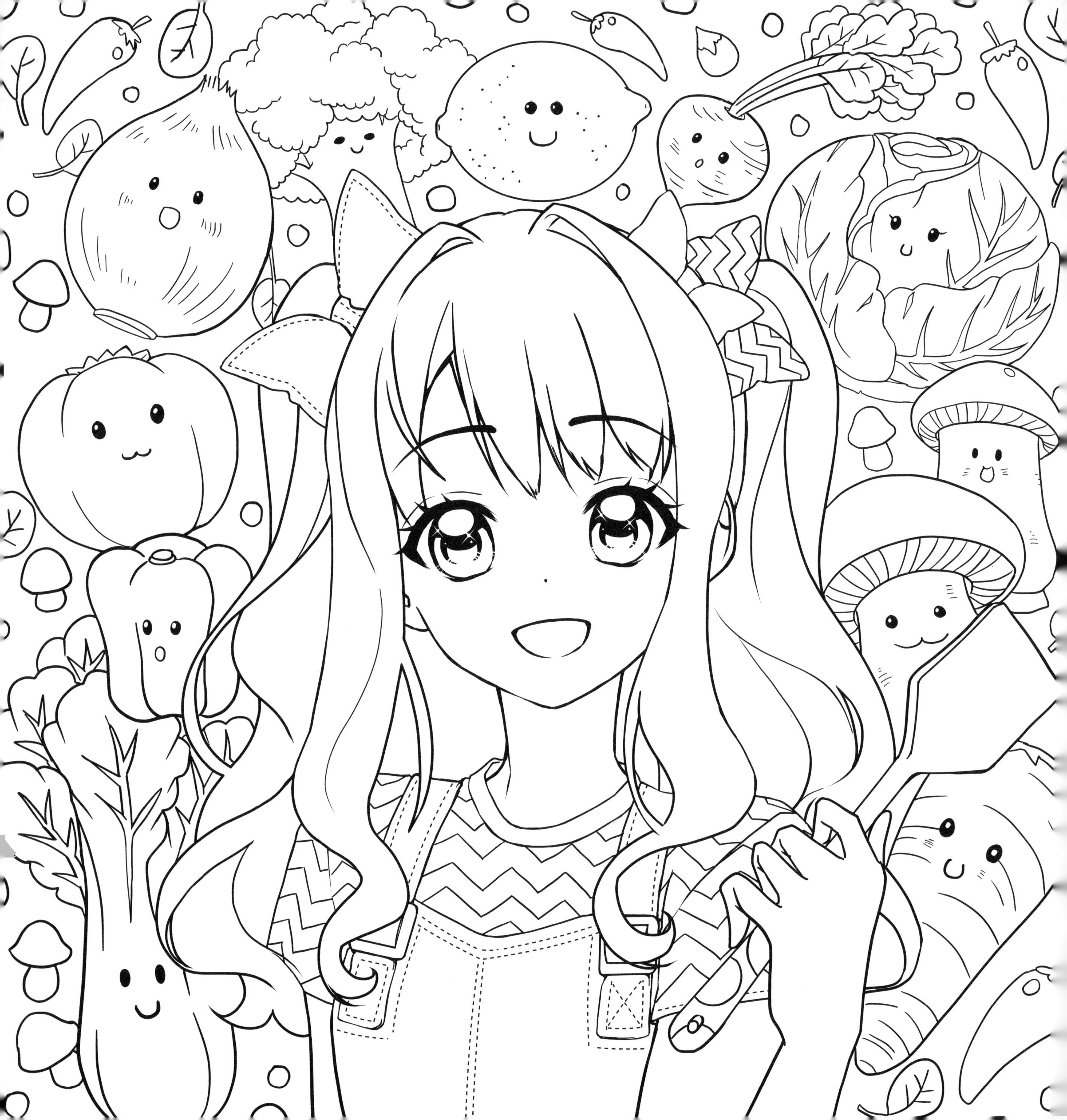

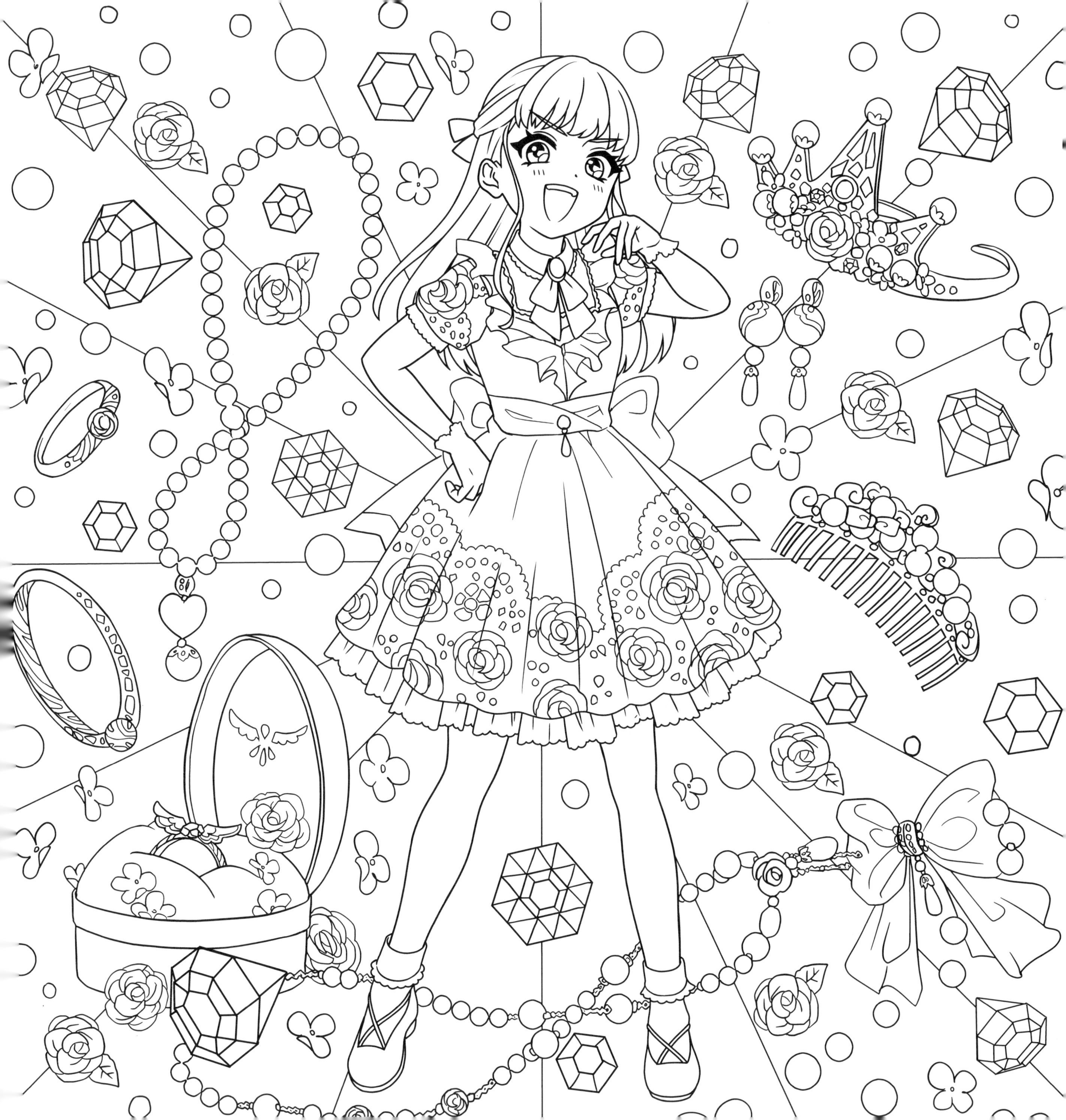

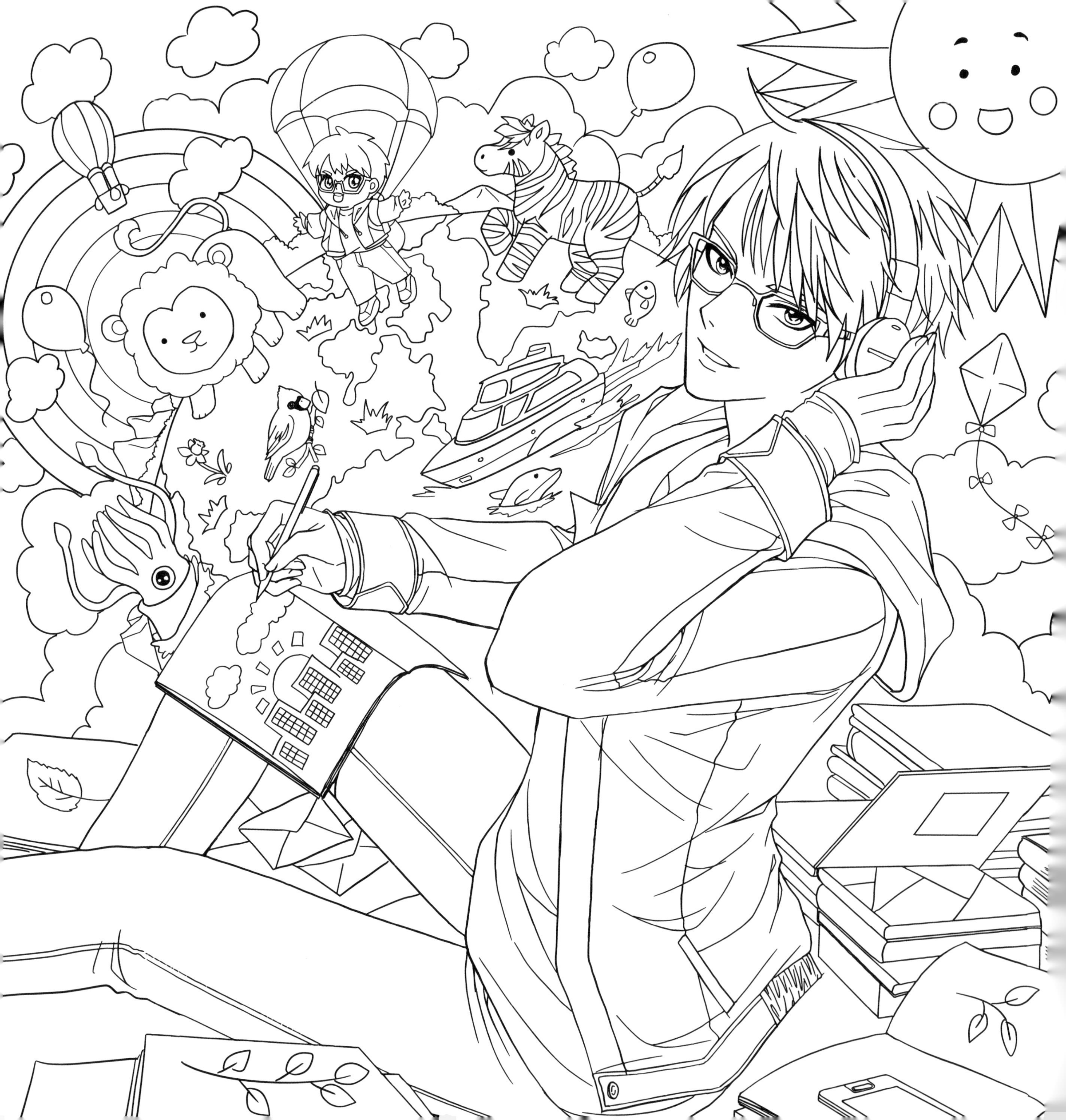

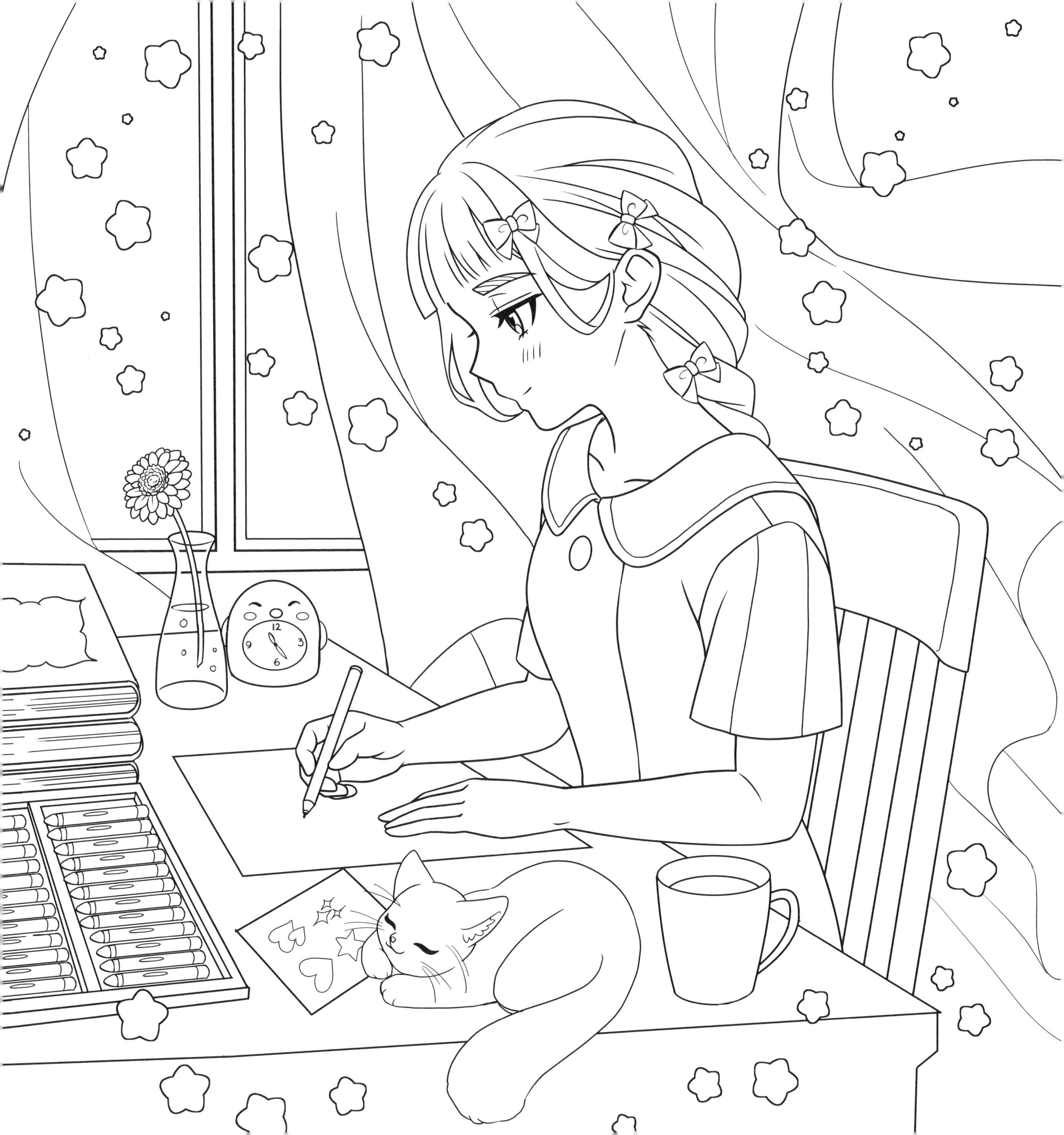

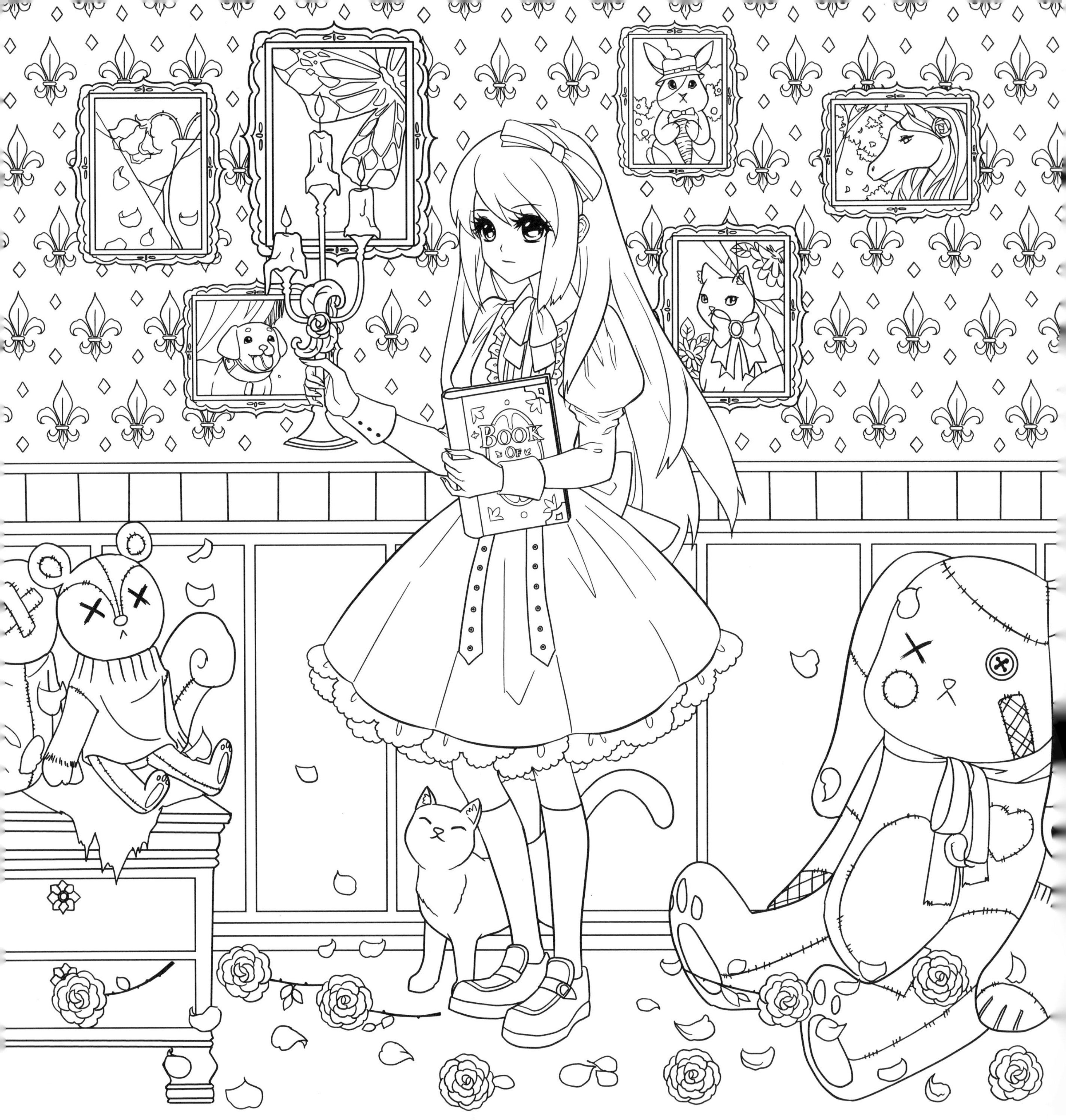
BOOK
OF

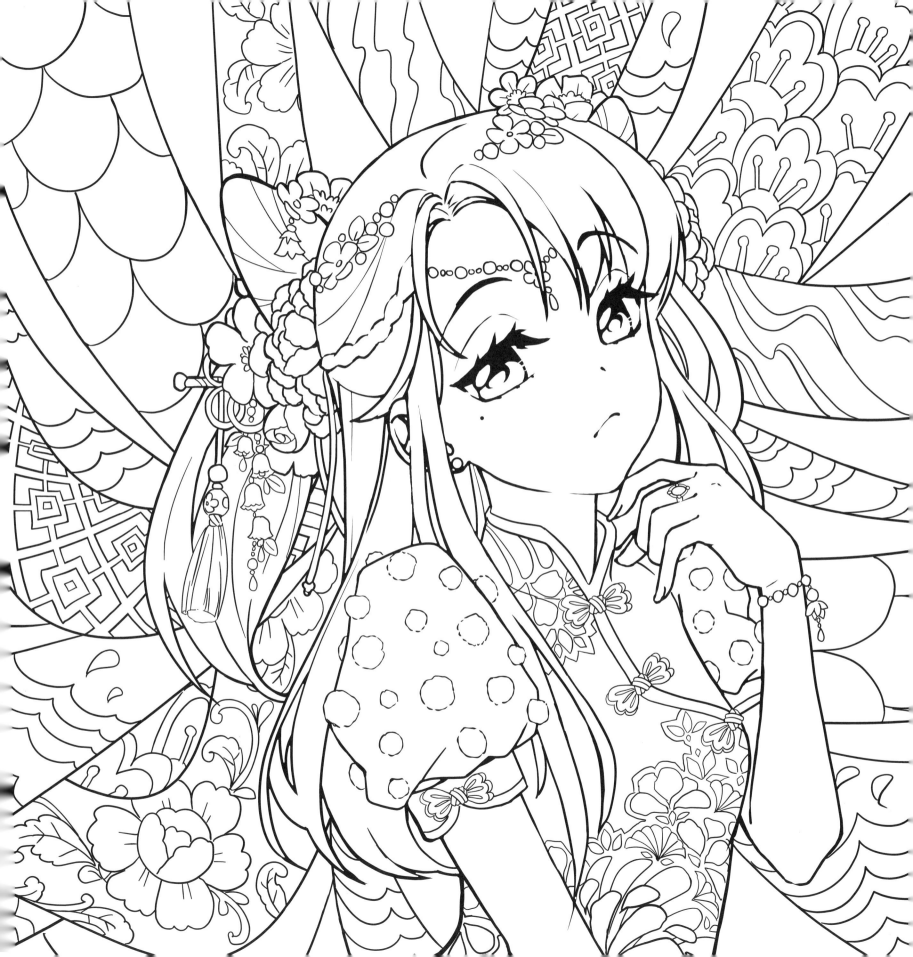

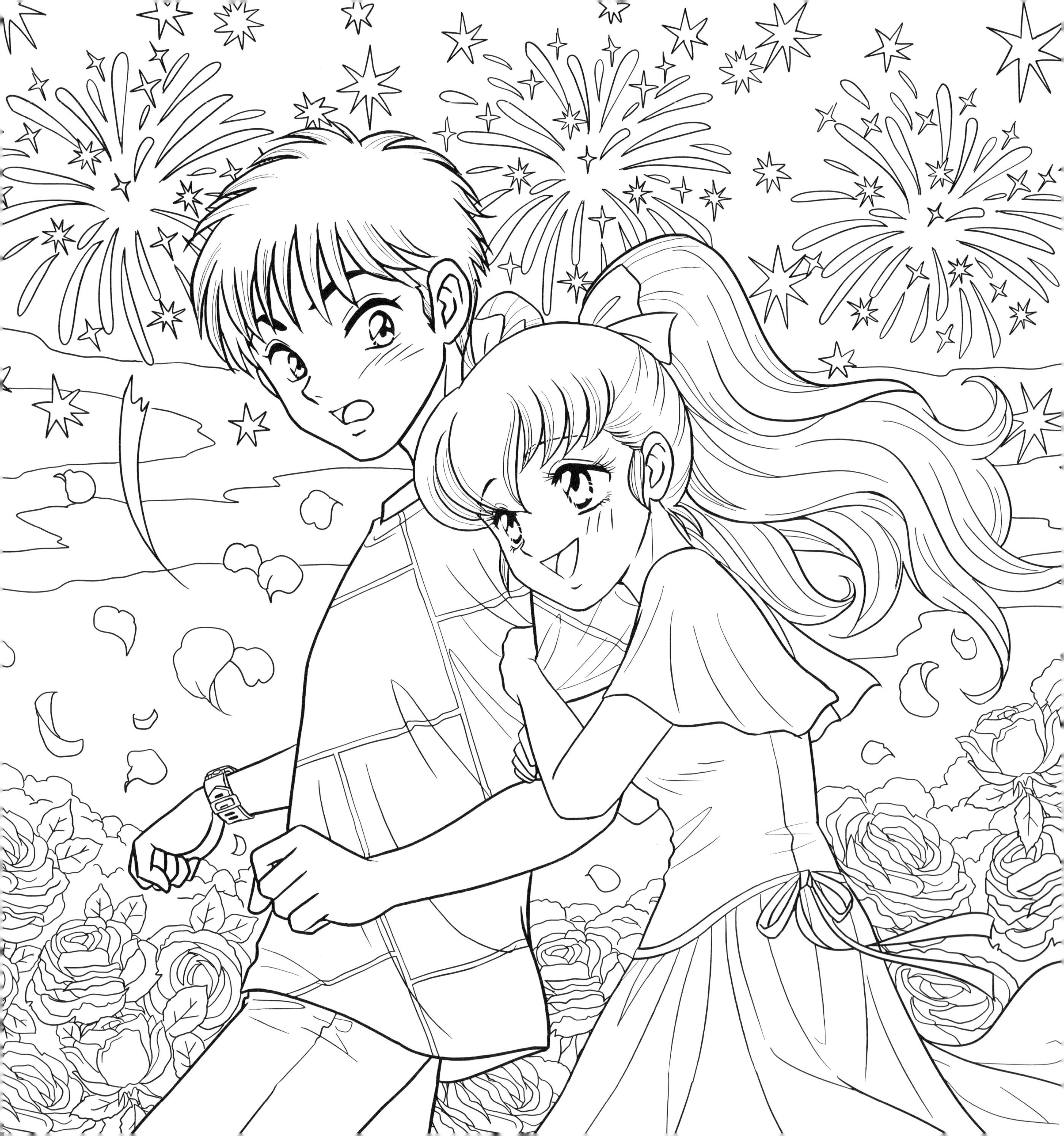

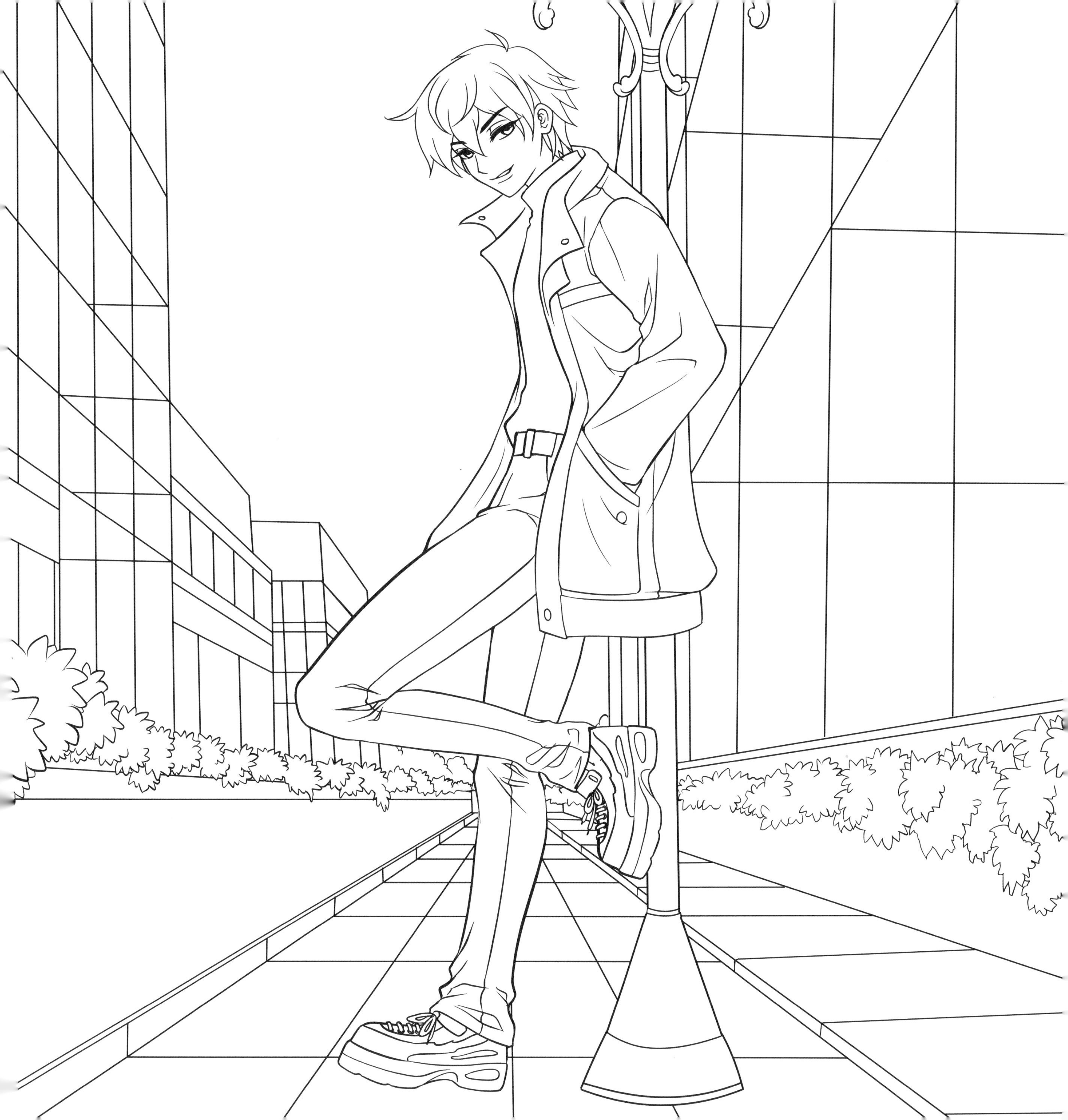

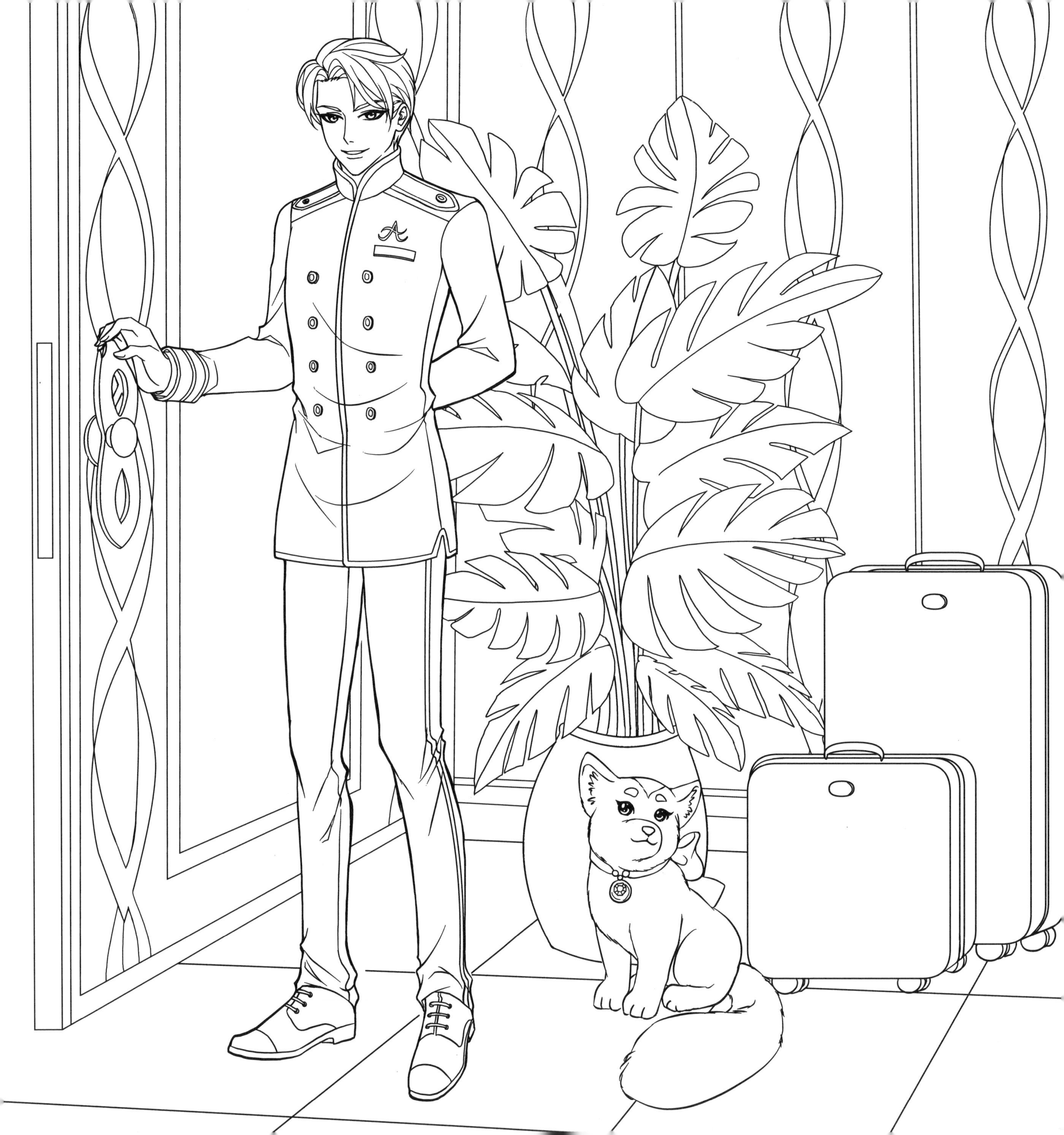

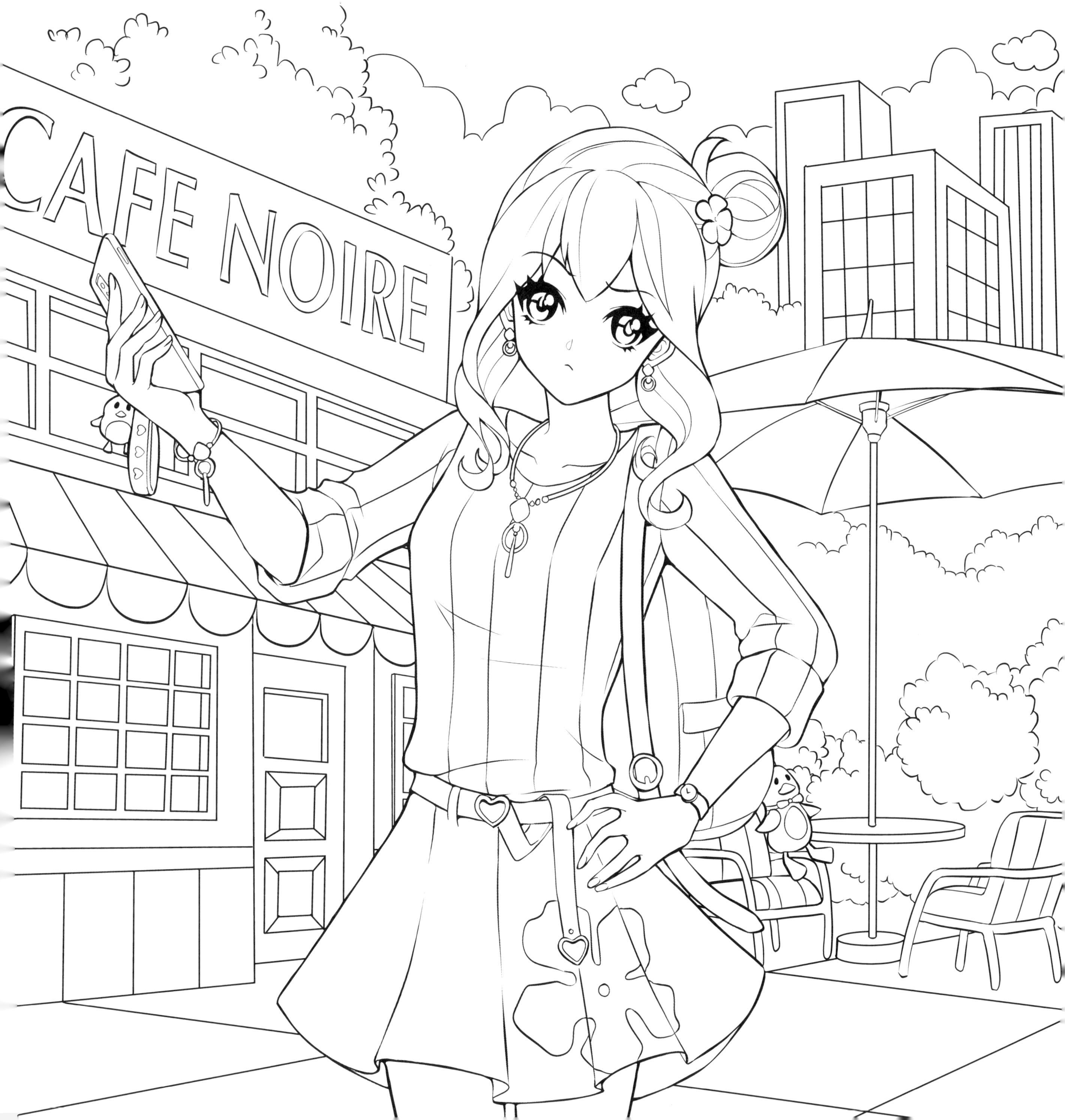
CAFE NOIRE

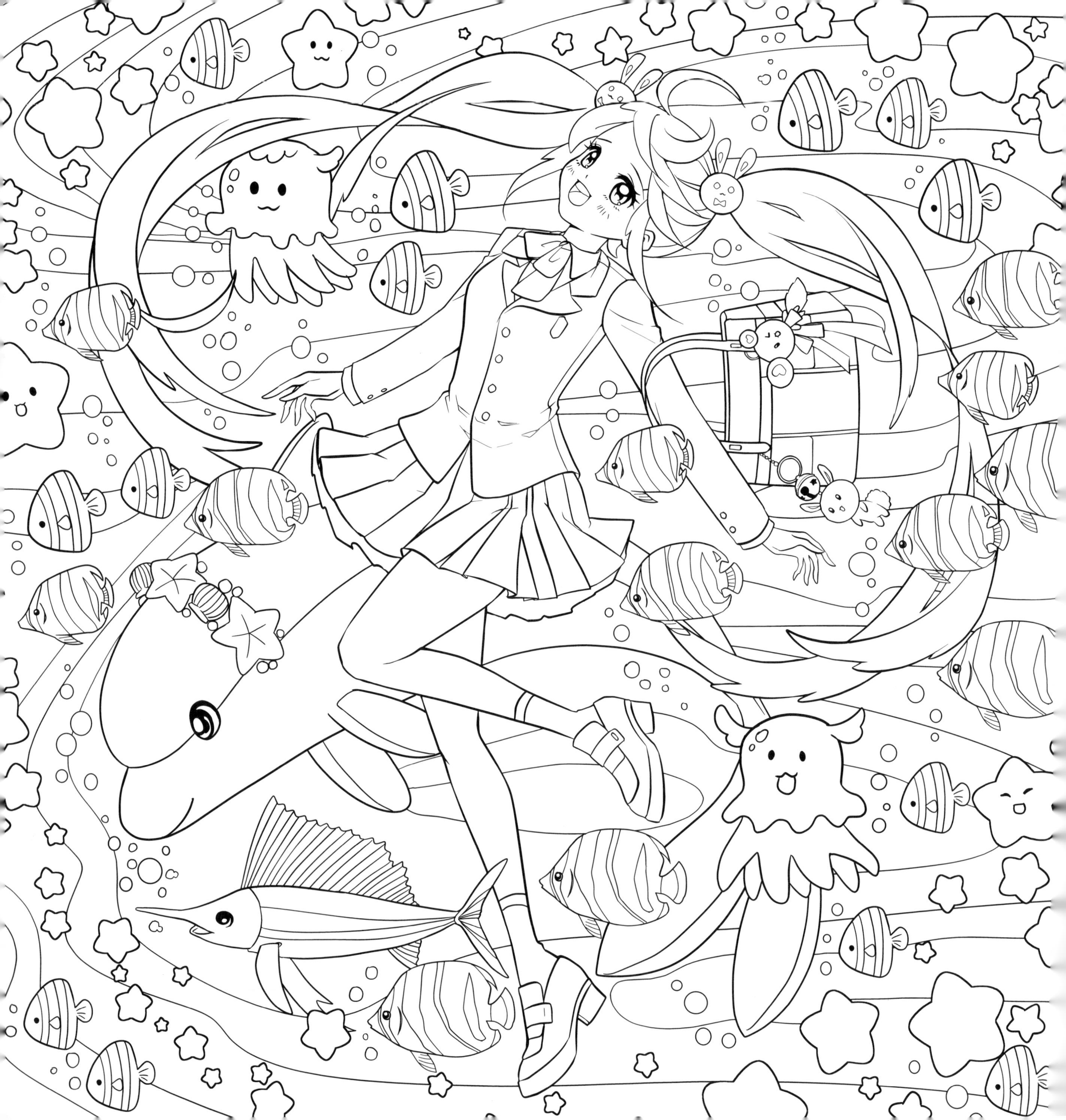

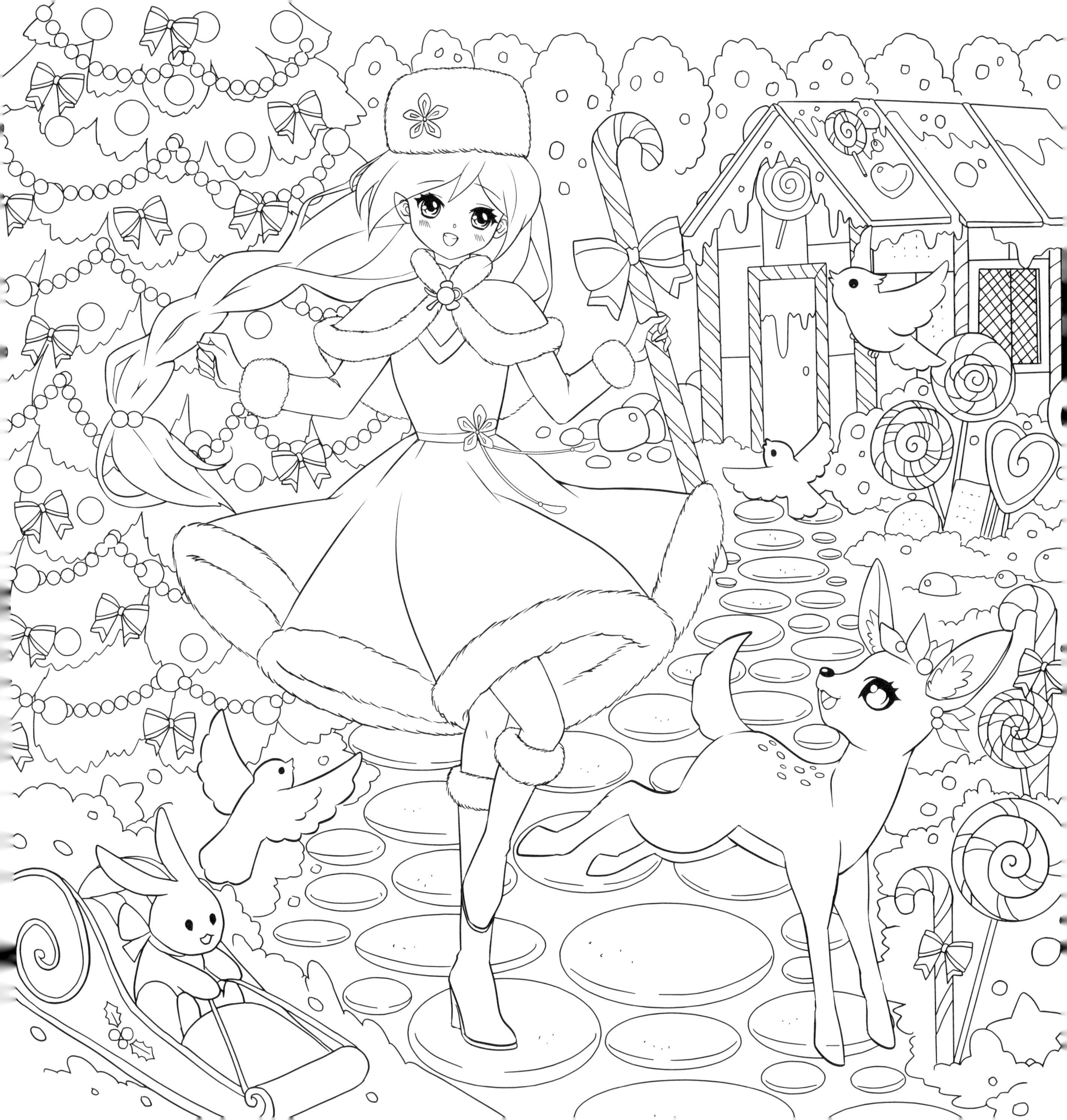

Enjoy Christopher Hart's Other Manga Coloring Books

DRAWING WITH Christopher Hart
The Manga Artist's Coloring Book
Fashion!
Fun Clothes & Characters to Color
MORE THAN 8 MILLION BEST SELLING AUTHOR BOOKS SOLD

DRAWING WITH Christopher Hart
The Manga Artist's Coloring Book
GIRLS!
Fun Female Characters to Color
MORE THAN 8 MILLION BEST SELLING AUTHOR BOOKS SOLD

DRAWING WITH Christopher Hart
The Manga Artist's Coloring Book
Girl Power!
Fun Female Characters to Color
MORE THAN 7 MILLION BEST SELLING AUTHOR BOOKS SOLD

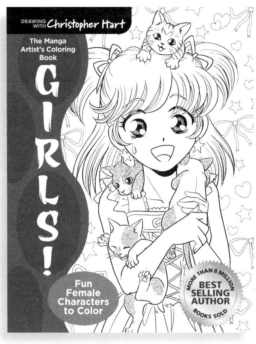